MANAG

IMI *information service*

yfor⸱ ⸱⸱ **16**

Sandyford
Dublin
Tel⸱

The skills of human relations training

A guide for managers and practitioners

Leslie Rae

Gower

Published by
Gower Publishing Company Limited,
Gower House,
Croft Road,
Aldershot,
Hants GU11 3HR,
England

British Library Cataloguing in Publication Data
Rae, Leslie
  The skills of human relations training.
  1. Employees, Training of   2. Interpersonal relations—Study and teaching
  I. Title
  658.3'1244   HF5549.5.T7

  ISBN 0-566-02529-9

Typeset in Great Britain by Graphic Studios (Southern) Limited, Godalming, Surrey. Printed in Great Britain at the University Press, Cambridge.

Contents

Acknowledgements

I am indebted to the many managers and others who have passed through my training hands and who have unwittingly contributed to my knowledge and experience of human relations and human resource material, and hence to this book. I am also indebted to the many psychologists, management trainers and consultants whose work I have tried to describe, and in particular to the behavioural influences on me by Peter Honey.

My gratitude must also go to my wife Susan for her encouragement, patience and typing assistance and to my young son Alexander who gave up games so that his daddy could work on the book.

At Gower Publishing I want to thank Malcolm Stern for once again managing the publication of a book of mine and having continued faith in me and Ellen Keeling again for her invaluable advice in tidying up the manuscript ready for publication.

WLR

Preface

The needs of people at work, from the youngest, newest, most junior employee to the most senior manager of the company, are many and varied. They range from learning basic clerical or manual operations, through a full range of technical and technological skills, to an ability to deal effectively with people.

Each of these different needs has to be approached in a way that is relevant to the type of need. There is little value in bringing together a group of brand new entrants and asking them to discuss how they should proceed with a job about which they know nothing. Similarly, with experienced managers finding difficulty in relating with people, little would be learned by simply showing them a film.

Ever since enlightened organisations realised that management was concerned with obtaining results not by people, but through people, it became evident that training was needed to help people to deal with other people. The different types of training also demand different skills from the trainers and it may be that the trainers who deal with people training – human relations trainers – need to be individuals with completely different views, reactions and approaches to other trainers. It is not simply a case of different techniques, but of personality and approach. It would be dangerous to say that either approach is more difficult than the other, but I have been a trainer in both modes and, apart from enjoying the people type of training more, I have found it more exhausting and more stressful for the trainers.

The purpose of this book is to describe in some detail the various approaches to people training – human relations training. Trainers with experience of technical training; new trainers; trainer-managers; and all managers with a responsibility for the development of their staff – I hope all these will find the book useful as a basic reference to methods and approaches. For those who desire more information or greater detail as a result of 'testing the water', basic references to wider and deeper sources of information are given. People at all levels will also find the book useful from their own viewpoints as course participants themselves: the book certainly tries to remove some of the mystique which surrounds many forms of people relationship training. This can only be for the good of all. If human relations training courses can always start with a minimum of suspicion and concern on the part of the participants, this can only improve the training and make it a more enjoyable experience for all.

Many trainers and indeed organisations have shied away from human relations training because some aspects of it have received a 'bad press'. What I intend to show is the range of training approaches available and how they are performed so that if one particular approach would never be used, it can be seen that there are other methods available. My own experience of human relations training has been wide, both as a trainee and, over the last dozen years or so, as the trainer or facilitator myself.

(This book is a companion volume to my book *The Skills of Training* published by Gower in 1983 and extends considerably the information on human relations training given there.)

A list of references and recommended literature appears at the end of each chapter. These lists are not intended to be exhaustive, rather they are representative of the reading material which I have found the most useful in my own learning. More extensive references are provided in the recommended books themselves.

For the sake of simplicity the generic 'he' etc. has been used throughout: in the majority of cases 'he' and 'she', 'his' and 'her', etc. are interchangeable.

The views expressed in this book are my own except where stated otherwise, and they are not necessarily the views of the Manpower Services Commission, my present employer.

Leslie Rae

1 The nature of human relations training

The many terms used in and about training can mean different things to different people and the phrase 'human relations training and development', far from avoiding this confusion, adds to it. Even the approach itself is known by a number of names in addition to human relations – interactive skills, interpersonal skills, social skills, life and social skills, people skills and so on. The common factor running through most of the titles either directly or implied is that the training is concerned with people rather than the more material aspects of work such as procedures, technical, manual and clerical operations and systems. Obviously, in what might be described as job-specific or functional training, the human element must be involved to some degree. A clear example of this human infusion is in training with computers. It may be a truism that the output of a computer depends on the input made by a human operator, but it is an accurate statement as anyone who has received a gas bill for £0.00 or a bank statement showing a balance of £32 million knows full well. Computers can commit an error, but the chances are that it is acting on the information supplied to it, and the supply of information is in the fallible hands of a human being.

We have now the basis for a definition of human relations training: that it is concerned with the development of people and their interactions with other people, rather than the concrete aspects of work. We have also seen that the divisions are not black and white, since in most forms of learning, other than self-learning in isolation, interactions between people are involved to a greater or lesser extent.

1

A human relations training event can now be defined within the constraints described. If it is necessary for people to learn the skills of interacting with each other, this is human relations training. Such events can include:

- interviewing techniques whether in selection, appraisal, counselling, discipline, grievance, termination or promotion situations
- interactive skills in group situations as either the leader or member of the group e.g. meetings, working groups, project groups
- skills of negotiation
- skills of consultancy
- training skills and techniques
- team building and development
- development of assertiveness
- development of action learning sets and quality circles and so on.

It will be noticed that many of these events include the development of skills and techniques associated with the effective operation of the individual. But the difference here is that in many ways the techniques are simply the vehicles to aid personal development rather than an end in themselves.

ORIGINS OF HUMAN RELATIONS TRAINING

The current approach by trainers and others directly associated with human relations training owes much to research over recent years by psychologists and psychiatrists. In fact, many of the training approaches would not have come into being without this observation and research. After all, the work of these professionals is concerned with the normal or abnormal behaviour of people, and as the result of constant observation of large numbers of people they have been able to demonstrate widespread patterns of behaviour. Many of these patterns have ceased to be purely aspects of research and have been applied in a variety of ways. A typical example of this application is Transactional Analysis, which started as psychiatric therapy with Eric Berne who observed patterns of behaviour among his patients. These observations were extended when it was determined that the same behaviours or ego states could be observed to a greater or lesser degree among the population at large. From this approach a technique of interactive behaviour was developed and is now practised widely in human relations training. This technique will be described more fully later in the book. Many other human relations approaches have similar psychological origins which have in many cases also produced a number of problems.

One of these problems is the very fact that the techniques have their bases in psychology: many people have a deep suspicion of psychology and psychologists and will reject without a hearing any technique which has any indication of such an origin. The wise trainer who is not completely sure of the reaction of his students will present the technique in a straightforward manner without any reference to psychology. This can often be difficult when a training group contains an individual who presses for information about the basis of the theory and its validation measures.

A problem that can become a danger for trainers involved in human relations training is a common syndrome based on the adage that within every trainer there lurks a budding amateur psychologist. The more the trainer is involved in activities in which people behave and react along patterns identified by the psychologist, the more interest in these behaviours he exhibits. It is a very short step from this interest to a deeper desire to extend his activities beyond his knowledge. In other words he tries to act as a psychologist without the necessary specialist training. This urge must be resisted at all costs, as there is nothing more dangerous than playing games with people without possessing the knowledge and skill to avoid hurting them, or even worse causing serious emotional damage.

One human relations course that I attended as a student was billed as a team development course, organised by a professional lecturer who offered public courses of this nature. The event turned out to be a badly-run, pseudo T-Group (of which more later) during which the 'trainer' sat with the group, most of the time saying nothing, but from time to time intervening with pointed and often offensive comments. The course had started after Sunday lunch and by the Tuesday morning an obviously level-headed and reasonably well balanced production manager had taken enough of the very personal remarks directed at him by the trainer. He left the course on Tuesday morning.

During the same course a rather quiet, likeable supervisor was encouraged to change into a high contributing, life and soul of the party, and by the end of the week had become a pain in the neck to most of the group. What the reaction of his boss and workmates was when he returned to work I hesitate to guess. The principal aim of the trainer appeared to be to reduce each member of the group to tears before the end of the week: he and I had an altercation towards the end of the course because he appeared to be annoyed that I would not succumb to tears to satisfy his objective. This type of human relations training by inept, unskilled, unaware and insensitive trainers has tended to give the training approach in general a bad name, whereas the majority of courses and trainers provide an effective and sensitive learning atmosphere and service.

A further problem associated with the psychological roots of most human relations training is the amount of psychological terms and jargon that have been transferred to the training. There can be no bigger turn-off for a hard-headed businessman or industrialist than to be told he is exhibiting an excess of negative socio-emotional behaviour. The Transactional Analysis technique referred to earlier attempted to rectify this problem by using words that were in everyday use only or were easily understandable. Unfortunately the very use of these words has produced a Transactional Analysis language as a result of the specific connotations of these everyday words and the differences from a lay interpretation. For example, the term Child in Transactional Analysis is used to refer to childlike rather than childish behaviour.

Consequently the trainer in the human relations field, although using training approaches based on sound psychological research, observation and models must:

- avoid trying to ape the professionally trained psychologist
- avoid the temptation to behave as an amateur psychologist
- avoid the use of the word psychology as much as possible if

the attitudes of his audience are not completely known
– use words which his audience can understand.

In spite of my recommendations to avoid reference to psychological models in a direct way, most human relations training is based on models and research of this nature. Consequently, if the human relations trainer is to be fully effective he must be aware of the research which is the base for his training. The range of models is extensive, but there is a small number of models which have stood the test of time and which are readily acceptable by the majority of learners. The trainer should have at the least an acquaintance with these models, and preferably an understanding and appreciation of them.

MASLOW'S HIERARCHY OF NEEDS

Probably the best known model of human behaviour is that produced by Abraham Maslow, a model referred to as Maslow's Hierarchy of Needs. Maslow saw human needs at various levels, the lower levels of which must be satisfied before the higher needs are attended to.

The lowest levels relate to man's basic physiological needs in terms of food, water, air etc., in other words the needs that man has to keep him alive. The basic need of a man who is dying of thirst is to satisfy that thirst: without this satisfaction he will have no interest whatsoever in any other achievement. The basic needs having been satisfied, he can then turn his attention to more long-term survival factors – shelter, clothing, job security etc.

The two lower levels relate to a major extent to the basic physical needs. With these under control, deeper desires can surface and involve the more emotional needs. Such factors as belonging, friendship and affection, with the involvement of other people will normally be the next satisfactions for which man will aim.

Similar in many ways, but at an even deeper psychological level is the next level which involves the need for esteem in terms of self-respect and the respect of others, competence, independence and self-confidence, and prestige.

The highest level of needs is that of self-actualisation, representing the highest achievement aim that man can have, in terms of self-fulfilment, self-expression and creativity. These needs may or may not be provided in an individual's work, but if they are not he will seek them away from work. The painters, writers, sculptors, sporting champions and entrepreneurs are operating at this level. The self-actualisation level is self-perpetuating and produces a permanent dissatisfaction with successive achievement. The artist who has produced a painting, strives to produce an even better painting; the writer who has created a literary masterpiece will not rest until he has completed an even better piece of work; the entrepreneurial businessman who has built up a successful enterprise will seek other avenues for business success, even though the obtaining of money is no criterion.

Maslow suggests that human behaviour will be motivated only by an unsatisfied need at any of the levels. The choice of level is not necessarily progressive from lower to higher and skipping of levels often occurs. Circumstances and pressures, social, economic, mental etc. will also have their effect. The practical application of the model is the indication that there is little point in attempting to motivate someone at a particular hierarchal level lower or higher than the one which is dominant at that time for that individual.

THE HERZBERG APPROACH

An equally powerful and widely recognised model is that of Frederick Herzberg and again relates to needs. Herzberg proposes two types of needs. The maintenance or hygiene factors are concerned with material needs which are continuous, progressive and never fully satisfied. If I breathe, I have to breathe again. If I eat, I have to eat again. The same considerations apply in the work situation. The hygiene factors of pay, working conditions and so on must be satisfied: however, these will not motivate, but if they are not satisfied the employee will become dissatisfied. Additionally, the factors are cyclical – as Herzberg describes it 'What have you done for me lately?' Similarly, the satisfaction of needs must be fulfilled increasingly: if there is an annual wage or salary increase, and one year the increase is not greater than the previous one, even though it is an increase it will be looked upon as a cut. So the hygiene factors cannot be regarded as motivators, they must be present before anything further can occur.

Herzberg's other factor is the motivational need. Too often the hygiene factors are used to try to motivate: such an approach is doomed to failure as a permanent encouragement. In order to motivate, Herzberg considers that the only motivating factors are those concerned with the needs for personal growth, achievement, responsibility and recognition. At work, these will be achieved within the job itself – job satisfaction, job enrichment and enlargement, more control over what is done and the opportunity to expand skills and knowledge.

McGREGOR'S THEORIES X AND Y

Another well established approach to human relations training is based on the work of Douglas McGregor who compared widely differing sets of assumptions about human nature. These differences are used in comparing approaches to management styles. He suggested that there are two contrasting approaches to management – Theory X and Theory Y. In Theory X man is seen as inherently lazy, prepared to work only when this is unavoidable, and loath to seek or accept responsibility. At the other end of the spectrum the Theory Y approach is that work is a natural human activity, so man is not lazy in his attitude to work, can enjoy work for its own sake, and that internal motivation will provide the necessary attitude.

The three sources of thinking in human relations training relate to the inherent qualities of man, but the human relations trainer will be more interested in the practical application of the various bases.

THE BEHAVIOURAL APPROACH

Essential to any form of human relations training or approach
is behaviour, as this is the only human aspect which we can
observe directly and react to. We can assume or theorise to the
nth degree about WHY one person is behaving in such and
such a manner: WHY Fred reacts to certain situations and so
on. The followers of different schools of psycho-analysis will
explain these reactions in terms of sexual frustrations, the
influence of parents or parent-figures in the individual's
formative years, or traumatic incidents during one's life. These
may or may not be true reasons for the actions or attitudes, and
the existence of so many possibilities suggests that there is
considerable uncertainty in determining the covert factors.
What we can be certain of are the overt, observable factors –
the actual behaviour of the individual. Whether or not the
sender intends the message, if someone smiles at me I react to
this behaviour and smile in return: if one of my proposals is
supported actively by another, I must accept that this support is
genuine unless it is accompanied by some other behaviour,
verbal or non-verbal, that denies the initial response. Most of
our actions are determined by our observations of the
behaviour of others and how we react to these behaviours. If
we try to guess at the motives behind the behaviours we may be
wrong as often as we are right. Of course the motives behind
some behaviours are obvious, but usually these motives
themselves become evident in the behaviour rather than
remaining covert factors.

The importance of behaviour, initially, in therapy and
subsequently in training, is largely based on the work of people
like Watson and Skinner in the early part of this century.

However, behaviour, the overt aspect of our personality,
must be rooted in the covert features of attitudes, feelings and
motives, and the psychoanalysts provide models for human
relations training. If the training atmosphere or activity takes
account of these models, then the resulting behaviour can to
some extent be anticipated or 'understood' so that behaviour
approaches can be modified.

The origins of psycho-analytical models can be found in the
work of such psychological experts as Freud who used the

analysis in therapy. The views of Freud and others led to the training applications and implications that:

- internal events affect external behaviour i.e. for every external effect there is an internal cause
- self-observation and analysis can help in the self-control of behaviour
- the past, the 'then and there' can influence the present, the 'here and now'
- an examination of the 'here and now' can lead to a determination of the root causes. This is an approach commonly and powerfully used in human relations training to bring to the surface the development of events in a group.

HUMAN RELATIONS TRAINING PHILOSOPHIES

It therefore becomes a necessity that the trainer or training manager who is to be involved in or managing human relations training must be not only aware of the basis of the approach, but must also have a securely determined personal approach. Many factors will vary this determination and the absence of right or wrong will produce personally decided approaches. External factors will come into an assessment of the training approach. Prominent among these will be the influence of the company or organisation if the training is to be conducted in-house. There is little mileage in the provision of training with an open and humanistic approach if the organisation's atmo-sphere is that of a closed and autocratic approach to its management and employees.

The trainer must above all else 'to his own self be true' and 'practise what he preaches'. Anyone who has been involved with a group of learners, particularly in the position of tutor at the head of a group, will realise how exposed this position is and how much the searching spotlight is on the tutor, however much he tries to avoid it. In such circumstances, acts or roles which are alien to the tutor will eventually be identified by the group and if these are seen to be in any way devious, tutor credibility will be lost. Similarly, if the tutor is preaching openness, democracy and self-directed learning and does not show and practise these himself, there is little hope that the group will accept them as appropriate approaches. The technical trainer in this respect has an easier task to perform, provided his teaching techniques are sound, but the human relations trainer, in addition to possessing the technical skills, must be himself a human relations person. This requirement means that the human relations tutor must have a personal philosophy that is in step with the attitudes he is teaching, and, as mentioned earlier, acceptable to the organisation in which he is working.

There is obviously no one philosophy that can be described as the universal norm, for many different reasons. Each trainer must identify the approach with which he can live and ensure that this is in step with the training line he has to take. Otherwise he should not be involved in human relations training. In a similar way, a need for all types of trainers, he must be in training with the sole purpose of developing the learner – anything else must be a bonus. Unfortunately trainers do exist who are in the position to satisfy their own aims and objectives, often self-centred aims. Human relations training offers much scope for trainers to satisfy these aims of enhanced adulation, both from the group and self-generated, and many opportunities exist to manipulate people to these and other ends. Such attitudes must be an anathema to the human relations trainer as so many opportunities arise to do real harm to the learners.

I have a philosophy to which I make no claim as the only or even the most appropriate approach, but it is the one which I try to maintain as both a human being and a trainer. It has been acceptable in the areas in which I have conducted human relations training but I will readily admit that it would be difficult to defend objectively.

The first element in my approach to human relations training is that I believe human behaviour is not a fixed and immovable part of a person's personality. Behaviour can be modified to make an individual's approach to situations more appropriate.

PERSONALITY V BEHAVIOUR

Behaviour is quite different from the personality traits of an individual and it is a foolish trainer who believes that he can modify personality. But many traits that are observable as behavioural aspects are only too often wrongly identified and accepted as inherent personality factors that are part of the warts on a person and so must remain. Many are simply behavioural aspects which can be modified if the individual is made aware of:

- the effect of the behaviours on others
- the reflection of the behaviours on himself in the eyes of others
- the existence of other behaviours that may be more appropriate.

Within this type of modification of behaviour, 'good' and 'bad' behaviour, 'best' and 'worst' behaviours are ineffective descriptions. More realistically there are 'appropriate' and 'inappropriate' behaviours. The span of behaviour must therefore be wide and above all flexible, and the basis of my own philosophy is *not* a singular approach to behaviour, but a multi-approach. Every situation demands a different approach, even though in many cases the differences are minor and can be variations within an overall acceptable approach. For example, it will be rare for the summarising behaviour of a chairman or group leader to vary in necessity from one meeting to another; in decision-making meetings the behaviour pattern will vary only infrequently from a seeking ideas, proposing, seeking clarification, giving information, supporting/disagreeing pattern. The concept of an overall behaviour pattern with variations according to the individual circumstances presupposes a recognised or acceptable general behaviour: we shall return to this theme at a later stage.

FEEDBACK OF BEHAVIOUR

Basic to a human relations training philosophy is the view that it is advantageous to most individuals to seek and receive feedback from others on their behaviour and its effects. This attitude is necessary rather than the stance – often based on defensiveness – that it is unhealthy to seek information about oneself and to welcome feedback of this nature is incestuous. If one wishes to, or has the need to improve by modification of behaviour, the prerequisite is awareness of one's present state. This can only be obtained by information given by others.

OPENNESS

A more difficult facet of behaviour relates to the extent of openness between people and within organisations, and this must of course be linked with the giving and receiving of feedback. A first premise for any human relations training must be that the more open you are with another, the greater likelihood there will be that they will be more open with you. Play your cards close to your chest, and so will they. But obviously life is not as simple as this. Apart from certain covert reasons for restricting the amount of openness, there will be occasions when it will be appropriate to limit one's openness: where disclosure of views, information or feelings would damage the other unnecessarily. The organisational atmosphere may inhibit certain levels of openness. This aspect is often evident in an organisation's openness in its employee reporting and appraisal systems. Some organisations who have reporting systems on their employees have a completely closed system in which the individual being reported upon may receive no information at all about the content of the report, indeed he may not even be aware that a report is being completed. Others have completely open systems, even to the extent that the person being reported upon has to sign the report signifying that he has in fact seen it. And there are many shades between these two extremes. One system I know has a report form, two items of which the person reported upon has the right to be informed about, but no rights to know exactly about the other aspects of the report. At the appraisal, however, the appraiser can, and indeed is expected to discuss the various aspects of performance. It is left to the appraiser to decide how detailed or general this discussion might be. Yet other systems have a reporting approach that is more or less open, but has very closed aspects once the appraisal has taken place with comments being added, which are never subsequently disclosed to the individual, favourable or unfavourable.

PLANNING BEHAVIOUR

A common approach by many in their interactions with others is to 'play it off the cuff', to 'take it as it comes' and similar purely reactive behaviours. This can be a highly successful method if the interactor is a highly aware individual who is also highly skilled at reacting favourably and appropriately to the turn of events. Unfortunately, the majority of individuals does not have this skill and even more unfortunately many people believe, erroneously, that they do have the skill. The basis of my approach is that most interactions are more likely to be successful if there is a considerable amount of pre-interaction planning wherever possible. The production of targets and objectives is a common and well accepted practice in practical situations, but for interactive situations it is rare that objectives of behaviour are set. Objectives of this nature are equally important in this type of event, particularly if the planner is prepared to be as flexible with his behavioural objectives as he should be with the more practical objectives.

Real life situations, in addition to training events, can so often demonstrate at best a considerable waste of time before the meeting of two sides gets down to real business, at worst a complete breakdown of discussion or negotiation. On many occasions these failures may be due to completely opposing, aiien views or entrenched positions, but many occasions will be due to both sides having objectives which neither discloses to the other. One classic occasion I can recall resulted in two groups spending an acrimonious forty minutes, arguing with each other and achieving no movement until by accident it was disclosed that both sides had exactly the same terminal objectives. Once this sharing of views and objectives had been achieved, no time was lost in reaching a satisfactory conclusion. This is not to suggest that every meeting should begin with an open disclosure of the objectives of each side, but there can be little doubt that many events would have an easier passage if there had been a greater degree of openness about objectives in the early stages.

'I AM NOT ALWAYS RIGHT'

One of the many human failings is to believe that I am always right, thus others are wrong: that if a problem exists it is the other person who has produced the problem, not me. Yet on so many occasions the neutral observer can determine the right or wrong and the originator of the problem. At an early stage in interactive development an individual must recognise that he may not be the one in the right and that to resolve the problem he must develop objective awareness. Similarly, if one is to attempt to modify the behaviour of others, he must be as far as possible like Caesar's wife and if necessary modify his own behaviour. Again, the basis of this activity must be self-awareness with a subsequent willingness to modify as necessary.

OPPORTUNITY FOR PRACTICE

The final facet of my human relations philosophy is that behaviour *can* be modified, but once awareness has been achieved, the opportunity to practise proposed modifications must be available. Modification practice is dangerous in a real life environment and if the modification fails the tendency is for the technique to be blamed with a consequent refusal to continue to practise. This suggests that practice should be undertaken in the relatively 'safe' atmosphere of a training event where failures or mistakes can be identified and discussed, then rectified in a further experience.

I hope that this description of what I believe to be human relations training and development has shown the comparison with the more practical and technical approaches. I believe that it is a much more difficult field in which to perform effectively than in the technical approach, not only because of the extent of knowledge, techniques and attitudes required, but principally because of the personal and interpersonal demands made on the trainer. Most human relations training requires the activities to take place in a group environment with a skilled facilitator present, but it can also be effective in the working environment with the assistance of an external consultant as facilitator or a company manager who is also skilled in interactive techniques. Training in a coaching mode can also be effective between a manager or supervisor and the employee on a one-to-one basis, particularly where the interactive needs are of a one-to-one nature.

2   The skills of learning

Whenever someone, whether student, employee or employer, needs to learn about something, a training need will probably exist. This training need can be satisfied in a variety of ways:

- reading
- attending lectures
- direct training 'on the job'
- action learning or similar events
- coaching by the boss or other expert
- self-development packages
- training courses 'off the job' and so on.

Each of these approaches to learning can be utilised in different ways. Research and experience shows that for different individuals one or a combination of the many learning methods is 'right' for that individual and less so for another. The subject to be learned can also be approached in different ways, the more appropriate method often being dependant on the type of learning necessary. For a learner who has never seen the piece of complex machinery which he will have to operate, it is reasonable to assume that reading a book about it will not be a very appropriate medium to use. It will certainly be of little effect for the learner who has a need to improve his oral skills to sit and listen to a long lecture on the subject – at some stage he will have to stand up and speak and receive feedback on his performance.

LEARNING PREFERENCES

When a large number of people are considered as a group or population, further indications about their learning requirements emerge. A considerable amount of research has gone into investigations of how people learn or prefer to learn. In separate research Burgoyne and Stuart, and Paul Temporal determined a rank order of the main sources of learning by managers. The ranking developed as:

1) Doing the job and learning through the experience.
2) Non-company education.
3) Living – the cumulative life experience of success and failure.
4) In-company education – deliberate training interventions.
5) Self-directed learning.
6) Doing other jobs.
7) Media influence.
8) Parents.
9) Innate learning.

It will be noticed that training courses although not too low on the list do not rank too prominently in spite of the prevalence of training events both in and out of company and the immediate reaction of most people to think of courses when a training need is identified.

The preferred methods of learning can be extended when training events themselves are considered as these can be produced in a variety of forms. Research and experience shows changes in preferred approaches at different stages in a person's career. In the early stages, usually when the trainee is young, has recently left some form of full-time education and has just entered employment, the preferred methods appear to favour a didactic approach, rather similar to the learning environment they have just left. This can be anticipated in view of a natural resistance to change and also the need to learn new procedures or instructions. As careers progress with developing knowledge and skills to middle-management levels, attitudes to training change appreciably. At this level there is strong resistance to any form of prescription in the training approach and an equally strong desire to exhibit intellectual and practical skills. Satisfaction of these wishes can normally be provided, with linked learning, by experiential approaches. These can take a variety of forms including syndicate or small-group working to produce answers to case-studies, work-related or general activities or exercises, or perhaps decision-making discussions. Above this level, the attitude to training can often depend on the training culture of the company in which they have developed. If their previous training has had a strong experiential bias, they are more likely to accept a continuance of this approach, perhaps modified to involve more work-related than general activities. If, however, the training culture has developed along more traditional lines of prescriptive courses, seminars by field experts and specialist conferences, the senior managers are more inclined to accept, and in fact demand a formal didactic approach.

BARRIERS TO LEARNING

Whatever the preferred methods at whatever stage, the trainer must be prepared to overcome inherent barriers to learning. In organisations where training has become the norm, there is only minimal resistance to attending training courses at whatever level, but in other instances when training is rare, a basic barrier exists.

MOTIVATIONAL BARRIER

This basic or initial barrier is concerned with the motivation to learn. For the process of teaching or learning to be effective, the desire or motivation to accept the need for the teaching or learning must be present within the learner. There are many motivating factors for people to learn; among others:

- the desire to progress within their chosen work
- the setting of sights on a specific higher level job
- security of job
- fear of losing face in the eyes of seniors, peers or subordinates
- a simple desire to be effective.

Motivation, in the view of many experts, cannot be forced upon people, it can only be self-generated. But the circumstances in which the learner is placed must have considerable influence on the self-motivation to learn. If what Herzberg describes as the hygiene factors are covered satisfactorily – wages are at least adequate, premises and other physical resources are satisfactory and so on – then the basic minimum requirements for self-motivation are satisfied. From this point, a variety of motivational encouragers must be employed, such as:

- the company must show that effective learning will be rewarded
- the company must encourage both learning and its application
- the company must give learners every opportunity to identify their personal best approach to learning and give them the opportunity to practise these approaches.

The trainers must also be involved in the encouragement of motivation. The hygiene factors of the training environment must essentially be satisfied, but such aspects as efficient and effective training methods must be considered; training must not only be acceptable technically, but also enjoyable; the trainers themselves must have credibility; and the end results must satisfy both the course and personal objectives.

To summarise, everything must be done to make the learner want to learn, to learn, and to apply his learning in practice.

Human memory is short and our capabilities of retaining certain skills can be variable. If a child at school is nurtured effectively, there is encouragement to the subconscious motivation to learn. The child will react favourably to good teaching and during these formative years will develop personal learning skills. But these skills, if not maintained or if discouraged by poor attitudes or poor teaching, can become rusty or cease to operate altogether. Such an individual, after years in an anti-learning wilderness, if placed suddenly in a learning situation, will resist the trainers' approaches to teach or at best find difficulty in adjusting.

Even if all previous exposure to being taught has been good, or not bad, the adult will experience adjustment difficulties.

Even the simple physical activity of once again having to sit in a 'classroom' will be difficult, the practice of taking realistic and meaningful notes will have to be re-learned, and the pressure of having to articulate his views in an acceptable manner could be difficult to overcome. All these little-used skills can hamper the learning process, even when the motivation to learn is present.

In the worst cases, there may be antagonism to learning as the result of poor previous learning experiences and these attitudes exaggerate the more normal difficulties cited above. Serious external barriers to learning can, unconsciously, stem from the trainer himself. One often quoted effect produced by the trainer is the result of his using an excessive amount of professional or training jargon with which the trainee is not familiar. The learner becomes so involved in trying to understand the words being used that the message is either ignored or not understood.

Even stronger barriers can be raised by the trainer, again unconsciously, and unfortunately sometimes nothing can be done to rectify this event. As an example of one of these effects, I can recall an occasion when I was one of a team of tutors running a course. After the second day I noticed that one of the students, although reacting favourably to the other tutors, seemed to 'switch off' whenever I came on stage or was unusually aggressive in his reactions to my attempts to project my teaching. It was equally clear that of the group of twelve, he alone reacted in this way to me, so I could only assume that my teaching approach was reasonably acceptable. I stuck this situation out for another day, and in the evening over a drink tried to determine what was the cause. To cut a long story short, I eventually discovered that I resembled closely, both in appearance and manner, a teacher in his school days whom he had hated as he was always singled out for ridicule by this teacher. Once we had talked this through, his whole attitude changed in the training room and he became one of my strongest supporters.

A natural barrier to learning of which the trainer must be aware is the fear of the trainees as to how they will be received in the group. This is particularly so in the case of the shy or inarticulate person who has the fear of making himself appear to be a fool. If this is a principal concern of some individuals they are unlikely to be receptive to learning as their own emotional problems will get in the way. When such feelings are present, and there are few new groups which do not exhibit some symptoms of this syndrome at the start of a course, either as a group or in some individuals, the trainer must be aware of these feelings. He must then adjust his training approach accordingly and not hinder the developing process by placing the course members in situations when inadequacies are exposed or highlighted.

UNLEARNING

An additional barrier that can exist, particularly in the case of 'older' learners, is the need to unlearn. The University of Life teaches us many things, unfortunately not always what we should accept as good practice. Necessity can teach us to cut corners for the sake of expedience, and these approaches can become the norm even when circumstances demand a fuller approach. In many cases, the new or correct methods demand radical change which because of natural human nature may be resisted strongly. Consequently, the training approach and method must be sufficiently effective and acceptable to overcome these resistances and widen the learner's mind so that he will be receptive to alternative ways of working.

LEARNING STYLES

It has long been recognised that different people learn in different ways and the barriers described are among the factors that produce this variance. But little investigation has been undertaken into the possibility of specific styles of learning. Training courses are often based on the approach preferences of the trainer, taking some account of the barriers to learning. However, every group consists of a collection of individuals, with the many possible variations that can exist between human individuals. It must be rare that a trainer is faced with a completely homogeneous group. But, the normal hetero-geneous group is treated as a single unit with a similar pace of learning, similar base levels from which to start learning, similar motivations and similar learning styles. It is hardly surprising that training courses do not have a completely effective record as means of learning. Obviously, there is success for those individuals whose learning methods correlate with those of the teaching and more enlightened training units recognise at least the varied base levels and pace of learning and can adjust their courses to take account of these individual needs. But for practical reasons, in many cases even these general adjustments are not possible, although a problem is recognised, let alone course adjustments to suit individual learning styles.

I believe that more account must be taken of these many differences in individuals if we are to produce completely effective training. Naturally there are many difficult problems in putting this into practice, not least of which is our ability to identify which learning styles exist and how to promote their effectiveness.

In recent years, Alan Mumford and Peter Honey have conducted research into the problems of satisfying the different training approach needs of individuals with their actual preferred style. This has led to the identification of four common styles of learning preferred by people and the construction of an instrument to identify their preferred learning approach. Naturally, some individuals will have the preference and the ability to learn in more than one mode: if so, all the better. But if from a large group of individuals, distinct learning styles can be identified for groups within the larger group, this will have strong implications for the method and approach to training events for each group.

There are a number of approaches to training, and particularly human relations training, and past problems may conceivably have arisen because some individuals may have found themselves in learning situations completely alien to them. In this alien environment we should not be surprised if they were not able to learn. I am sure that most trainers will have run courses that were eminently successful for 90% of the trainees attending. But for some reason there was one individual who appeared to learn little, may even have been antagonistic in his attitude to the course and the tutors, and resisted every attempt by the tutors to bring him round to a more receptive attitude. I have certainly experienced such cases and have been puzzled by them. Of course, the reasons for this attitude may lie in one or more of the barriers cited earlier. But they may lie in his rejection of the approach used simply because the learning method was foreign to his preferred style.

Human relations training is much more prone to this effect than the more technical or procedural events, since to a greater extent in human relations training we are appealing to the reactions from an emotional base. But similar considerations must also apply when we are considering such training approaches as self-development or distance learning. There would be little value in recommending to an individual a self-development approach of reading and analysing a specified book, if it was determined that his strongly preferred approach to learning was to get up and try something out to see if it worked. This concept is not an unfamiliar one as it is well accepted that there are differences of ability in groups of people – manual, intellectual, social and so on.

Honey and Mumford have produced four basic styles of learning which can be identified by discrete descriptions and have also produced a questionnaire which is intended to identify the preferred style or styles of learning.

ACTIVISTS

Activists are the people who enjoy doing something, even at times simply for the sake of doing. They revel in innovations, but having innovated, tend to become bored quickly and look around for something new to try. Watch the 'activist' trainer who gives his group a task to perform, a questionnaire to complete. He scarcely knows what to do with himself while others are engaged in doing. One can almost read his thoughts – 'I wish they'd get on with it', 'Why are they taking so long?', 'Should I leave the room and let them get on with it or is there something useful I can do here while I'm waiting?'

REFLECTORS

The reflectors are interested in new concepts and ideas, but want to stand back and think about the details and the implications. They like to look at all angles and are cautious before making a move. If locked into their reflective mode they can become very annoyed with the activist who wants to get going, and vice versa.

THEORISTS

This type of person must also reflect, but to the deeper extent that they insist on knowing and understanding the basic data and assumptions, the theories and models on which the ideas are based. They think in objective, rational, logical ways and are disturbed by subjective approaches and impressions. Their attitude is 'If it can't be explained, I don't want to know'.

PRAGMATISTS

The pragmatists are activists who are certainly interested in trying out new ideas, but only if they can see a direct and specific application. They are essentially practical, down to earth people who can involve themselves fully in practical decision-making and problem-solving activities – as long as there is a real end product which can be put to good use.

The implications for trainers in this approach would appear to be important. If identification of the preferred learning style or styles can be made, learning events can be tailored to suit the individual or groups of similar individuals. It was suggested earlier that some people who may be required to teach themselves might be recommended to read a book – the activist is less likely to accept this approach than the theorist. In a very experientially biased course, particularly if it is reasonably unstructured, the reflectors and the theorists are less likely to accept the activity than the activists and the pragmatists. The theorists will want to know why they are doing it, what is the model on which it is based, and so on. The reflectors and the theorists could become annoyed with the activists who will want to get on with the activity and can't be bothered with all this pussy footing determining aims and objectives, procedures and parameters, identifiable end results and so on. But when the time comes to analyse the activity the reflector comes into his own, probably again to the annoyance of the activist who wants to move on to something new.

MIXING

Even in the best of all possible worlds we cannot always select who comes on our courses and consequently we can expect a heterogeneous selection of course members with a full mixture of learning styles. Unless the format of the course is such that, having identified the learning styles present, the full group can be divided into smaller groups with similar learning styles, the problems will have to be accepted. However, even with this mix all is not lost: at the very least the course content can be modified and balanced to satisfy the various approaches. This is very much a compromise, since, although all the members will not be completely satisfied, all will at least have something on which to work in their own preferred way. But if the group can be divided according to the learning style, each group can be put on the path of learning in the way that will appeal most to them.

Identification of individual learning styles can assist the trainer in other ways, particularly when the group has a complete mix of learning styles. Many courses require syndicate or small group working and one of the trainers' perennial problems is how to mix the trainees in the most effective manner possible. On many occasions the mixing is a matter of chance – selection is made on a geographical basis, a male/female division, similar or different jobs, or many other variations. But by basing the division on the learning styles, a grouping can be produced with a reasonable chance of achieving the desired objectives.

A natural division which duplicates a real situation is to select for each group at least one of each learning style. Thus, in each group we could have at least one activist, one reflector, one theorist and one pragmatist. In this way a group would be produced that would be similar in many ways to groups which are formed by chance in the working world. A group of this nature can be observed behaving, in the artificial world of the training course, to a very large extent as if they were working back in their workplace.

A number of other combinations is possible. If, for example we wished to demonstrate to the group the need for high reactors and high contributors to modify their behaviour in order to achieve the task effectively, a group of activists could be selected. Conversely, if the objective might be to encourage more activism in a group of reflectors or theorists, a singular grouping of people with these preferred modes might be made.

One common objective in human relations training is to encourage the modification of an individual's behaviour. Fulfilment of an objective of this nature has a prerequisite of knowledge of the individual's learning style. Identification of style may show a variety of preferences: the results may come out strongly weighted preferences for reflection, for example. This may be satisfactory for the individual and his learning approach in most situations, but there will be occasions when the reflective style will not be appropriate and in some groups there will be the need to modify this reflective behaviour. Awareness of the style will alert the individual to modifications which may be necessary. In considering modification there may be no ideal learning style or behavioural profile, but there can be little doubt that the individual with a greater balance between his styles, rather than being heavily weighted in favour of one style or another, has the better chance of using the most appropriate behaviour in a variety of situations.

Identification of the styles is obtained by the completion of a questionnaire containing 80 statements which the individual has to mark according to whether he agrees more or disagrees more with the statement. The scoring is carried out by analysing the markings in a simple uncomplicated way. The markings produce scores in the range 0 – 20 for each style – Activist, Reflector, Theorist and Pragmatist. Honey and Mumford have used the questionnaire with over 1,300 managers from a wide range of commercial, industrial and public organisations and as a result have produced norms which, within the statistical limits, determine the level of preference of each style. The levels of preference are stated as 'very strong, strong, moderate, low and very low'. Although the numbers are small and research is continuing, norms have also been suggested for specific groups, for example trainers, sales managers, production managers etc.

LEARNING MODELS

The work of Honey and Mumford was preceded by the approaches by other investigators who aimed at identifying an individual's preference for a particular learning style. Several models have been produced giving an experiential learning theory which has four or more principal stages.

Stage 1. This is the stage in which the learner experiences a 'here and now' event. This may be some form of experiential training activity in which the learner performs a task, usually in a group and either as the leader of the group or one of the group members.

Stage 2 is the stage in which data and information are collected about what occurred during the event. A typical method of collecting this information is for each participant to complete a summary audit of what they observed or did during the event.

During *Stage 3* the participants can share the information collected by the individuals in the group and produce a full analysis of the task process and/or behaviours. The appropriate and inappropriate activities are identified, there is a sharing of views on the effects of interactive behaviours, and the usually conflicting or incomplete views of each member on the objectives and terminal agreements of the event are made public.

Stage 4 is the opportunity for individuals to consider how they and the group might improve their performance by modifying their approach to the task and interactions with each other. These decisions are made on the knowledge gained and shared in the previous stage and the agreements made.

Stage 5 is also Stage 1 of the cycle being repeated with the performance of a new concrete event, but on this occasion with the modifications for improvement being tried out. This new activity is then analysed and the whole process is repeated for as long as necessary. The model can be summarised as in Figure 2.1.

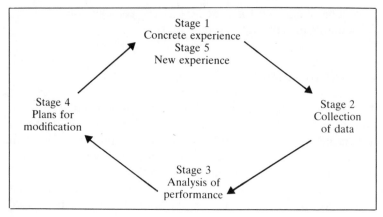

Figure 2.1   Learning model

Kolb in 1975 produced a model of this nature and followed it with the development of a Learning Style Inventory which was intended to identify and measure an individual's preference for a particular learning approach. Like Honey and Mumford at a later time, Kolb produced four basic learning styles. He labelled these styles – converger, diverger, assimilator and accommodator. In order to identify an individual's styles, Kolb used a questionnaire which contained 36 words to which the participant had to respond. Unlike the statements of Honey and Mumford, the words were not directly related to managerial activities and consequently the Inventory could be accused of an unrealistic approach. In fact in 1980, Freedman and Stumpf published a criticism of the approach which certainly cast doubts on the validity of the instrument. Producers of inventories and instruments of this nature must of course be prepared for such critiques since it is doubtful whether any pen and paper exercise will ever produce a 100% valid result, based as they must be on subjectivity. People who complete questionnaires of this nature may:

- complete the questionnaire honestly, but with misguided or unaware views of what they do, say or feel
- give the responses they feel they should

- give the responses they feel the questionnaire deviser requires
- have a different interpretation of the word, statement or question from others completing the same questionnaire or even the deviser of the questionnaire
- give completely honest and accurate responses
- complete the questionnaire in a random manner.

The Learning Styles Questionnaire of Honey and Mumford may suffer from these same subjective objections and may be open to criticism in the same way as that of Kolb. I have used the LSQ on a large number of occasions with no cases at all of rejection by the participants of the results and I have been happy to use the preferences as indicators to help me during the training event. However, I accept the possible influence of subjectivity and consequently treat results as indicators only, to be supported by other evidence.

The comments in this chapter may suggest to those involved in training or providing learning events that learning attitudes are a minefield with too many hazards existing for them to take into account. However, there can be no doubt that there are different types of people who have different learning styles and have various barriers to learning. The skilled trainer will be aware of these possible problems and methods of approaching groups in order to ease the learning event, and will be on his observational toes so that he can be aware of the reactions of his students.

REFERENCES AND RECOMMENDED READING

Boydell, T. and Pedler, M. (1981): *Management Self-development*. Aldershot: Gower.

Freedman, R.D. and Stumpf, S.A. (1980): 'Learning style theory: less than meets the eye', *Academy of Management Review*. July.

Honey, P. and Mumford, A. (1982): *The Manual of Learning Styles*. Honey.

Kolb, D.A. and Fry, R. (1975): 'Towards an Applied Theory of Experiential Learning', in C.L. Cooper (Ed.) *Theories of Group Processes*. Chichester: Wiley.

3 Observing human behaviour

The greater part of human relations training, whether it is concerned with the interactions within a group, between groups or between individuals has as its base the observation of the behaviour of the participants and the effects of this behaviour on others. In the group events there can be behavioural interchanges between individual and individual within the group; between an individual and the rest of the group; and the group as a whole within itself. In one-to-one interactions the observable behaviours exhibit themselves as those of each individual and their mutual reactions.

Behaviour is not of course the only process in an interaction. When a group comes together it does so for a purpose – the performance of a task – not simply the performance of behaviour. These tasks can include problem analysis, decision making, brainstorming, open discussion and so on, and in general training programmes the performance of the task and the practice of particular techniques may be the more important points at issue. However, when a group has come together for the purpose of developing and improving interactive skills, human behaviour must become the most important factor in performance and the consequent observation.

The links between task performance and behavioural factors become even stronger in one-to-one interactions and in training sessions of this nature the observational methods must carry an almost equal weight. Consider for example a training event concerned with interview training for people new to this type of work. Some tutor input on the techniques and methods of the effective interview will almost certainly have initiated the learning event. Commonly, practice involving role playing by the trainee interviewers will follow this input. Practice is of little real value if it is not observed for the purpose of subsequent feedback as appraisal of the interaction. We shall be considering later who performs the observation and gives the feedback, but somebody will be doing so. In the practice interview three points may need to be observed:–

1) The format of the interview as a whole, e.g. the opening phase, the investigatory phase, the decision-making stage, and the closing of the interview.
2) The techniques used by the interviewer, e.g. the use of open, closed, multiple or leading questions, the use of reflecting techniques and so on.
3) A wide range of behavioural aspects which could include the amount of talking by the interviewer compared with the interviewee; the relative amounts of use of the various techniques and categories of behaviour; the non-verbal aspects of behaviour used; tones of voice and methods of expression.

Consequently the trainer must decide what forms his observations are to take and for what purpose: how the observations will be made and recorded: how the observations will be fed back to the participants: who will do the observation and feedback. If the observations are to be recorded, decisions must also be made as to the form in which they will be recorded and, if the observers are inexperienced, what training in observation will be necessary. It will be too late for decisions of this nature to be taken after the event, as can so easily happen in the stress of an interaction, and the observers must have sufficient notice of and training in their roles in the interaction.

One difficult question which has to be faced at some time by human relations trainers is the psychological level at which observation and feedback is performed. The most straightforward approach is at the overt behavioural level, the behaviour which can be observed and to which others react. The much more difficult level is the psychological one which tries to take account of the covert aspects of motives, attitudes and feelings, the internal factors that may be exhibited overtly as observable behaviour. Unfortunately the observable behaviour may or may not demonstrate the internal motives. Consequently assumptions of motives may have to be made, based on a variety of observable signals. These assumptions may be correct, but the odds are at least even that they could be wrong.

One instance I can recall was when I was a participant on a training course, on which, prior to my attendance, for personal reasons, I had decided to act as devil's advocate on certain occasions and as the awkward member on other occasions. Both these roles were completely alien to me whenever I became a course student. Very soon the remainder of the course members had identified me as an awkward so and so, who because of my nature could be depended upon to behave in the role which had been observed. When I changed my role to one of a supportive and helpful nature, this change was interpreted as a change in my nature because I had realised the effects of my negative approach. Obviously all these observations were far from the truth and reflected my overt behaviour only, not my covert feelings and motives for behaving in that way. If the observations were intended to reflect the reaction of people to my behaviour, there were no problems as this certainly occurred. But beyond this my motives never became evident or even suspected to the others. Such are the problems of attempting to assess the true feelings of an individual.

Again, it is the trainer's responsibility to decide which approach he should take, but if he attempts to delve into the psychological, covert levels he must be aware of the dangers expressed earlier of his developing into an amateur psychologist.

Methods of observation can cover a wide range of approaches, including self-assessment, simple approaches, sophisticated instruments, observational methods that can be used by acting as a member or leader of a group, or ones that require considerable expertise and a remoteness from the event.

MEETING AUDITS

Perhaps the simplest assessment approach is a self-observational method which has the advantage of, at the very least, making the individual consider his actions in an objective manner rather than the more subjective considerations which are usual. Many managers or other leaders of meetings or group events either rarely consider the success or value of their events, or accept without evidence that things are going well. Even worse they accept that things are not going well, but do nothing positive to remedy the situation. On how many occasions has the feeling been expressed after a meeting 'That meeting was a bit of a disaster, wasn't it. I wonder what went wrong?'. Once the feeling has been expressed or thought, the interest passes and nothing more occurs. The next meeting is held with similar results and similar post-meeting thoughts, and unfortunately with a similar lack of positive action.

A natural action would be to ask the meeting directly how its members felt about the process and success of the meeting, but unless the leader has a very open and supportive relationship with the individuals of the group, it is doubtful whether much real feedback will result.

One method of avoiding this difficult situation is, at the least, to put oneself into a position whereby searching questions in an objective mode have to be asked. A questionnaire such as the example given in Figure 3.1 can be evolved using questions which are intended to concentrate thought on the process that has occurred. After the meeting the leader can use this performance audit to polarise his views on what actually happened. Although there must still be an element of subjectivity, since the individual is answering his own questions, a real thought process is being invoked and objectivity is being sought. Once the answers have been written down, and in most cases it is beneficial actually to write the answers so that there is less chance of self-deception, if they suggest that all is not well, consideration can be given to what actions are necessary to remedy the failings or take advantage of the helping factors. The questions, of course, need not be those shown in Figure 3.1: some situations may require different questions or questions perhaps in a more specific form.

POST-MEETING QUESTIONNAIRE

Q.1a (If there was an agenda) How clear was the agenda for
the meeting?

Very clear |___|___|___|___|___|___|___| Unclear

Q.1b (If no agenda) Would you have welcomed an agenda
for the meeting?

Yes [ ]   No [ ]   Not sure [ ]

Q.2   How clear were you about the reasons/objectives of the
meeting?

Very clear |___|___|___|___|___|___|___| Unclear

Q.3   How successful was the meeting in achieving those
objectives?

Very successful |___|___|___|___|___|___|___| Unsuccessful

Q.4   How much were your views listened to
a.   by the Chairman
Totally |___|___|___|___|___|___|___| Not at all
b.   by the other members
Totally |___|___|___|___|___|___|___| Not at all

Q.5   How would you describe the chairmanship?

Autocratic [ ] Democratic [ ] Abdicated [ ]

Benevolent
dictatorship [ ] Any other [ ] (please describe)

Figure 3.1   Meeting audit

The natural, and indeed desirable extension of the self-
analytical use of this form of questionnaire is to involve the
other members of the meeting or event. After all, they are the
ones who are probably most involved in making the event a

success or failure. Approaches to having the audit questionnaire completed can vary, depending on the inter-relationships
between the leader and members or among the members
themselves. After the leader has explained, perhaps at the end
of a meeting, what the questionnaire is about and why its use is
being proposed, and its use has been agreed by the group, the
questionnaire is distributed to all, including the leader. One
method of attempting to achieve honesty and realistic feedback
is to suggest that the questionnaire be completed anonymously
and handed in to a neutral person for collation of the results.
The subject for the next meeting of the group will naturally be
the collated results of the questionnaire, emphasis being
usefully placed on the apparent problem areas. As the group
members have identified the problem areas, they can then be
invited to suggest ways in which the problems might be solved
or the meetings improved. On most occasions, provided that
the leader demonstrates his willingness to take account of the
criticisms and suggestions for improvement, the views of the
members will surface in an open and constructive atmosphere
with positive end results. Although initially the audit was
conducted anonymously, it is rarely that individuals will not
identify themselves at the discussion stage with comments,
particularly if that individual sees that he has support from
other members of the group.

An attempt such as the one described can of course represent
a risk to the group leader, as the information and comments can
be critical of the leader who may not be prepared for such a
reaction, or even may resent criticism. If there is any danger
that the leader will not be willing to accept the views of others,
an audit should not be initiated. But the obvious benefits must
be considered in terms of a decrease of ignorance and self-
deception.

The post-meeting questionnaire is used extensively in training situations to help the participants to concentrate their
thoughts on the activity in which they have been involved, and
to guide their thoughts to those areas which they will find useful
to consider. This is useful as a precursor to a group discussion in
which the activity is analysed in a variety of ways, the particular
direction of the analysis being determined by the desired
objectives. If the intention is to concentrate on the methods

used in the activity, the questions can be aimed towards such elements as the extent and success of the planning stage, how and how well the leader organised the group and so on. If the activity techniques require attention, impressions can be sought on how well the questioning techniques were used. If behaviour and its effect is the principal reason for the activity, such questions can be included as 'Who helped the group most during the activity?', 'How?', 'Who hindered the progress of the group?', 'How?' etc.

SIMPLE CONTRIBUTION SCORING

There are, however, more direct methods of observations of processes and behaviour, the simplest of which, as its name implies is Simple Contribution Scoring. In this approach the observer has a piece of paper, not necessarily even a complete sheet, on which is written the names of all the people involved in the meeting or event. As the meeting progresses, a stroke is placed against the name of the participant each time he or she makes a contribution – that is to say, says something whether it is in the form of a question, statement or any other form of verbal behaviour. Stroking continues throughout the meeting until, at the end of the meeting, a statement of the total contributions made is available. Figure 3.2 demonstrates an example of this observational instrument.

The analysis of the meeting shown in Figure 3.2 shows the level of contribution activity for each participant, whether high, medium or low, or in the case of one member, very low. The

John	‖‖‖ ‖‖‖ ‖‖‖ ‖‖‖ ‖‖‖ ‖‖‖	
	‖‖‖ ‖‖‖ ‖‖‖ ‖‖‖ 111	53
Fred	‖‖‖ ‖‖‖ ‖‖‖ ‖‖‖ 1	21
Charlie	‖‖‖ 111	8
Joan	111	3
Sam	‖‖‖ ‖‖‖ 1111	14
Mary	‖‖‖ ‖‖‖ ‖‖‖ ‖‖‖ ‖‖‖ ‖‖‖	
	‖‖‖ ‖‖‖ ‖‖‖	45
Rita	1	1

Figure 3.2   Simple contribution scoring

level of contribution of members can itself be useful information to the leader of a group or chairman of a meeting group
which meets on a regular basis. Often such leaders have a
subjective view about the activity levels of their members, in
terms of quietness or otherwise, and do not know exactly *how*
quiet or *how* active they are. Indeed on so many occasions,
usually when the leader has become very involved in the task
rather than performing a real leader/chairmanship role, he may
not even be aware of the relative activities of various members.
The Simple Contribution Scoring analysis at least gives him this
information in quantitative terms.

However, this form of analysis does little more than state the
number of times a participant speaks in stark numerical terms.
It does not show the quality, duration or sequence of the
contributions, let alone any indication of what was said or how
it was said.

In the example shown we know that Rita spoke once only,
but not how long her contribution was nor how important.
Similarly with John and Mary: it is evident that they were high
contributors, but their high number of contributions may have
all been very short or not relevant to the discussion. Analysis in
this form cannot give this information, but what it can do is to
raise questions in the mind of the leader. The questions will
certainly be raised if the leader was not aware of the
contribution level and may include questions of whether Rita
needs to be encouraged to contribute to a greater level or
whether she should even be present at the meeting. It appears
from the analysis that John and Mary may have had more than
their fair share of the meeting time, perhaps in non-productive
altercation. The analysis certainly suggests to the leader that he
must, at the next meeting, keep a closer eye and control on
these two members.

The Simple Contribution Scoring form of analysis can be
extended to some extent to provide further information. One
of the criticisms cited earlier was that no indication was given of
the duration of the contributions. A variation to indicate this
information can be produced by placing a stroke, not for every
contribution, but for every ten seconds of a contribution – ten
seconds can reasonably accurately be estimated. A further
variation which will identify the sequence of contributions can

be to record numbers instead of simple strokes. So the first person to speak will have '1' recorded against his name, the second '2' and so on. This type of information is often highly significant, particuarly if it is linked with a simple timing particularly for the late contributors.

The exact method of recording the contributions will need to be chosen by the group leader or the observer, depending on the reasons why the analysis is to be performed. The simpler approaches can be particularly useful to the leader of a new group to allow him quickly to identify some elements of his new group.

One objection which is often raised by people hearing about this form of analysis for the first time is that the participants of the meeting will see the observer completing the analysis, and will react with suspicion. However, in most cases these fears can be overcome. If the scoring is being performed by the leader of a meeting, it is not unusual for the leader to be taking some form of notes as the meeting progresses, either to use these as a basis for his summaries as the meeting moves through its various stages, or to ensure that he has a grasp of all the proposals made on a subject, or to supplement the minutes or action notes of the meeting. So meeting participants are accustomed to the leader making some form of note. Also, the scoring itself requires a minimum of deviation of the leader's attention from the discussion: all that is required is an identification of the speaker – the contributor – finding his name on the scoring sheet and entering a simple stroke.

If there is still concern, particularly about the secrecy of the observational record, the activity can be brought into the open at the start of the meeting by a discussion about what the leader would like to do. This discussion could take the form of a statement of the leader's wish to look objectively at the mechanics of the meeting in order to improve the meeting's effectiveness.

This open declaration of scoring the members' contributions has the danger of producing the 'Big Brother' syndrome. If the members know that their behaviour is being observed and recorded, they may behave unnaturally: the normally highly active members may reduce their contribution rate to avoid scoring too many strokes, and the quieter members may feel that they had better contribute in order to appear on the record. When one thinks about this, one realises that there is little wrong in a reaction like this – after all, in many cases this behaviour pattern is the one we are wanting to achieve.

But often, the unnaturally modified behaviour patterns are not maintained. The 'Big Brother' effect can be short-lived, particularly when the participants become interested and immersed in the discussion. Then they either forget about the observation or ignore it as being secondary to their need to contribute to the subject. The observer has several options open to him. If it appears that the modified behaviour pattern is being maintained throughout the meeting, the record can be kept and its results used for a discussion at the end of the meeting. This discussion can take the form of questioning whether there were benefits from the changed behaviour patterns of the meeting and how the group might benefit from the continuance or development of these patterns. If however, as is more commonly the case, the behaviour reverts to the normal pattern, two scoring sheets can be used; one would cover the first ten minutes or so of the event, when the unnatural behaviour is being exhibited, and the second for the period subsequent to this when behaviour had returned to normal. The first record can be thrown away as not representing the real behaviour of the group and therefore not relevant.

SOCIOGRAMS

It is desirable on occasions to observe a group in such a way that not only is the level of contribution analysed, but also the flow pattern of the discussion. To do this, a directional sociogram can be used. This instrument is in effect an extension of the Simple Contribution Scoring approach, but with an added element.

At least three variations can be used. The first method has as its starting point a sheet of paper on which circles or other reference symbols are drawn indicating the individuals of the group and their physical positions relative to each other. As the discussion progresses, lines are added to this initial skeleton chart. If a contribution is made directly by one member to another, a line is drawn joining the two members, with an arrow added to the line to show the direction of the contribution. In the example shown in Figure 3.3, member B has communicated directly with member A on four occasions and A with B on three occasions. If the contribution is not made clearly or directly to another member but to the group as a whole, the line is drawn outwards. In this way a pattern of the flow of communication between members and the focus on particular individuals can be shown.

A second variation, one which I prefer because of greater clarity, involves the use of marks on single lines, rather than a line for each contribution. As in the first example, a sheet of paper with reference points for each member of the group is needed at the start of the observation. But before the start of the discussion a single line is drawn connecting each member, and smaller lines are drawn from each member towards the outside of the pattern.

Once again the flow between the members is recorded, but in this approach by entering half an arrow on the line joining the two individuals, or in the case of a contribution to the group, on the line out from the member. If a second contribution is made to the same individual, the second part of the arrow is entered. Consequently, a complete arrow indicates two contributions in that direction. An additional luxury can be obtained by indicating also the number of interruptions in terms of who interrupted whom. For this purpose a simple stroke is placed across the line relating to the two individuals. For example, in Figure 3.4 C interrupted A on three occasions, the three occasions only in fact when C communicated directly with A!

Figure 3.4 demonstrates clearly the information which can be obtained from a sociogram of this nature. The relative levels of contribution can be obtained as with the Simple Contribution Scoring, but the pattern shows clearly that in this meeting there were virtually four separate meetings in progress. Members E, F and G had formed a triad and almost every one of their contributions was directed at each other, never to the group as a whole and rarely even to the Chairman A. Members B and C were having a discussion as a dyad, with only limited reference to the group and the chairman. D was in an isolated position in which nobody talked to him, except perhaps to interrupt him,

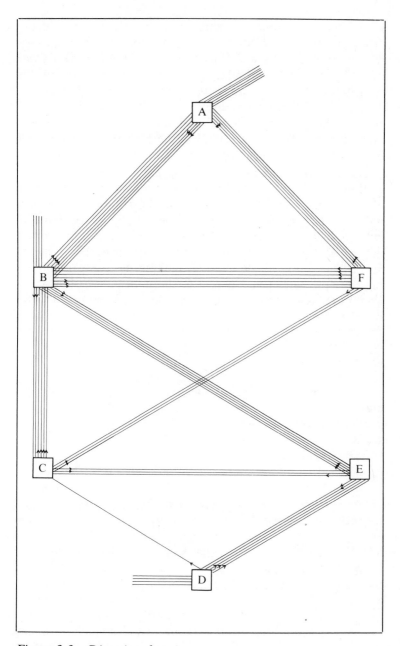

Figure 3.3   Directional sociogram

so for the short time he remained as a real member of the group, most of his contributions had to be to the group as a whole. And these were obviously ignored! The chairman A was in a position very similar to D and made most of his contributions to the group, only to have most of these ignored. To people who are experienced and skilled in leading discussions or chairing meetings, a situation such as the one observed might appear to be unrealistic. But the sociogram in Figure 3.4 is actually one that I produced of a real discussion group.

The flow of interactions shown in a sociogram can also be demonstrated in a matrix format. In the matrix, the members of the group are shown on both the horizontal and vertical indices, the record of contributions being placed in the intersecting square. The contributions made to the group by an individual are entered in the vertical column headed 'Group' against the name of the member making the contribution. In the example shown in Figure 3.5, the information shows that Fred spoke to Joe on eight occaions whereas Joe spoke directly

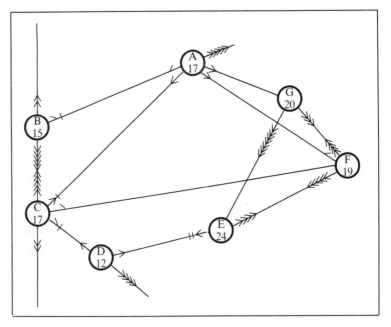

Figure 3.4   Directional sociogram

		TO						
		FRED	JOE	MARY	BILL	GROUP	TOTAL	% FROM
FROM	FRED		8	10	2	6	26	40
	JOE	4		6	6	4	20	31
	MARY	2	0		2	0	4	6
	BILL	6	5	2		2	15	23
	TOTAL	12	13	18	10	12	65 / 65	100
	% TO	19	20	28	15	19	100	

Figure 3.5   Matrix sociogram

to Fred on four occasions: Bill spoke to the group twice only, whereas Mary spoke to the group as a whole not at all.

The information provided by a sociogram of whatever form shows the number of contributions made by each individual, the flow pattern between members, any focus on any particular members, and such additional information as the amount of interrupting of whom by whom. In these respects the sociogram clearly extends the information which is provided by the Simple Scoring analysis, but still does not provide information on the quality and duration or sequence of the contributions.

Unlike the Simple Contribution Scoring analysis, it is almost impossible for the fully participating leader, chairman or even member to complete a sociogram. It really needs someone outside the group to take on this task. This reintroduces the question, in real life working groups, of the openness of completing such instruments of observation. There is obviously no problem on a training course, as the students are quite accustomed to the trainer making some form of note as an activity is taking place. Only once in the past seven years of interpersonal skills courses during which I have sat aside from the group completing an interaction analysis, have I been asked what I was doing. However, even in the training situation, if the trainer is directly involved in the discussion or activity, he cannot complete the sociogram himself. In cases such as this, a colleague who is known to the group and who is often present in any case, can perform the task.

On many occasions it is necessary to observe, record and analyse behaviours to a much deeper level than is possible by using the methods described so far. This is particularly the case in training situations where the feedback that has to be given must be extensive and all encompassing. Group training events in human relations training certainly require this approach and for the feedback to be realistic and acceptable it must be objective and complete. A variety of approaches is available and it is the responsibility of the trainer/observer to select the one with which he is the most confident.

GENERAL OBSERVATION

At the general end of the spectrum of methods available is the purely observational approach in which the observer is as aware as possible of what is occurring within the group and is taking note particularly of critical incidents. At the end of the meeting the trainer is able to lead a discussion with the group on what has occurred, what the participants themselves have observed and what additional incidents have been observed by the trainer. Much depends on the general awareness and observational skills of the trainer and his skill in presenting this type of information to a group. Observations of this nature must be to a large extent subjective and there is the danger that because the trainer is concentrating so hard on observing, he reads more into an incident than actually occurred.

Initial decisions must be made by the trainer on which areas of the activity he will observe. Observations can include the level of contribution and participation, the aspects of influence, the decision-making procedures used by the group, the performance of the task itself, the maintenance functions of the group, the development of atmosphere within the group, the techniques and behaviours of the leader and so on. Obviously no single trainer can observe all of these at the same time, but essentially he will have determined beforehand the objectives of why the activity is being held, and the observations will be restricted to be in step with these objectives. The essentially subjective nature of these observations can of course be supplemented by more objective aids such as cassette or tape recorders, or video cassette recorders operating through direct video cameras or closed-circuit TV systems.

Useful as these observational methods are, considerable reliance is placed on the skills of the observer and the level of his objectivity. More objective and analytical methods and measures are available and these have the advantage of providing a permanent record which can be maintained for progressive research. Many versions of this type of analytical instrument exist and have varying degrees of complexity and usefulness.

INTERACTION PROCESS ANALYSIS

One of the earlier observational instruments, produced by Bales, appeared on the scene more than thirty years ago as Interaction Process Analysis. The basis of this analysis is to record the content of the group interactions in terms of the behaviours exhibited. The behaviours are classified in a number of categories which relate to problems of orientation, evaluation and control, and questions and answers within these areas. The three category groups symbolise the classical progress of a group through the decision-making process.

> *Orientation.* During this phase the behaviours are principally those of informing, clarifying, repeating, confirming, seeking information or clarification, seeking confirmation or repetition.
> *Control.* Giving suggestions and directions, providing solutions, and seeking suggestions and solutions.
> *Evaluation.* Giving opinions, evaluating, analysing, expressing wishes or feelings, and asking for opinions, seeking evaluation and analysis, and seeking expression of feeling.

These three elements represent the task-dimension of the interaction. But Bales also recognised the behaviours which could be described as of a social or emotional nature. This is shown in his social-emotional dimension in which behaviours are either positive or negative and are categorised into three groups – decision making, managing tension and integration.

Decisions. As a positive element, this category includes the behaviours of agreeing, passively accepting, and understanding. In the negative mode it includes disagreeing, showing passive rejection, withholding help.

Tension management. On the positive side these behaviours of showing tension release are exhibited as joking, laughing, and showing satisfaction, whereas as showing negative tension, the behaviours include withdrawing and seeking help.

Integration. The behaviours which illustrate positive solidarity are raising the status of others, helping and rewarding, with the negative behaviours of deflating the status of others, defending or asserting self.

In practice, to use Bales' Interaction Process Analysis, an analysis sheet is completed during the interaction, scoring the behavioural contributions of each individual into the dimension categories. A typical analysis sheet of a one-to-one interaction would appear as shown in Figure 3.6.

CATEGORY OF BEHAVIOUR	INTERVIEWER	INTERVIEWEE
Task-dimension:		
Gives suggestions	1111	1
Gives opinion	⧌11	1
Gives orientation	⧌11	11
Asks for suggestions	1	
Asks for opinion	111	11
Asks for orientation	11	⧌111
Social-emotional dimension:		
Shows solidarity	11	1
Shows tension release		
Agrees	1	1
Shows antagonism	111	⧌
Shows tension	1111	⧌111
Disagrees	111	⧌11
Totals	37	36

Figure 3.6   Interaction process analysis

In the example shown in Figure 3.6 the behaviours categorised show that the interviewer has taken a very prescriptive and antagonistic approach which has produced a similar reaction from the interviewee. Most of the task-dimension behaviours were on the part of the interviewer who lost no opportunity to state his own views and propose courses of action. This telling emphasis has produced mainly socioemotional reactions from the interviewee who reacted negatively to the interviewer and showed tension, antagonism and disagreement. A pattern perhaps of how not to conduct an interview, unless this was the deliberate intention of the interviewer.

The Bales approach to interactive analysis has superficially the advantages that:

- behaviours can be categorised and scored
- a large number of behaviours can be summarised within acceptable bands
- the analysis can be used as a method of feedback so that the individuals can consider any behaviour modification necessary.

However, many practising trainers have found difficulty in applying the analysis because:

- it is more complicated than it appears initially
- not all behaviours can be categorised in the groups selected
- the categories appear tidier than they are
- categorisation can require interpretation (i.e. assumptions) rather than reliance on observation of overt behaviours only.

KLEIN'S INTERACTION SCHEDULE

Klein modified Bales' Analysis and produced some twelve years later her Interaction Schedule. This later approach to the analysis of interactions leans heavily on that of Bales and although the Schedule is based on a task-dimension range of behaviours, two aspects are identified – facts and values. The giving of facts is treated as the impersonal aspect of behaviours and can be categorised as the asking for or giving of information. Klein said that values, on the other hand, are personal, express an individual's personal judgement and are not verifiable. Although values are recognised as an aspect of behaviour they are not separated in the Schedule, since Klein felt that people express ideas which are a combination of facts and values.

The dimensions and categories in Klein's Schedule are fewer than those of Bales and have a notation element expressed in positive and negative terms. Figure 3.7 summarises this approach to behavioural observation and analysis; in practice an interaction would have the members' contributions categorised using the notations information+, agrees– and so on.

Criticism of Klein's Interaction Schedule are similar in many ways to those made of the Bales approach and researchers and practitioners have found the major problem in both the approaches to be the correlation of observer results. When more than one observer records an interaction, different results of what was observed can be obtained, often with alarming differences. Rackham and Honey also found that a number of significant behaviours which could be detected by other means were not being picked up by these analytical instruments. My own experiences with them have been similar and during an interaction I have found myself having to make value judgements of covert aspects in order to categorise a contribution. Problems of this nature contaminate the objectivity of an

Asks for information	inf –
Gives information	inf +
Asks for views	vi –
Gives views	vi +
Makes explicit proposal	pro
Disagrees	agr –
Agrees	agr +
Expresses hostility	expr – h
Expresses withdrawal	expr – w
Expresses friendliness	expr + f

Figure 3.7   Klein's Interaction Schedule

instrument designed to be used in an area that has sufficient inherent difficulties without introducing additional ones.

REFERENCES AND RECOMMENDED READING

Argyle, M. (1969): *Social Interaction*. London: Methuen.

Argyle, M. (1972): *The Psychology of Interpersonal Behaviour*. London: Penguin.

Bales, R.F. (1950): *Interaction Process Analysis*. London: Addison-Wesley.

Cooper, C.L. (Ed.) (1981): *Improving Interpersonal Relations*. Aldershot: Gower.

Dyer, D.A. and Giles, W.G. (1974): 'Improving Skills in Working with People: Interaction Analysis', *Training Information Paper* No.7. London: HMSO.

Klein, J. (1963): *Working with Groups*. Hutchinson University Library.

Phillips, K. and Fraser, T. (1982): *The Management of Interpersonal Skills Training*. Aldershot: Gower.

Rackham, N., Honey, P. *et al.* (1971): *Developing Interactive Skills*. Wellens.

Rae, W.L. (1983): *The Skills of Training*. Aldershot: Gower.

Scheine, E. (1969): *Process Consultation*. London: Addison-Wesley.

Stewart, V. and Stewart, A. (1978): *Managing the Manager's Growth*. Aldershot: Gower.

4 Analysing human behaviour

The observational instruments of Bales and Klein were described in the previous chapter and it was shown that, certainly for training practitioners, there were a number of problems in using these instruments effectively. It was also mentioned that Rackham and Honey encountered these problems. It is only too easy to criticise any work, but much more difficult to produce something effective to take its place. This chapter describes one such approach which is now widely used and which I use extensively in a variety of situations in the human relations training in which I am involved.

Neil Rackham and his associates joined Peter Honey and his colleagues who were working on supervisory training in what was at that time British Overseas Airways Corporation. In 1968 problems were being experienced with the evaluation and assessment, and hence the real value, of BOAC's 'Administrative Skills' training and a new approach was wanted by the trainers. A number of approaches to the problem were considered and the most promising appeared to be some form of interactive analysis. The instruments of Bales and others were tried but were eventually rejected for the reasons stated earlier and it was decided that a new analytical instrument was needed.

CRITERIA FOR CATEGORY SELECTION

A realistic and logical approach demanded that any analytical instrument had to satisfy a number of criteria before it was acceptable. The importance of the criteria hinges around the categories used in the observation and recording, for it was principally on this basis that the other analytical instruments were rejected. As the training under consideration was group training, the criteria established related to group activities, but it was found eventually that they were suitable for other interactive situations.

The criteria for the inclusion of a category in a behaviour analysis instrument, determined by Rackham and Honey, were five in number.

Criterion 1. *Possibility for change.* It is very interesting and useful in behavioural research to observe all behaviours occurring, whatever they may be. But to perform behaviour analysis for practical training purposes there is very little point in observing and recording behaviours which cannot be modified or changed by the person displaying them.

Criterion 2. *Meaningfulness.* The category of behaviour must be understood by both the person exhibiting the behaviour and the person observing it. If the observer does not understand it, he will have difficulty in observing and identifying it, then subsequently discussing it with the person observed. If the person observed does not understand it, he will reject it in feedback and the basic purposes of observation and analysis will be undermined. I can visualise reaction of a hard-headed supervisor who is informed that he is exhibiting an excess of negative socio-emotional behaviour.

Criterion 3. *Reliability.* When two or more observers watch an interaction there must be a statistically significant correlation between their results in terms of the numbers of contributions recorded and the distribution of these categories throughout the interaction. This criterion itself relies heavily on:

Criterion 4. *Degree of differentiation.* The categories must be sufficiently distinct from each other so that confusion is kept to a minimum. It is an excellent criterion to have in mind when constructing a behaviour analysis instrument, but problems can arise in practice. Although the difference between the categories is clear in the mind of the observer, the behaviour of people is not equally clear and concise. Many contributions are made in a manner so woolly and obtuse that the listener has considerable difficulty in taking in what is being said (I suspect that the speaker is often in the same position!). In cases like this, clearly distinguished categories help, but do not produce the absolute answer.

Criterion 5. *Relationship to outcome*. This is particularly relevant in a training situation in which the behaviour must be applicable. In any interaction there will be behaviours that will be important to the outcome, just as there will be behaviours that will have little or no effect on the outcome. It will obviously be a wasted effort observing the latter behaviours.

BEHAVIOUR CATEGORIES

Using these criteria, Rackham and Honey, after considerable experimentation, eventually produced a set of thirteen categories which formed the basis of an analytical instrument for the observation of behaviour in groups. They called this instrument 'Behaviour Analysis' or BA as it is commonly abbreviated. A list of this nature does not prescribe that a user of Behaviour Analysis is restricted to this range alone; in fact a major advantage of BA is its flexibility. The range of behavioural categories is extensive and, bearing in mind the criteria for selecting categories, an observer can select those which best suit his purpose and objectives.

In using BA, a full understanding of the behaviour categories is of paramount importance as, not only do they define the scoring entries of the analysis, but they also represent discrete behaviours exhibited by people.

The thirteen categories in the general purpose BA are proposing, building, supporting, disagreeing, defending/attacking, blocking/difficulty stating, open, testing understanding, summarising, seeking information, giving information, bringing in and shutting out.

Let us look at what these categories represent in behavioural terms.

Proposing. A behaviour which puts forward an idea or suggestion for a new course of action. The proposal can usefully be signalled by 'I propose that . . .', but more

commonly proposals appear as 'I think we should . . .', 'Let's
. . .', or 'I suggest that we . . .'.

Building. This is a supportive proposal which extends or
develops a proposal made by another person and which
enhances the initial proposal. Building behaviour is
important as to exhibit it one must have listened carefully to
the original proposal. Let us take the case of a proposal 'Let's
go to the cinema tonight'. Building could take place on this
proposal in the form of 'Yes, there's a cowboy film on at the
Odeon, and as we all like cowboys we can go there'. Building
is not limited to one follow-up proposal and much value can
be obtained by a number of group members each building on
a proposal. In our example, further building could take the
form of 'And we could go to the first house so afterwards we
could go and have a Chinese meal'. Opportunities to build
may be almost limitless and result in a weighty and
substantial agreement from what may have been a weak
initial proposal.

Supporting. Supporting behaviour is one in which a conscious or direct declaration of support is made with another
person or his views. The verbal support can take the simple
form of 'Yes, I agree' or 'Yes, I support that', or may be a
much longer contribution in which the individual says the
same thing as the initial contributor, but uses different
words.

Disagreeing. The obviously different view to supporting on
which there is conscious and direct disagreement with the
concepts and views of another, even the simple 'No I don't
agree with that'.

Defending/Attacking. These behaviours occur with a statement of opinion against another in which is contained a value
judgement of the other's views or emotive words, phrases or
tones of expression. A statement such as 'I might have
expected *you* to say that' could be taken only as an attack on
one's manner and approach. The resulting behaviour would
be likely to be an attack in return, and so on in an ascending
attack/defend spiral until the attack is terminated either by
one of the 'fighters' opting out of the fight or backing down in
some way, or the chairman stepping in to stop the destructive
behaviours.

Blocking/Difficulty Stating. This category covers a range of behaviours which in general add nothing to the activity and do not help it along. A classical 'block' is 'We're just going around in circles'. This contribution although indicating the actual state of the group's discussion, does nothing to help to move it on in a positive manner. If the participant had wanted to make his contribution more useful and positively helpful, he could then have said 'So what I suggest we do is . . .'.

Facetious or funny remarks are also included in this cateory. There are, however, occasions when the humourous comment can be very useful in a group event by relieving tension. But it is a question of scale and degree: if every contribution by an individual is a block, that individual's value to the group and his acceptance by the group decreases with every funny comment.

Difficulties can also be stated in a similarly unhelpful way, although not going so far as to disagree, and certainly not giving a positive aid to the event. Such comments as 'Well, I can see the way you propose will be tough', 'We're not going to be finished in time if we go on like this' and so on are typical difficulty stating contributions.

Open. Open behaviour is that in which a speaker admits an error or omission, or apologises for his actions. The behaviour can range from the simple 'Sorry' to 'Yes I'm afraid it's all my fault as I should have seen that reference in the report'. Open behaviour need not always be as negative as these examples. It can be a useful and positive strategy to employ if one is in an attack/defend spiral and realises the futility of this position. In a case such as this, *in order to progress the event,* one member might back out of the fight saying something about realising that certain things should not have been said. On some occasions it may be useful to accept the blame for something for which you were not responsible, again *in order to progress the event.* Obviously it would be unwise, for the sake of one's career prospects, to do this too frequently.

Testing understanding. This is a very useful behaviour which serves several purposes. A typical testing understanding contribution starts off with 'From what you have been saying, if I have got it right, you are suggesting . . . .'. The repetition of the original contribution allows the checking of understanding of what has been said; gives others in the group the opportunity to check that *they* have understood; checks with the original contributor that he said what he had intended to say, and that you had been listening to him. It also gives the opening for any misunderstandings to be corrected or omissions to be rectified.

Summarising. This category is very similar to testing understanding but without the direct checking back. It is a statement in a compact form that collects the content of discussion and decisions made to that stage of the event or of a previous event. To be effective a summary must be complete and accurate. It is similar to testing understanding in that it gives the opportunity for both the leader and members to check that they recall everything that needs to be recalled. It is likely that insufficient summaries occur during an event at appropriate stages, reliance usually being placed on the end summary, if there is one, to remind members of everything that has happened.

Seeking information. The questioning behaviour which in a restricted category BA includes the seeking of information, clarification, ideas, views, feelings, opinions and thoughts.

Giving information. The stating behaviour in which views, information, thoughts, opinions, facts and feelings are offered.

Bringing-in. A gatekeeping category of behaviour which is a direct and positive attempt to involve another in the discussion. It is usually linked with a question and names the person invited to come in. So 'What do you think, George?' leaves George and the other members in no uncertainty that his views are being sought, not Fred's.

Shutting-out. This behaviour on the other hand excludes or attempts to exclude another. This exclusion can be made by:

- interrupting someone before they have finished speaking
- members participating in side discussions

  – a member making a contribution when another member
  has been brought in.

All these shutting-out activities say that the ones who are
doing the shutting-out are not listening to other members
and that they have something more important to say.

USING BEHAVIOUR ANALYSIS

The practical application of BA in observation of a working
group is for the observer to use a BA form similar to the one
shown at Figure 4.1. This example uses 13 categories as
introduced by Rackham and Honey and consists of a sheet with
vertical columns for each of the participants in the group and
horizontal rows for each of the categories used.

As the event proceeds, each speaker or contributor is
identified and the contribution he has made is allocated a
category. A stroke is then made in the box at the intersection of
the individual's column and the category's row. This process
continues for each contribution made, with the strokes or
scores building up to produce a record of the event. A
completed analysis will show:

  – the level of contributions made during the event by each
    individual
  – the categorisation of each individual's contributions
  – the total level of contributions in the group
  – the categorisation of the group's contributions.

Two particular points need some explanation. It is normally the
intention for one stroke to be entered for each person's
contribution, namely the important or significant part of the
contribution. If the stroking was not limited in this way, the
number of strokes for a long contribution could get out of hand.
One could envisage a long contribution in which the
contributor starts by supporting a comment previously made,
continuing with several aspects of giving information and
opinion, a partial disagreement, a hesitant proposal, more
information giving and ending up by saying 'What I have been
trying to say [for the last 10 minutes] is that I fully support Joe's

BA 1
NAME W. L. RAE   ACTIVITY DISCUSSION 1600–1640 h.

	JOHN	MICHAEL	BRIAN	JOAN	MARY	RALPH	TOTALS
PROPOSING	6	15		1	12	4	38
BUILDING	3			1	3		7
SEEKING IDEAS, INFORMATION	21	6	1	6	16	19	69
GIVING IDEAS, INFORMATION	12	22	12	14	14	25	99
SUMMARISING	7				1		8
SUPPORTING	5	1	8	5	4	6	29
OPEN		1		1		2	4
DISAGREEING		6		2	2	1	11
ATTACKING, BLOCK, DIFF'Y STATING	1	8		2	6	6	23
BRINGING-IN	10			1	2	1	14
SHUTTING OUT	6	15	1	6	8	14	50
TOTALS	71	74	22	39	68	78	352

Figure 4.1   Behaviour Analysis form

proposal'. It is likely that a single stroke in the supporting column would suffice for that contribution.

On the other hand, there will be occasions when all parts of a contribution appear to have a similar importance or weighting. For example 'I propose that we continue with the procedure unchanged. What do you think about that as a course of action, Fred?' Here we have a proposal linked with a seeking views and a specific bringing in of Fred. In an instance such as this I would score a stroke for each of the three categories included. So BA is not as mechanistic nor as black and white as may appear on first acquaintance.

The other occasions when scoring becomes a little more

complex are with the bringing in and shutting out categories. Bringing in normally involves a direct invitation to comment by naming an individual or individuals, and this action is invariably linked with a seeking behaviour – 'What do you think, Mary?'. In this case, the observer would score two strokes: one for seeking information, the other for bringing in.

Similarly, if a shutting out occurs in the form of an interruption, the stroke is scored in the shutting out category, plus one in the category of the contribution made by the shutter out. For example, if, after the shut out or interruption, the person who has interrupted goes on to say 'No, what I propose is that we . . . . .', in addition to scoring a shutting out, a proposal would also be scored for that individual. Of couse, this second stroke could relate to any of the other categories being used in the BA form.

MODIFICATIONS OF BA

One of the major advantages of BA is its flexibility, also one is not constrained to use the original categories. In fact one is encouraged to use other categories which may be more appropriate to the event being observed. When I first started using BA I stayed for a time with the original categories of Rackham and Honey until I was at home with them through practice and experience. At a later stage I felt the need, and saw the possibility, of being more precise in my analysis of certain situations. Obviously, if a category has to encompass a number of allied, though slightly different behaviours, a more general picture is being produced than may be desired.

Many of my personal modifications to the original categories are the result of comments by participants in my training events, and I now use a BA with 16 categories.

DISAGREEING

Let me take as an example the first category which I modified. This was the behavioural category of disagreeing. After I had used the category for some time, some confusion arose particularly in feedback discussions on how this behaviour should be viewed. Disagreement in itself is not an inappropriate behaviour on most occasions and if we strongly disagree with someone and do not say so, we are usually acting non-assertively and denying our rights to express our views. The main criterion appeared not to be the disagreement but the form in which it was expressed. If I disagree with someone or their concepts and baldly and bluntly say 'No, I don't agree with that', I am likely to be forced to give my reasons, may resist giving my reasons although questioned repeatedly, may be attacked for just disagreeing, or either of us may withdraw from the interaction. None of these resultant behaviours can be called particularly helpful.

However, if instead of simply stating my disagreement I did so and also clearly and logically explained and presented my reasons for not agreeing, there would be a much greater likelihood of having a positive response from the person with whom I had disagreed. The result would still be in the form of the disagreement, but in this case the approach would be constructive in which the objectives would be to arrive at agreement or at least acceptance. We are considering in this situation behaviours which can be described in the broad sense as negative on the one hand and positive on the other.

In my modification of BA I include two categories instead of the single 'disagreeing' of Rackham and Honey. One category is in fact termed 'disagreeing' and is defined as bald, blunt disagreement in which the reasons are not given. The other category is 'disagreeing with reasons' in which as suggested although disagreement occurs, the reasons for doing so are explained fully and rationally.

PROPOSING

Another category which I have also divided into two categories is that of 'proposing'. Recent research by Honey has shown that proposals can be made in two forms. The basic proposing category as defined by Rackham, described the proposals in the form of a statement. For example 'I propose that . . .' or 'I think we should . . .' are typical of proposals which attempt to prescribe what should be done. But proposals can be put in the form of a question: 'What do you think if we . . . . .?' Honey's research has shown that the questioning method – given the category title 'suggesting' – has a greater likelihood of being accepted than statement proposing, a 42% likelihood compared with a 25%.

SEEKING IDEAS

The third modification I have introduced is an additional questioning category 'seeking ideas'. My general observations of group events have shown that when a task was to be performed it was rare if anyone enquired whether there were any ideas or suggestions as to how the task should be tackled. Usually what happened was that the leader or a dominant member came up immediately with a proposal, and on many occasions, whether the proposal was the best one or not, it was accepted without question. However, when ideas were sought it was more common for a number of proposals or suggestions to be offered, with subsequent discussion and agreement. Inclusion of this category confirmed this subjective view and has proved a valuable aspect for discussion when behaviour modification and improvements are being considered.

Obviously, other categories could be added. For example, proposing could be divided into procedure proposing and content proposing; or seeking information could be divided into seeking information, seeking views, seeking opinions and seeking feelings and similarly in the giving category. However, although the greater the number of categories the better defined are the behaviours, the more the categories the greater is the difficulty for the observer to keep up with the interaction and score the contributions effectively. Most people, with reasonable training are capable of coping with a BA of about 11 categories, and my experience on training courses in which BA practice is included, is that a high proportion are capable of obtaining a correlation of .75 or more with a minimum amount of practice following an effective input session.

A different difficulty experienced by obervers new to BA is related to the number of members in the group being observed. With experience, following training, an observer should be able to cope well with a group of six. With groups containing more than six the difficulties of observing efficiently increase, although not proportionately. After all, even in a group of 20 only one person is speaking at a time, *most* of the time. The real problems occur in the larger groups when the activity rate becomes high, a number of people are speaking at once or quickly after each other, or there is a high shutting out rate.

The use of BA is valuable and effective on an individual training course, but even without setting out to undertake serious research a considerable amount of useful data is collected when BAs are obtained for a number of activities.

BEHAVIOUR PATTERNS IN MEETINGS

Neil Rackham and Terry Morgan have conducted research using BA into the behaviour patterns exhibited by groups to determine whether effective groups exhibit particular behaviours in identifiable patterns. The principal emphasis was on the chairmanship function, but information about members also emerged.

The set of behaviour categories used in these studies differed little from the 13 category analysis described earlier, but included the splitting of the proposing category into procedure and content elements as mentioned earlier. But before an effective study could commence, two aspects had to be clarified.

The objective of the study was to determine whether any particular behaviour pattern was observable in meetings with effective chairmanship. In order to satisfy this objective, criteria for the definition of effective chairmanship had to be established. These criteria, or more correctly views, included such values as perceptions of the fairness and efficiency and a good track record of experience in chairing different kinds of meetings. It was agreed that these criteria, and many others that could be used, would be highly subjective and in some cases naive. Forty seven chairmen selected from a number of companies were observed in meetings using the criteria and the 31 achieving the highest scores were selected for further study. At least one meeting of each of the 31 chairmen was attended and a BA completed. Table 4.1 summarises the behaviour pattern observed and also shows the behaviour exhibited in the meetings by the other members.

Table 4.1

Behaviour profile of chairman and non-chairmen

Category	% of behaviour by	
	Chairman	Others
Content proposals	1.8	11.1
Procedural proposals	9.6	2.4
Building	3.2	2.0
Supporting	5.8	15.5
Disagreeing	2.0	8.4
Defending/Attacking	0.1	1.1
Testing understanding	15.2	3.1
Summarising	11.5	0.7
Seeking information	29.1	16.3
Giving information	21.7	39.4

Reproduced from *Behaviour Analysis in Training* by courtesy of the authors Neil Rackham and Terry Morgan (published by McGraw-Hill Book Company (UK) Ltd: now out of print)

The results show an interesting series of comparisons between the chairman and member roles and behaviour patterns which emerged, although care must be taken in using these results in an absolute manner in view of the small sample and the relatively subjective criteria.

Proposals were rather higher from members than from the chair. This would be a welcome approach as the objective of most meetings should be to obtain the views, ideas and proposals for action from the members rather than the chairman. Also the larger proportion of the chairman's proposals were concerned with the running of the meeting rather than the content.

Building was seen to be a behaviour common to both chairman and members but with a slightly higher rate in the case of the chairman. This should be a desirable situation as it signifies that the chairman is listening to the members and their proposals and is using his experience to help these proposals.

The seeking behaviours of testing understanding and seeking

information came out particularly high for the chairman, 44.3% of his total contributions against 21.7% giving information. Seeking and checking the views of his members must certainly form a large part of a chairman's profile, otherwise his inappropriate approach would be reflected in him frequently giving his own views. In most meetings this is not the reason for his being there; if it is the reason, one queries whether there should be a meeting at all.

Summarising emerged, naturally, high at 11.5%, but perhaps from some points of view it may appear too high. I have been present at meetings when the chairman did produce a large number of summaries, and the reaction from the members was 'I wish he'd get on with it instead of keep on going back to what we have agreed'. On the other hand, general observation of many meetings, particularly ineffective ones, suggests that summarising does not normally occur so frequently – perhaps the reason why on so many occasions people are unsure about what has been agreed at the meeting.

The assumption must be that if these were effective chairmen, then these meetings were also effective and the members behaved in a reasonably effective and appropriate manner. The behaviour patterns for the members will therfore suggest an appropriate behaviour pattern, in general terms, for members at meetings.

My own observational data approaches the subject from a different angle. I made no attempt to identify effective meetings and simply recorded the behavioural patterns I observed over a range of decision-making meetings, both on training courses and real-life working meetings. Observations were made of 104 such meetings in the Manpower Services Commission, meetings of other industrial and commercial organisations and also meetings of social organisations. The meetings which related to training courses were those on interpersonal skills courses at a stage before members had received any behavioural feedback and before they had considered any approach to modification of behaviour. The results of these observations are shown in Table 4.2.

The first conclusion which can be drawn from Table 4.2 is that the behaviour pattern for chairmen in the population studied is nearer the pattern established by Rackham than for

Table 4.2
The use of behaviour categories in 104 observed decision making meetings. (% of contributions)

Category	Chairmen	Members
Proposing	10%	5%
Building	1	1
Seeking information	33	14
Giving information	29	55
Summarising	3	1
Supporting	5	6
Open	1	1
Disagreeing (modified definition)	1	1
Attacking, blocking etc.	2	4
Bringing in	10	1
Shutting out	7	10

members, where direct comparison can be made. Proposing by chairmen appeared at 10% compared with 11% in the Rackham study, but this value is somewhat diminished when the 5% proposing rate of members is considered.

Building by both chairmen and members is lower than the Rackham result and this low rate is confirmed by the participants in events who accepted that on these occasions they were not really listening to and taking account of the views of others as much as they should have been doing.

The ratios between seeking and giving, for chairmen, are of the right order, but are badly out of step in the case of members and, although for chairmen the amount of support to maintain neutrality was at the right level, for members direct verbal support was low.

The low level of support among members and their low building content, linked with a relatively high level of such behaviours as disagreeing, blocking, attacking, shutting out and giving information confirmed the low level of listening to others and taking account of their views.

The more appropriate behaviour patterns exhibited by the population surveyed when they are chairmen, reflected the situation that they were mainly of managerial level and were more accustomed to chairing meetings.

BA IN OTHER INTERACTIONS

The discussion of BA so far has been concentrated on the observation of groups and their interactions, but BA techniques can be applied equally to one-to-one interactions. In fact application in this area of observation can be much easier; the observer has to observe only two people. The smaller number of people reduces the numerical problems of the observation, and quite often the contributions made in such interactions are longer in duration. One of the objections aimed at BA when used in group observation is that the observer is so involved in the analysis that he is unable to observe other aspects of the event – this is not strictly true, however, for when an observer becomes experienced in the technique, the analysis does not demand his complete attention. However, for less skilled or less experienced observers the objection has some substance. Another objection is that BA produces an analysis of the content only, not the process of the interaction. This also is quite true, but it must be accepted that BA is used for a particular purpose and with specific objectives, namely to observe and analyse the content of an interaction. If we wish to observe the process we must use an analytical instrument designed for that purpose. There is no observational instrument which can do both tasks fully and effectively.

However, in the one-to-one interactions, as a result of the reduction of pressure on the observer, he is able to be aware of other aspects of the interaction – whether they are non-verbal contributions, the process of the interaction or the effective use of techniques.

If BA is to be used as the observational instrument, a number of variations from the group interaction format are both possible and desirable. The specific categories employed will be in step with the type of interaction observed and the objectives for performing the analysis.

JOB APPRAISAL INTERVIEWS

One of the interview situations for which I have used BA as an observational instrument is job appraisal interview training.

Because I wished to observe for feedback purposes a number of specific behaviours, in addition to more general behaviours, the categories I used were:

- prescribing
- suggesting
- building
- asking for ideas
- asking open questions
- asking closed questions
- asking multiple questions
- asking leading questions
- giving information
- supporting/agreeing
- disagreeing
- testing understanding
- summarising
- negative behaviour (blocking, attacking, difficulty stating)
- shutting out.

Although this list of categories is extensive, 15 in fact, I found little difficulty in coping with the BA in addition to observing the structure of the interview. This was, of course, due to the reduced constraints in having to observe only two people, as described earlier.

Figure 4.2 shows the results of an actual training appraisal interview and demonstrates the behaviour pattern of a not very effective interviewer. The interviewer obviously took a very prescriptive line and made little attempt to really involve the person being appraised. The interviewee made several attempts to break into the appraiser's statements, but with little success and slowly opted out of the interview.

Rackham and Morgan have applied their research approaches using BA to appraisal interviews. Once again the main problem was not in the analysis but in a determination of appraiser effectiveness with which to compare the results. Some of the criteria used were whether the appraisal was judged by the interviewee to have been worthwhile and useful; an improvement in performance by the subordinate following the appraisal, in terms of the number and significance of the

	Appraiser	Interviewee
Prescribing	7	
Suggesting		1
Building		
Asking for Ideas		1
Open questions	2	5
Closed questions	18	5
Multiple questions	9	
Leading questions	12	
Giving Information	28	5
Supporting/Agreeing	1	1
Disagreeing	14	14
Testing Understanding		
Summarising	1	
Negative behaviour	15	12
Shutting out	8	18
	115	62

Figure 4.2   BA of appraisal interview

changes; and finally the action by the interviewer following the
interview. Using these criteria 117 appraisers were identified as
'expert' and a further 61 appraisers were considered on a
random choice basis and classified as 'average'. The 'expert'
group was eventually reduced to 93, of whom 61 produced two
tapes each of appraisal interviews conducted by them, and 32
who produced one tape each, a total of 154 interviews. The
taped interviews were analysed by BA and the summary results
are shown in Table 4.3.

Table 4.3
Behaviour differences between expert
and average appraisers

	% of total behaviour	
	Expert appraisers	Average appraisers
Proposing	8.1	16.2
Building	4.7	1.8
Supporting	11.7	8.3
Disagreeing	7.2	6.8
Defending/Attacking	0.2	1.3
Testing understanding	8.3	3.1
Summarising	6.4	2.3
Seeking information	15.1	12.7
Seeking proposals/solutions	6.4	2.0
Giving internal information	14.9	12.0
Giving external information	17.0	33.5

Reproduced from *Behaviour Analysis in Training* by Neil Rackham and Terry Morgan by kind permission of the authors (published by McGraw-Hill Book Company (UK) Ltd: now out of print)

The summary analysis of Table 4.3 shows a variation of behaviour between the 'expert' and 'average' appraisers in terms of the 'expert'

- making fewer proposals
- using more building behaviour
- testing understanding more often
- summarising more
- asking more questions
- giving less information.

Similar BA approaches can be used to analyse other types of one-to-one interactions, using categories similar to those chosen for the appraisal interview or others selected for varying objectives.

PRESENTATION OF DATA

It is of little value obtaining data if it is not used and the obvious use is to present it in an acceptable form to the people observed. Of course, the actual BA form can be shown as it stands if we are considering singular incidents, but a different approach is necessary if comparisons are required over a number of events.

One obvious method is to present the information in graphical form, and using this approach different behaviours can be plotted against others. The results of the full group can also be included to show members how they stand in relation to others in the group. For example, the difference between the behaviours of giving information and seeking information has valuable implications. These behaviours can be plotted on a graph to present the data in a comparative manner. Figure 4.3 demonstrates this method.

My own approach differs in presenting to my groups on interpersonal skills courses the collection of BA data which has accumulated over a number of activities. Figure 4.4 on page 71 shows an example of the data feedback sheets used with my groups; one is produced for each member of the course.

Each activity in which the member participated is shown with the scoring of the categories from the BA observation. Both the raw numbers of the scoring are included and more importantly, these numbers translated into percentages of the individual's contribution. The figures at the bottom of each activity show the individual's total contributions against the total contributions by the group for that activity. The figure in brackets is the hypothetical average number of contributions in the group for that activity. The final column is the average figure for all the activities giving in crude terms the behaviour pattern for that member.

From the foregoing it will be seen that the observation and analysis of behaviour can take many forms, some simple, some complicated; some giving limited information, others producing a mass of complex data. However, no single form of analysis can produce total information and the different approaches must be considered as aids in the build up of a variety of possible information. Behaviour Analysis, for

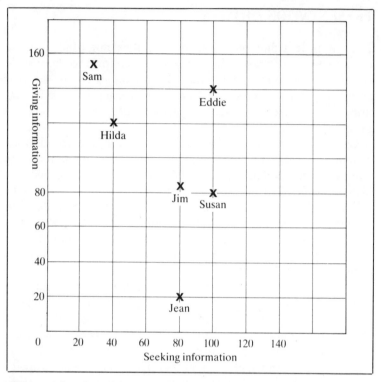

Figure 4.3   Graphical representation of data

example, although providing much valuable information cannot be the only approach and will need to be supplemented by even subjective general observation.

COMPUTER APPLICATION IN DATA PRESENTATION

One of the unfortunate consequences of providing the participants of an interactive skills course with sufficient behavioural data for them to make realistic interpretations on which to base their modifications plans is the amount of data generated. The behaviour analysis of one event is interesting and useful, but it is necessary to provide data over a number of disparate events to produce a behavioural profile for an individual. Immediately the problems of data reduction and provision are multiplied.

Table header: **Activity** (columns A–F)

Category	A	B	C	D	E	F	Average
PROPOSING	2 / 2%	6 / 11%			3 / 16%	1 / 3%	2 / 5%
SUGGESTING	1	1 / 2%					– / –
BUILDING	1	2					– / –
SEEKING IDEAS	1	2					– / –
SEEKING INFORMATION	14 / 14%	9 / 17%	3 / 10%	1 / 3%	4 / 21%	1 / 3%	5 / 11%
TESTING UNDERSTANDING	2	1					1 / 2
GIVING INFORMATION	43 / 43%	23 / 43%	19 / 63%	24 / 77%	7 / 37%	16 / 43%	22 / 50
DISAGREEING WITH REASONS	11				1	1 / 3	2 / 5
SUMMARISING							– / –
SUPPORTING	5 / 5	3 / 6	1 / 3	1 / 3	1 / 5		2 / 5
OPEN	1 / 1			1 / 3			– / –
DISAGREEING	1 / 1					1 / 3	– / –
ATTACKING						2 / 5	– / –
BLOCKING	9 / 9	2 / 4	7 / 23	1 / 3	3 / 16	7 / 19	4 / 9
BRINGING IN	1 / 1	1			2	2 / 5	1 / 2
SHUTTING OUT	12 / 12	6 / 11		4 / 13	5 / 5	6 / 16	5 / 11
Bill	$\frac{101}{396}$ (59)	$\frac{53}{250}$ (36)	$\frac{30}{390}$ (56)	$\frac{31}{249}$ (35)	$\frac{19}{145}$ (21)	$\frac{37}{289}$ (41)	44

Figure 4.4   Presentation of behaviour patterns

71

If a group of eight people has been engaged on a decision-making activity over a period of an hour, the total number of contributions made by the group could be of the order of 480. So we have 480 bits of information about behaviour. But the 480 contributions will be distributed among the eight participants in an irregular manner – say

15   60   45   72   84   25   93   86

Within each individual's total, the number of contributions is divided among the categories of behaviour, the number of categories to be observed having been decided by the analyst.

However, because of the variations in the number of contributions made, these raw numbers are of very little direct use. The individual whose total score was 15 made only 3 proposals whereas the one with 93 contributions made 12. The general implications of this difference are obvious, but to make realistic comparisons the raw numbers have to be converted into ratios or percentages. Thus, the 3-proposal rate of the 15-contributor becomes a proposal rate of 20 per cent of that individual's contributions, whereas the proposals of the 93-scoring individual are shown in their proper perspective of only 13 per cent of those contributions. These calculations have to be made for each category, for each individual – probably some 70 to 80 calculations minimum for each event analysed. If this conversion activity is multiplied by the number of activities analysed, say 7, with other calculations such as the summation of figures, we are considering a total number of calculations of the order of about 650 or more. This represents a considerable number of work-hours if the reductions are to be processed manually. Sometimes this has to be performed in this way with the resultant reduction in 'spare' time for the facilitator during the training event.

Fortunately the availability of computers and micro-computers in the home, office, hotel, conference and training centre is increasing and this facility can be brought into use to eliminate much of the drudgery of manual calculation. Quite simple programs can be provided for the computer to supply the calculations described above. Many more analyses are possible; for example, much wider comparisons can be made of the uses of different behaviours between people or within the repertoire of individuals. A greater degree of comparison of the individual's behaviour vis-à-vis the group profile can be made and different elements of an individual's profile can be demonstrated, rather than the simple overall average produced by manual reductions.

The variety of data feedback formats possible with the computer is very large and there can very easily be the temptation to a maximum output of information. This may be necessary for behavioural research purposes, but in the practical training situation the information must be limited by

- the amount that the trainer can cope with in guiding the learner
- the amount the learner can take in without being confused.

In practice I have found a very suitable range of information to be that described earlier as being produced by manual methods plus perhaps one additional piece for comparison, but obviously this limited information can be produced much more speedily and with less effort on the part of the trainer than if it had to be produced manually.

Figure 4.5 shows a typical printout of this nature for a number of activities, and in effect it duplicates a number of behaviour analysis sheets but with some comparative percentages included.

The vertical column 1 contains the behaviour categories observed during the group activities, and columns 2 and 3 the number of contributions made within the group as a whole; column 3 shows the raw number of contributions against each category and column 2 shows these numbers expressed as a percentage. Columns 4, 5, 6 and 7 show the contributions of each participant in the group under observation. Against each category for each individual three figures are shown. B is the actual raw number of contributions made in each category. A is this figure expressed as a percentage of that individual's total contributions. C is the figure shown at B expressed as a percentage of the group's contributions in that category. For example, in the category 'blocking' the group had 47 contributions of this nature, representing 3 per cent of the group's total contributions. Within this category, Tom's contributions of 13

Behavioural analysis (1)	IPS Course 24 Group % (2)	Total (3)	Activities 1-6 Tom (4)	Dick (5)	Mary (6)	Group A Jane (7)
PROP	11	160	(A)8	12	5	14
			(B)25	60	10	65
			(C)16	38	6	41
SUGG	2	22	1	3	1	–
			4	15	1	2
			18	68	5	9
BUILD	1	19	2	2	–	–
			6	12	–	1
			32	63	–	5
SKG ID	1	14	1	2	1	–
			2	10	1	1
			14	71	7	7
SKG INF	10	143	1	21	–	4
			20	105	–	18
			14	73	–	13
TU	2	33	2	4	1	–
			6	22	3	2
			18	67	9	6
GVG INF	40	600	39	32	63	38
			125	160	139	176
			21	27	23	29
DIS/REASONS	7	102	11	3	2	10
			35	15	4	48
			34	15	4	47
SUMM	1	7	–	1	–	–
			1	6	–	–
			14	86	–	–
SUPP	8	114	9	8	16	1
			30	42	36	6
			26	37	32	5
OPEN	1	13	1	–	4	–
			2	1	9	1
			15	8	69	8
DISAG	3	46	2	–	4	7
			6	–	8	32
			13	–	17	70
BLOCK	3	47	4	1	1	6
			13	4	2	28
			28	9	4	60
ATT	1	19	1	–	–	4
			2	–	–	17
			11	–	–	89
BRING IN	2	27	1	4	1	1
			2	21	1	3
			7	78	4	11
SHUT OUT	9	134	13	4	3	14
			41	22	6	65
			31	16	4	49
		(D)1500	320	495	220	465
			(E)21	33	15	13

Figure 4.5   Behavioural data printout

actual blocks represented 4 per cent of his total contributions and 28 per cent of the blocking contributions made within the group.

D is the total number of contributions made within the group followed by the individual raw number of contributions for each participant. *E* shows the total contributions of each learner expressed as a percentage of the group contributions.

Of course, the computer is capable of a much more extensive analysis than shown in this example and for research purposes the program would be written to take acccount of this. However, even the limited analysis demonstrated gives considerable information on which a learner might base any behaviour modification plans.

The computer is a mixed blessing, offering advantages and disadvantages. The principal advantage is clearly the facility for speedy and complex analysis once the program has been written and the behavioural data fed into the computer. This latter requirement is, however, the principal disadvantage since, as with any program, the data have to be coded and fed into the computer. Because of the large volume of small amounts of data required to be coded and entered, the preliminary operations can take up a considerable amount of time. In fact, by the time this action is taken, much of the simple analysis could have been performed by a skilled, manual operator.

REFERENCES AND RECOMMENDED READING

Cooper, C.L. (Ed.) (1981): *Improving Interpersonal Relations.* Aldershot: Gower.

Dyer, D.A. and Giles, W.J. (1974): 'Improving Skills in Working with People: Interaction Analysis'. *Training Information Paper No. 7.* London: HMSO.

Honey, P. (1976): *Face to Face.* Institute of Personnel Management.

Phillips, K. and Fraser, T. (1982): *The Management of Interpersonal Skills Training.* Aldershot: Gower.

Rackham, N. and Morgan, T. (1977): *Behaviour Analysis in Training.* Maidenhead: McGraw-Hill.

Rackham, N., Honey, P. et al. (1971): *Developing Interactive Skills*. Wellens.

Rae, W.L. (1983): *The Skills of Training*. Aldershot: Gower.

Rae, W.L. (1978): 'Behaviour Analysis in ESA Training'. *Industrial and Commercial Training*, 10 (5).

Stewart, V. and Stewart, A. (1978): *Managing the Manager's Growth*. Aldershot: Gower.

5 Interpersonal skills training

Although human relations training can cover the wide range of subjects mentioned in Chapter 1, most of this training includes both particular skills in the use of techniques and the behaviours associated with them. For example, training in discipline interviewing looks at the structure of such an interview, the technical side of an interview – methods of questioning, reflecting and so on – and the behaviours necessary to induce the appropriate reactions from the inter- viewee.

The purer form of human relations training is concerned with the behaviourally interactive factors only, the behaviour – what is causing it, what it is and what effects does it have. Factors of this nature are more universal in application and can link with any other more technical approaches. Training in this mode is commonly referred to as interpersonal skills, or equally interactive skills, social skills or even simply human relations.

The approaches to interpersonal skills training are even more numerous and more varied than the descriptions applied to them, and vary considerably according to the philosophy and personal approach of the individual trainer. This, of course, is one of the problems of acceptance that human relations training has experienced. There are many human relations trainers who are absolutely sincere and skilled in their approaches, but there are a number who present this form of training for what may be described as selfish reasons. Rarely do events run by the latter group produce credible and effective learning experiences and the reputation of human relations training suffers. Fortunately these cases are rare.

Because of the many variations possible, one cannot suggest a set approach to interpersonal skills training, nor even a recommended format. It may be useful if I share my own experiences in this form of training over a number of years. This sharing of experience may help you to decide on your own approach to human relations training. Just as many of the methods I use are not original, feel free to borrow any of my ideas which may be new to you. After all, training is based on plagiarism and would have made no progress without this healthy exercise!

The interpersonal skills course with which I have been involved for some years now, has changed considerably over this period of time. Some of the changes have been the result of consistent feedback from the participants, others from my own feelings and observation of what I considered to be effective and appropriate. Apart from the major changes to the format and content, there has been an almost constant change in more minor aspects. In many ways each course in interpersonal skills is different as each group is a collection of different individuals and consequently each group develops differently during a course. These variations are for me one of the major attractions of interpersonal skills training – each course, each group is different in some way or other and consequently you cannot become bored as with a repetitive form of training. However, this variation and indeed uncertainty of what lies ahead with a group, may not appeal to all those who may be responsible for human relations training, preferring a more predictable and 'safe' atmosphere for their training events.

There has also been a more personal reason for some of the variations. In my trainer's 'tool kit' I have a large number of exercises and activities which are appropriate for this type of training. After using a particular activity for two or three courses, I change the activity for the next two or three courses, not because the initial activity does not satisfy the objectives for the overall activity, but I know that if I had to sit through the same activity again, *I* would become bored! Additionally of course there is always the possibility that a constant activity may become known prior to the course to the potential participants and in some cases may consequently lose its impact.

My interpersonal skills training approach has undergone three important changes during the principal period it has run. The present Mark 3 is in my view the most effective in most cases, but Mark 2 has not been completely superseded as in some cases it may be a more appropriate approach.

INTERPERSONAL SKILLS MARK 1

Mark 1 was the most adventurous and as such was not a complete success in helping the people who came for help. I think that this was due to the setting of objectives which could not be achieved in the short period of a week.

The stated objectives for the Mark 1 course were to:

1) Increase the awareness of an individual in his own behaviour.
2) Increase the awareness of an individual in the effects of his behaviour on others.
3) Increase the awareness of an individual in the behaviour of others and the effects of that behaviour on himself.
4) Increase the awareness of an individual in the behaviour of others and the effects of these behaviours on others.

These awarenesses would relate specifically to working in groups and one-to-one interactions, particularly counselling interactions.

5) Give the participants the opportunity and means to modify their behaviour where this might be appropriate.
6) Increase awareness of intergroup behaviour and relationships and give the course members the opportunity to improve, as necessary, any problems in this area.

The content of this version of the course included a number of group activities intended to encourage the participants to behave and to observe the behaviour of each other; guidance on the techniques of counselling interviews was followed by one-to-one practice of this form of interaction; at least two opportunities for intergroup interactions; and encouragement

to consider and practise modificatio   viour. All this was
contained in a week's course comn   day Monday
and finishing at midday Friday.

The course normally contained 12   e   who for most of
the time were separated into two groups   6 each under the
facilitative guidance of a trainer. Most of the technique input
sessions were conducted with the whole group and, with the
exception of an early activity, the activities took place in the
small groups. The division into two groups enabled behaviour
analysis to be performed on each group and encouraged more
intimate relationships to develop than would have been
possible in the group of 12. The existence of two groups
working separately most of the time and the development for
each group of a group identity and cohesiveness, set the scene
for intergroup interactions with varying elements of competition and conflict.

The one-to-one counselling interactions were preceded by an
input session on the structure and techniques for an interview
of this nature. To save duplication, the input session was
conducted with the complete group. Again, the division into
two, almost stranger groups was beneficial as it allowed a
pairing of a member from each group for the practice
interviews, closely simulating real life. Case studies were used
initially in the practice, but the members were encouraged to
introduce personal problems for counselling, if they felt that
they could open to this extent.

The format of the course had many advantages and at the
least the members were introduced to a wide range of
interpersonal situations. However, it was in this wide range of
situations and events that the principal disadvantages occurred.
Primarily, because of this wide range and the restricted amount
of time, although an introduction to many interpersonal events
was possible, there was insufficient time to deal effectively and
fully with any of them. Even more problematical was the
disadvantage that although awareness of behaviours and the
problems which could arise were ventilated and an increase of
behaviour was exhibited, there was rarely the opportunity for
any attempts at modification.

Although the participants made no criticisms about the latter
disadvantages as seen from the point of view of the course

arranger, there were comments on the restricted time available for the various aspects. On a number of occasions, discussion had to be cut short to allow necessary movement to the next section of the course, and at the one-to-one stage, typical comments about the counselling were: 'Great, but we wanted more time to get down to the personal problems we have and to counsel them through. And, OK counselling interactions, but what about dealing with grievance, discipline, selection and appraisal interviews in the same way?'. Obviously there was insufficient time to include these aspects and there was no possibility of extending the time allowed for the training.

The inclusion of too much material and too extensive objectives is a common failing when introducing a new form of training. But it was all good experience and I took account of the lessons which emerged from the practice.

INTERPERSONAL SKILLS MARK 2a

These lessons learned during the Mark 1 course resulted in Interpersonal Skills training course Mark 2, or as will be seen later, really Mark 2a.

The main modification made to the Mark 1 version to produce the Mark 2 course was to find more time for a smaller range of topics. The reduction was achieved by omitting any specific reference and activity which was relevant to one-to-one interactions. The point was made however, that much of the appropriate behaviour exhibited in a group could be transferred to the other interactive modes. It was, however, recognised that one-to-one interpersonal interactions were as important to many people as were group behaviours. Consequently a separate learning event was produced to help with this important field of human relations. The new course included the behavioural aspects, the structures and techniques of dealing with problems relating to individual employees: counselling, grievance, discipline and correction, and the handling and resolution of conflict. Appraisal interviewing was covered in a separate course which looked overall at the reporting system.

But back to Interpersonal Skills Training Mark 2. The

objectives originally set were now reduced and more time was released for group activities, and more particularly the analysis and discussion following the activities. This appraisal was conducted principally by the participants, with the tutor/facilitator coming in only if invited or if he felt that, from his privileged observational viewpoint the group had failed to be aware of a particularly significant event or incident. The additional time also permitted a greater amount of flexibility and on most occasions the group was invited to prescribe its own time limits for many of the activities, and certainly for the appraisal periods.

The physical structure for the course remained, with a total of 12 members who were divided at an early stage into two groups, each with its own tutor and 'home' room. Much less emphasis was placed on the need for the groups to come together for common sessions and the groups remained apart for a large proportion of the week. The separation of the groups was a useful aid in attempts to achieve one of the remaining objectives – the behaviours and interactions between groups.

At the start of the course, the group was approached for introductory purposes as a full group, but immediately after the opening session it was divided into the two, pre-determined 'family' groups. Within these groups the members performed one or two 'getting to know you' types of activities during which the initial stages of group development and cohesiveness were able to develop. But before the end of the first day, the two groups were brought together for a full group decision-making activity. A number of structured exercises were available for this activity, most of them based on the requirements for a group decision from information held but shared among the group. The information supplied to each participant is different. Different, not to the extent of being false, but each participant does not receive *all* the necessary information. However, all the necessary information is held within the total group. A typical exercise of this nature is entitled 'Urania' and involves a group acting as a selection committee deciding on the most suitable applicant for a particular job from the details provided.

This activity, although performed in the full group, acts as a catalyst in introducing intergroup interactions. The division into two groups early in the course and the initial 'family' group activities exhibit themselves in a division in the full group activity. The participants have usually seated themselves in close proximity, at least the group which had remained in the room to which the other group had to return for the activity. This divisive orientation forced the incoming group to take the seats remaining, usually together. The division was exhibited within the full group by mutual support among the members of a 'family' group and some element of conflict with the 'other' group.

During the third day of the course, the aspects of intergroup rivalry were demonstrated, and effectively encouraged, by an intergroup activity. This activity was the Controlled Pace Activity introduced by Neil Rackham.

CONTROLLED PACE ACTIVITY

The process of a controlled pace activity can take a number of forms, but has as the universal basis the negotiation of a specific aspect between two groups, but negotiation with a number of constraints.

The first constraint is the location of the two groups in separate rooms with an additional constraint that any communication between the groups can be in writing only. This restriction in itself controls to some extent the pace of the negotiation, but there is a further control in the requirement on the groups to categorise each written contribution.

Earlier in the course, the course members had been introduced to Behaviour Analysis and the language of behaviour categorisation. When one group sent a message to the other group, before sending the message the group was required to categorise the contribution and record it. On receipt of the message, the receiving group, before reacting to the message had to agree the category they considered to be represented by the message. The agreed category was then recorded and each individual of the group was required to produce a reply. The various replies would be considered and one, or a composite message, would be agreed. However, before this reply was sent it would be recorded and categorised. The whole process was then repeated as many times as necessary until the negotiation was completed.

Following the activity an in-depth discussion took place in which the progress of the process was analysed from the records of the categorised messages. An important aspect was always the misinterpretation of a message by the group receiving the message, compared with the category in which the sending group thought their message was contained.

Commonly, the atmosphere between the groups hardened as proposals and counter-proposals flowed between them. Obviously this conflict was encouraged by the separation of the groups, the dangers of misinterpretation of the written word and the two group identities which had developed. All of these built up into an intergroup suspicion which produced a very realistic and lively interaction.

In an activity of this nature, the subject of negotiation does not need to be a serious one, but it must be real, negotiatable and enforceable. As the activity was held on the course immediately after lunch, the brief given for the negotiation was: 'At the tea break this afternoon, there will be seven cups of tea. Your task is to negotiate who shall receive the cups of tea and to negotiate alternatives for those who will not receive a cup. The results of this negotiation will be enforced'.

As there were twelve course members, this meant that many variations in the negotiation were possible. The subject of the negotiation appears so simple and almost childlike. Some courses very quickly resolved the task in spite of the constraints, but the vast majority fell into the traps and made the negotiation difficult and protracted. I wonder how many readers can imagine a group of twelve adults arguing, in writing, over who should receive the tea or acceptable alternatives from 2 pm to 4.30 pm, as happened on one occasion! In order to achieve this painful process, typical messages included such contributions as 'Rubbish'.

The final event which was intended to demonstrate and give practice in intergroup behaviours and interactions, took place on the Thursday afternoon. Each group, again separated in their 'family' rooms, but with no constraints imposed, were asked to perform four tasks.

1) To produce on newsprint twelve adjectives describing the other group.
2) To produce on newsprint twelve adjectives which the group thinks the other group will use to describe themselves.
3) To produce on newsprint twelve adjectives which the group thinks the other group will use to describe them.
4) To produce on newsprint twelve adjectives describing themselves.

The groups were then asked to exchange with each other whichever lists they wished and then take any action they felt necessary.

The possible results varied widely from the two groups getting together to co-operate before the lists were completed, to almost complete secrecy on what each had produced. The interactions resulting from this activity at times continued almost to the end of the course the following day.

When the Mark 2a course was being appraised for success or otherwise, the results of the intergroup interactions became the major cause for concern. On occasions so much conflict arose, conflict which was difficult to resolve and build upon in the time available. This resulted certainly in awareness, but no opportunity to practise behaviour modification. The intergroup problems also produced the danger that individual behaviour modification fell apart in the trauma of the intergroup conflict before it had been consolidated.

None of these conflicts, interactions and problems is undesirable in human relations training terms, but to resolve them and permit practice of more appropriate behaviour, time is necessary. Within the constraints of the course, this time was not available. Also, the introduction of intergroup events could be considered to be artificial and could disrupt the internal development of each group and individual in a prescriptive manner. All these problems occur in real life, but in that environment not every behavioural problem has to be solved within five days!

With these problems in mind, further modifications were considered and the result was Mark 2b. It had become obvious during the progress of the Mark 2a version that two aspects of the course needed attention – the problems related directly to intergroup events and the time restrictions which interfered with the opportunities for behaviour modification practice. The Mark 2b version was maintained, with minor variations for some two years or so, and was found to be a successful model to follow.

INTERPERSONAL SKILLS MARK 2b

DAY 1

The course in this version, which is still used when it has been assessed that it is the most appropriate approach for a particular group, has a similar initial construction to the earlier version. After the introductory session, the full group of twelve is divided into two groups of six each with a facilitator, and unless the groups decide otherwise, they do not come together again. In effect we have two courses running side by side with two tutors, but unlike two separate courses there is always the facility for interactive events. The two groups follow a basically similar pattern, certainly to the same end result, but specific detailed operation can and does vary considerably between the groups.

Once the two groups have separated, the development process of the group is started. A natural starter is to have the group members introduce themselves in some way. The traditional method of doing this is known in the training world as the 'creeping death'. Starting at one end of the row, U-shape, or whatever in which the trainees are seated, each member introduces himself. This introduction continues in sequence to the last member of the group. This method is rarely successful as once a speaker has introduced himself his listening to others is reduced as a result of his relief in having got his turn over. While a member is waiting to speak his listening is reduced as he is thinking more about what he is going to say himself.

A variation of the creeping death can have rather better results, although there are still problems. The same procedure of sequential self-introduction is followed, but, instead of following the absolute sequence, the tutor leads the introduction by selecting individuals to speak. The selection in this case is random and consequently the attention of individuals is held to a greater extent as no one knows who will be picked on next. Of course, there is still the problem that once a randomly chosen introducer has spoken, he may switch off.

A number of other approaches were considered and eventually an effective model was developed. Following the emphasis of the course as a trainee-centred event, the introductions activity was turned over to the trainees and they were given a brief to discuss and decide upon an acceptable (to them) method of introductions, and then to perform it. This approach served two purposes: one of course effected the introductions in a way which was acceptable to the group; the other as an initial event in starting the individuals talking to each other, behaving as individuals and a group, and developing as a group.

Continuing the objectives mentioned above – talking together, behaving and developing – the next activity is one particularly designed to start the opening-up process. The group is given a selection of topics on which to hold mini discussions, control of the depth of discussion being vested in the group, as is the time control. The range of possible topics is wide and can include such subjects as:

- objectives for coming on the course
- major interpersonal strength or problem
- things they like or dislike doing or saying
- feelings on entering a new group
- feelings on entering this group
- feelings about the group at this early stage and so on.

By the end of the mini topics activity the group has started positively on the steps to a more open development, each individual has a reasonable amount of information about the attitudes and feelings of the others, and all are rather more ready to disclose a little more than purely superficial information. The end of the activity usually signals the end of the first day.

DAY 2

During the activities of the previous day, the group has usually not performed very effectively. Usually the failings are in the areas of a poor use of time, ineffective organisation, quite often in not electing a leader or chairman, and most of the other barriers to effective group working. In order to help the process of easing the group development, the group is invited to reflect on the activities of the previous day, to determine the factors that helped or hindered the process, and to produce guidelines for the group to work to for the remainder of the week. The guidelines produced are posted prominently in the training room as a constant reminder during the course.

Other than requiring the group to complete the task, no constraints are placed on the group, including the use of time. As a consequence no timetabling is introduced since each group requires a different amount of time depending on how much they need to consider and agree on their guidelines.

This flexibility is the keynote of the Mark 2b course, not in terms of the tutor opting out, but so that the group can become aware of the need to use time effectively by the efficient use of the group process. In an atmosphere of this nature, no specific programme can be set by the tutor, for, in addition to giving the group control over the time they use over activities, the group is also invited to make the week as learner-centred as they wish. Obviously the tutor must have a general plan available to lead to achievement of the objectives, but having made the offer of group direction, he must honour this agreement. He must also make himself available as a resource to the group either as an expert in particular aspects or to provide activities.

However, in this early stage of the course, few groups are willing to take the lead and look to the tutor for a certain amount of guidance. This is a natural sequence in the classic development of a group, so the tutor must have a plan of movement to offer. He must also be aware of the dangers of his over-involvement which might result in the group's over-dependance on him which might delay their development.

At this stage a further activity is offered to allow the group to operate as a developing group, use the guidelines produced and use the activity to increase awareness of group processes and behaviours. A common activity offered at this stage is one which asks the group to consider a number of factors which make for effective group or team working and, after agreeing the factors by consensus, compare these agreed results with the present state of the group itself.

An activity of this kind can either be an end in itself or can lead the group to take up for discussion and agreement other aspects of their own existence. The latter reaction is quite common and the group makes considerable progress during the remainder of the day in terms of awareness of their interactions, increased openness of personal disclosure and feedback.

Feedback is encouraged at the end of the day with the offer by the tutor of an activity which gives members an opportunity to give positive and direct feedback to each other on how they are viewed by others. It is rare for this activity to be refused, for by this stage in the course the members are usually hungry for as much information about themselves as possible.

The activity takes the form of each member completing on each other member of the group a rating for a number of behavioural aspects. Typical behaviour categories on which they can rate each other can include 'helpful–unhelpful', 'active–inactive' and so on. Categories similar to those used in Behaviour Analysis can also be used. A number of instruments of this nature exist with a variety of approaches, some very safe, some very emotive. The views are given in written ratings which are then exchanged so that each member can summarise the views of him as expressed by his peers. An example of 'Wad some Pow'r the giftie gie us'.

The information given in this way must, by necessity, be restricted in view of the relatively short time that the individuals have known each other. However, even this short period of acquaintance is often longer than that with many people with whom one comes into contact, and who form immediate impressions.

Discussion on the summarised information is left to the group and usually the members are content, after a short discussion, to take the results away to contemplate privately.

DAY 3

Following individual contemplation overnight, supplemented by some informal exchange of reactions in the bar during the evening, the members are usually ready to have a discussion as a group on the results. They are given their head on this discussion and the depth of comment will depend on the level of open feedback the group has achieved.

By this point of the course, the group is usually at an uncertain stage of its development, is searching for a number of answers, and is not sure how it can progress. It feels that it should know more than it does and should be able to do something positive.

This is the point when the tutor can usefully come out of the shadows and present a practical input session on behaviour awareness and methods of behaviour analysis. A description of BA and practice in this technique gives the members a common behavioural language and a method of increasing observational awareness. The session also prepares the group members for the feedback in BA terms on their behaviour during the week, that is programmed for later in the day.

The group then takes part in either an activity of its own choosing or one provided by the tutor. The actual activity has little importance. What is significant is that during the activity the members are now aware much more of their behaviour, are signalling their behaviours or making them more apparent and starting to behave in a more appropriate manner. Even more significant is the group's appraisal of its activity and the increased openness of feedback given one to the other. Equally important, the feedback is starting to be given in more acceptable terms. Rather than saying 'You have annoying mannerisms', the feedback is more likely to be in terms of 'When you do certain things, these stop me from behaving effectively'. The time is now ripe and the group is ready and wanting more definite feedback on its behaviour, as a group and as individuals.

From the start of the course the tutor has taken a very low key approach and, apart from providing activities for the group to use, has intervened at significant junctures only, usually when the group is in danger of missing an important happening.

But in addition he has been completing a BA of every group activity, discussion and appraisal session in order to build up a behaviour pattern for each individual as the course has progressed.

The general advice given to all new tutors is that feedback should follow immediately after the event and this is certainly sound advice for most situations. However, I believe that this general approach should be treated with some caution as far as behaviour analysis is concerned. I see dangers in giving immediate BA feedback in the early stages of an interpersonal skills course, particularly on a course such as the one currently being described, and also on many other kinds of courses where behavioural feedback is necessary. Until the session which includes a description of BA and its uses, the members are not aware of the significances exposed in BA and consequently are not in a position to take full advantage of the data. But more importantly, the observation of one event can give a completely misleading impression of an individual's overall behaviour. On that singular occasion the individual may have been active or inactive, highly reactive or non-reactive for a variety of reasons – lack of interest, lack of knowledge, illness and so on. It is only when the BA data collected over a number of activities is collated that a more universal image of the individual's behaviour *pattern* can emerge. This pattern must of course be produced as an average behaviour in which there can be wide variations, but it does give a strong indication to the person as to his more preferred behaviour.

The behavioural data gathered to this stage is now presented to the group members. Presentation is preceded by a short input about behaviour patterns and their appropriateness, and the patterns of the group and individuals are displayed so that information can be shared and compared. This display is of course only with the group's agreement, but I have never encountered disagreement since by this stage the group and individual attitudes have developed to permit a high level of openness.

Individual data sheets have also been prepared and these are distributed following a discussion on the portrayal of the group information. The individual data sheets are usually in the form of Figure 4.4 (page 71). It is normal for some discussion to follow the issue of the data, after its initial digestion and often recovery from shock. This discussion usually leads to the questioning of the group about what the individuals feel they might have to do now in terms of behavioural modification as a result of the information they now hold in addition to any other feedback they have received.

The evening of this day of the course is usually one in which the individuals consider their data and, with or without informal discussion with their colleagues, assess the implications and start the process of considering behaviour modification.

DAY 4/DAY 5

On the morning of day 4 of the course the members usually reconvene in a contemplative mood and are motivated to consider seriously plans for behaviour modification. This is encouraged and the suggestion is made that they take time off to consider, to produce plans and to write down these plans. Many of the items are common to the group and encouragement, if necessary, is given for the group to share the plans and perhaps produce a group plan. Sharing of information and modification plans is often essential as much of the inappropriate behaviour can be seen in the behaviour patterns of all or most of the group. The plans can be retained as individually known plans or can be posted on the walls of the training room in a sharing experience.

In a typical course information may show that all are high on blocking and shutting-out, very high on giving information, low on seeking information and very low on seeking ideas and building. Most of the group may decide as individuals to modify all these behaviours. Very little group harm would result if blocking and shutting-out and some degree of just giving information were reduced. But to balance these there would be a greater need to have more seeking ideas, seeking information and building. The consequence could be that everybody would be asking everybody else what they thought, and as building requires initial proposals, the generation of ideas would suffer. An anomalous and ridiculous situation. The personal modification plans, for at least the remaining time on the course, must therefore be balanced with the needs of the group, although modifications to the behaviour pattern of an individual can be borne in mind for his return to his real life work groups.

Opportunities must be given for the members to try to put into practice their new insight into their behaviour. In addition to any activity which the group itself decides to perform, there is usually time for a major activity suggested by the tutor. This is titled 'Where are we now?'. The objectives of this activity are, taking into account all the feedback and data the members have been given or have given each other, that they should:

- consider the stage of development of the group and individuals
- identify the elements which have helped or hindered this developmental process
- give each other realistic and helpful feedback
- practise plans for behaviour modification
- consider what improvements still need to be made and how these can be produced.

This activity usually continues to the end of day 4 and frequently spills over into day 5, the last morning of the course. It is also during this activity that the groups who have been working along separate paths all week may decide to come together to operate as one large group and practise their behaviour in a new environment. Commonly, however, one group only has progressed to this stage and its proposing advances are rejected by the other group during day 4 afternoon or even day 5 morning. The rationale for rejection is usually expressed in terms of the group still needing time to examine its own problems rather than have the addition of intergroup or large group complications.

DAY 5

The morning of day 5, when the course ends at midday, cannot be pre-planned in any way as so much depends on the progress of each group. It can take the form of, as suggested above, an intergroup activity; a large single group activity; or more commonly the two groups separately continue their 'Where are we now?' activity. Alternatively, either as two groups or one large one, such subjects as the clarification or extension of events which have occurred during the course can be raised, or some action can take place on aspects not covered or those over which there is still some doubt.

But whatever the sequence of events, the tutor's contract with the groups is that before members leave they will have arranged time to sit down to produce 'Action Plans', which can put into effect back at work the learning achieved during the week.

An interpersonal skills training format of this nature puts considerable stress on a tutor, or more correctly facilitator. He cannot plan a programme to which there will be strict adherence; he must have the ability to sit quietly for long periods but to be in an observing role ready to intervene *when he judges it is relevant to do so*; he must be skilled in BA and the production of factual analysis to feedback; he must be skilled in giving feedback; he must have a wide range of relevant activities to offer or suggest; his own interpersonal skills must be high or defensible if apparently inappropriate on occasions; and he must have the skill of not intervening and prescribing even though the group appears lost or to be taking the wrong direction. And many more attributes . . . . . .

6 A model IST course

Towards the end of 1981 I decided to assess the operation of my interpersonal skills training for a number of reasons:

- training needs to be constantly re-assessed
- the Mark 2b model had been operating for some time
- I was uneasy about some aspects of the course
- however successful any form of training may be, it can always be improved.

Much of my concern was subjectively based as, within the many constraints of evaluating human relations training, any validation and evaluation which was performed had shown that the training was achieving a good measure of success. But I felt that several areas existed where improvements might be made, based on my own observations of the process and the accumulated comments of many participants.

The first area which gave me some cause for consideration was that, as with the majority of courses, the early stages were very slow and the participants did not seem to be really coming to terms with what they were learning until the end of day 3. This hesitation in itself is acceptable since it demonstrates the difficulties learners have in coming to terms with behavioural attitudes and practices. But for progress to be made in an acceptable way, a considerable amount of time is necessary. This period of time was not available nor was an extension of the time available for the training.

The second concern was related to the closing stages of the course. The learning events, appraisal of activities and other feedback means are excellent in improving the awareness of the participants in all the required directions. But the crunch of human relations training, in company with most other forms of training, is not just what is learned, but what action is taken following the learning.

During the Mark 2b course some little time is given to behaviour modification and there is a varying amount of time given for practice, most of the time restrictions being due to the activities of the members themselves. As mentioned earlier, the 'Where are we now?' activity continued on occasions almost to the closing minutes of the course. This problem of restricted time following the awareness stage was the subject of many of the comments made as criticism of the course.

In summary, time seemed to be the major problem and constraint. The course could not be extended in time, so other ways of approaching the problem had to be sought. One solution that was favoured strongly among the ones proposed, was to introduce a greater degree of control into the process, but without being over-prescriptive, without curtailing much of the freedom of the members and without introducing many more formal sessions.

The benefits to the course organisation of this possible solution were that a more structured approach would be possible, the learners would have a clearer idea of what was still to come, a greater emphasis could be placed on 'what do you do now that you are aware' and the transfer of learning could have a more prominent place in the learning event.

The principal – perhaps only – disadvantage was a restriction on the flexibility of the course, but although this had seemed to be an advantage in earlier versions of the training, flexibility had turned out to be the major disadvantage.

A programme was produced and one method of checking it out was to discuss it with people who had attended the previous types of course. Without exception, although these views had to be treated with some caution, they said that they felt it would produce a better learning course than the one they had attended, even though they had appreciated the almost complete learner-centredness. So the Mark 3 version was introduced in 1981. This version, after several minor modifications, is still running successfully. However, as mentioned earlier, if during the progress of the course, a modification of the approach is necessary, with the agreement of the group, the Mark 2b version, or a modification thereof is introduced. In view of the more structured approach the two-group division was found to be not necessary and normally the course now consists of eight participants with one tutor. The restriction to eight students is controlled by the optimum size of a working group and the reasonable number of people on which behaviour analysis can be completed over a long period.

The programme which follows shows the changes made for the Mark 3 version. The activities and sessions marked * are new material and are described later in the chapter.

DAY 1
2.00 – 3.00   Introductory session and explanation of the programme.
3.15 – 4.00   Introductory behaviour activity.*
4.00 – 5.15   Mini topics discussion.
5.15 – 6.30   Learning styles questionnaire.*

DAY 2
9.00 – 11.30   Working in teams activity.
11.30 – 12.30 Group appraisal of activity.
12.30 – 12.45 Group effectivness audit.*
2.00 – 3.00   Behavioural, decision-making activity.
3.15 – 4.30   Group appraisal of activity.
4.30 – 5.00   Discussion of awareness and perception.
5.00 – 6.30   Exchange of views on observed behaviours within group.
Evening.   Individual consideration of feedback from remainder of group.

DAY 3
9.00 – 10.45   Co-counselling activity.*
10.45 – 12.30 ⎫ Input session on behaviour awareness and
2.00 – 2.45   ⎬ observation, including techniques of behaviour analysis. Session includes practice in conducting BA using taped meeting extracts.
2.45 – 3.45   Preparation for joint meeting activity.*
3.45 – 4.45   Joint meeting activity.*

4.45 – 5.30   Group appraisal of activity.
5.30 – 6.30   Discussion of models of effective and appropriate behaviour and feedback of observed behavioural data.
Evening.   Individual consideration of BA data feedback.

DAY 4
9.00 – 10.00   Planning behaviour modification.*
10.15 – 11.30 Objective setting in interactions, including case study practice.*
11.30 – 12.15 Feedback and discussion of case study results.
12.15 – 12.45 Group effectiveness audit.
2.00 – 2.45   Preparation for 'Where are we now?' activity.
2.45 – end   'Where are we now?' activity.
Evening.   Individual preparation for learning transfer.

DAY 5
9.00 – 10.00   Clarification and bringing up to date session.
10.15 – 11.30 Learning transfer and action planning.*
11.30 – 12.00 Course roundup and validation.

INTRODUCTORY BEHAVIOUR ACTIVITY

This approach is yet another version to replace the 'creeping death' type of introduction, but in this case one which puts the onus on the participants and fulfils an additional objective of starting the group talking and opening up with each other.

The opening session of the course ends at a natural break stage with a cup of tea, taken away from the training room. While the group is engaged in this 'activity', the tutor places the members' nameplates on different seats in, with a group of eight, three sub-groups of 3, 3 and 2. The placement selection is purely random and is produced by shuffling the nameplates and dealing out, as it were, three hands.

When the group returns and the members find their new positions, usually without argument, they are given the task of determining why the sub-group selection was made in the way that has given the members their new locations.

Sufficient time is then given for the sub-groups to discuss the task and come to some conclusions. In the majority of cases the individuals disclose to each other a reasonable amount of information about themselves in order to try to determine the common factors. Usually about 15 minutes or so is necessary for this stage.

A useful discussion can follow the activity in which it can be determined:

- what conclusions were reached
- how these conclusions were reached
- the processes involved in reaching the conclusions
- the feelings of the members when they returned to the rearranged room
- the reactions of the members to the tutor for having done this to them.

When these issues have been resolved, the final question to be raised is whether the group requires anything else in the way of introductions. Usually this is requested, so the group is asked to decide what form of additional introduction it wants, and then to carry out what it has decided. It is not surprising in view of the early stage of the group development that most groups opt for a fairly traditional type of introduction, and in fact voluntarily operate the 'creeping death' approach. However, a recent group decided that it wanted no further introductions as it appreciated that any comments would be superficial and felt that real introductions would emerge as the course progressed.

The reactions of groups to this approach are normally that they accept the activity, discuss themselves and come up with a variety of solutions for the moves, including the right answer. However, the tutor can always expect surprises. On a recent course, when the group returned from tea, one of the members on seeing that his nameplate had been moved refused to sit in his new seat. Perhaps 'refused' is too strong a word as this implies that the tutor tried to force him to change – this was not so. In fact, I immediately agreed to his not changing and gave the impression that I had considered the non-move and saw that it would make no major difference to the 'overall plan'. What became interesting was that immediately after the activity the member was challenged by several other members as to why he had taken that stance and they showed that they had felt embarrassment for me. A very open discussion resulted from this and information and feelings emerged which would not normally have emerged at that stage of the course.

LEARNING STYLES QUESTIONNAIRE

This particular audit of the preferred styles of individual learners introduced by Peter Honey and Alan Mumford has been described in Chapter 2. On my course, the questionnaire is presented with a minimum of description. Following completion of the questionnaire the results are scored by the members themselves, but with the group agreement the results are shared and are posted on the training room wall for the duration of the course so that reference can be made as required.

In my experience, it is very rare that individuals reject the results to any significant degree. If this occurs, quite often the attitude is reversed at a later stage in the course when the individual becomes more aware of his behaviour and attitudes. One particular case I can remember was of a course member whose audit indicated a very strong preference for the Theorist mode, compared with low preferences in the other three styles. He did not accept this result, but as the course proceeded this preference of behavioural style became more and more evident. Every time he spoke in any discussion the contributions were invariably in the form of typically theorist contributions:

- 'Why should we proceed in that way. Is it the best?'
- 'Tell me what has led you to that view?'
- 'Let's hang on for a while and see if that's the best way of doing it and find out if it has been done successfully in a certain way before.'

This approach became so evident that he was challenged by the remainder of the group and he responded that he had already come to a self-admission that his original judgement had been wrong, and, typically, was awaiting the right moment to disclose this.

During the discussion on the results of the LSQ it is suggested that the group members might:

- consider during the week whether any very strong or very low preferences might usefully be modified so that the other styles and approaches might be considered for strengthening to produce a more balanced approach
- look at the mix of styles used during the week when sub-groups were to be selected and thus enable observation of the effects of this method of mixing.

The satisfaction of the first suggestion can be assisted by the enactment of some form of structured activity in which the participants are required to take on roles based on the styles which are foreign to them. For example, a strong Activist is required to become a low contributor and to listen to the others to such an extent that his major contributions will be building behaviour. A strong Reflector could be the member required to provide the greatest number of ideas during the activity. The Theorist might be given the brief not to express disagreement, difficulty stating or delaying tactics of any form, but to urge and support action. The Pragmatist can be required to be supportive of ideas even though he may not see any practical use for them.

GROUP EFFECTIVENESS AUDIT

One of the objectives of the course, although perhaps not a major aim, is to build the group during the week into some form of team and in so doing to give the members the opportunity of observing the aids and hindrances to this development. It would be unreal to consider full team development in this situation as in most cases the group is a 'stranger' group, or, at best, a 'cousin' group. If the group were to be a complete 'family' group or existing developing team, a different approach could be taken.

One useful monitoring approach to the development of the

group is to introduce a check at different intervals into the state of the group. A questionnaire is used for this purpose, asking course members to rate the state of the group at that point in time on a number of factors. The factors include reactions to the use of time by the group; the amount of trust existing in the group; the involvement of the members; commitment to the group and so on. The rating can be made by a scoring on a scale of say 1 to 7.

During the Mark 3 course the questionnaire is completed on the Tuesday morning of the course, but without any immediate sharing of the results or discussion about the exercise. The tutor, however, collects the audit questionnaires and summarises the results on an OHP transparency which is in the form of the questionnaire itself.

The same questionnaire is completed on a second occasion, usually about midday on day 4. On this occasion the results are added to the summary of the earlier audit and any movement, in whatever direction, is discussed. In most cases the movement is towards the higher end of the rating scale, but usually some individuals show a downward movement. By this stage in the course there is generally little hesitation in volunteering information by the individuals who have rated differently from the remainder. And similarly there is little hesitation in giving reasons for the rating.

At this point in the course, the model of group development is introduced. My preferred model is the one based on five normal stages of development in most groups.

Stage 1 of the group development is the stage in which a group finds itself when it comes together for the first time as strangers or relative strangers. This phase is characterised by formality, suspicion and assessment. Most disclosures are usually at the superficial level, career and job topics being foremost with little or no really personal details being offered or even sought. Such a state of affairs must be natural, since, if the others in the group are strangers, one doesn't really know who they are, what their power bases are and how in some way they might be able to affect your job. So you keep quiet until you find out whether or not it is safe to make certain statements.

Even if the situation is entered with the intention of being open from the start there is no guarantee that this will be the most appropriate approach. One personal experience occurred when I was attending a human relations course tutored by someone I had not previously met and the members of which would be strangers to me. There would be one exception to this unfamiliarity with my fellow course members and this was a colleague who was also attending the course. We assessed before the course that we would almost certainly be asked to introduce ourselves and state our personal objectives for attending the course. We had both quite legitimate reasons for attending in that we wished to improve our own skills in this field. But we were also trainers and were attending to assess the value of this type of training – a different approach from our own – and, again as we were trainers, we would be on the look out for techniques, methods, activities and approaches that we might use ourselves! The question was, to what extent should we disclose all our objectives and motives.

We decided that we should try to be as open as possible right from the start and during the introduction period which in fact occurred, we both disclosed the objectives cited above. There was little reaction at the time, but as the course progressed and the other members started to become as open as we had decided to be, we were accused that our only motives were to pick holes in the course and had no intentions of behaving in any appropriate manner. This developed to such an extent that the group banded against us to protect the course tutor – in spite of protestations from the tutor that he needed no help or even protection. I learned a lot on that course about openness!

In stage 2 of a group's development the more overt characteristics of the individuals in the group begin to emerge, and those who have concern about leadership or dominance begin to show these traits. Disclosure is still very much at the formal and polite level, but there is a movement towards the more personal aspects being disclosed and personal feedback beginning to be given. Disagreements and their existence become apparent, but generally are either not fully disclosed, or if they do emerge, the disagreement is accepted without challenge.

Stage 3 is characterised by the increasing openness of the group, but generally in more negative than positive ways.

Disagreements and conflict emerge and are discussed, but this discussion can take an emotional rather than a rational approach. Consequently resolution of these differences is rarely fully achieved. If procedures and methods have been agreed, these are followed inflexibly even though the members themselves realise that the approach is inappropriate.

Stage 4 is the breakthrough point in the group's development and the human relations trainer is looking to entry to this stage if his event is to have any success. Once the stage is reached, real procedures with appropriate flexibility are produced and operated. The differences and conflicts which still exist are brought out fully into the open, but now are resolved. There is considerable group loyalty and cohesion and the group is very willing to experiment with different approaches. Feedback, particularly at the feelings level is much more freely given and received.

The final stage is most unlikely to be achieved in a training group, particularly one of short duration, and will rarely be achieved in working groups, certainly because of the normal changes of personnel in most working groups. Even without changes of members or restrictions due to artificial environments or constraints of time, the 'mature' group can very infrequently evolve fully. The demands at this level are of complete openness and trust, freely given feedback, complete flexibility of methods and approaches, and appropriate relationships with other groups. Problems and difficulties of both a task and people nature will still occur, but these will be approached from the point of view of complete acceptance that individuals and events can never be perfect.

APPRAISAL OF GROUP ACTIVITY

Although in previous versions of the course, activities were always followed by a discussion to obtain an appraisal and feedback on the process of the activity, these discussions had restrictions. There was rarely time to do the discussion justice and the session was usually allowed to be free ranging and completely under the control of the group. On many occasions this worked well, but on an equal number of occasions it did not, the group taking refuge in flight from real feedback. In the Mark 3 version, in order that discussions might be contained reasonably in terms of time and content, a time constraint is introduced and guidance is given on the lines of the discussion. This guidance normally takes the form of a set of questions to be answered by each individual. The answers are then used as the basis of the discussion, following such lines as:

- the awareness of the objectives of the activity
- the success or otherwise of the process used
- who or what helped and hindered
- what were the best and worst features of the activity process
- what will be done during the next activity to ensure a more effective operation.

Of course, no complete limitations are placed on the group who if they decide to approach the appraisal in a different way, are free to do so. But experience shows that most groups are very happy to follow the guidelines, particularly in the early stages when they are still a little unsure of themselves.

FEEDBACK CO-COUNSELLING

The exchange feedback of views about each member has been the normal practice for most of the time the course has been in existence and the activity is retained for the final day 2 activity on the Mark 3 version. But it was felt that full value was not resulting from the previous free discussion of the results. Consequently the members, after immediate reaction discussion, are asked to consider their feedback as an individual voluntary activity during the evening and to plan further discussion with a colleague.

The following morning the members paired off, the learning styles indicators being used for this purpose – activist with activist, reflector with reflector and so on. The group is reminded that so far it has received feedback in the form of the learning styles preference, the appraisal feedback following the activities which have taken place, and the mutual feedback in a written form of the previous evening. It is then suggested that for the next 90 minutes or so the pairs co-counsel each other on the basis of this information.

In practice, the individuals obtain considerable value from this discussion, much more than if the discussion were to be held in the group. The like pairings help this process since, in addition to the material to discuss, the two people will have some aspects of their personality and approach in common. One comment which is often made to me after the activity is, 'Before we started I didn't think we would have much to talk about. But now I wish we'd had longer!'

A short discussion in the whole group follows the paired activity, on their reactions to the co-counselling – what they thought of this approach as a technique which they could use, how the pairs had processed the activity, what had emerged (if the participants wish to disclose) and so on. But the principal value of the exercise is found in the paired discussions themselves.

JOINT MEETING ACTIVITY

This particular activity combines several objectives. As it follows closely the input session on behaviour awareness and Behaviour Analysis, there is the opportunity for the course participants to discuss the value of the techniques and their drawbacks. This is achieved by dividing the group into two sub-groups, one charged with looking at the benefits of behaviour observation, the other with objections and disadvantages.

As the course is divided into two groups for this purpose, an element of intergroup interaction and behaviour is introduced, and it is always surprising how a group which has been developing so well as a cohesive unit, can so easily divide in competition with the other half.

The sub-groups are given time to prepare their cases and how they intend to proceed with the meeting. The details of the actual meeting are deliberately left vague so that the groups need to consider this aspect of their coming together and the

techniques of objective-setting, including behavioural planning, can be introduced in a natural manner. Finally, as the
group now has a greater awareness of behaviour and a common
language and technique to describe the activities and
behaviour, the course objectives are enhanced.

After the period of planning in the sub-groups, the two sides
come together for the joint meeting. In the brief given to both
sides there was an implication of a debate to decide the pros
and cons. However, this was implied only and the actual
content of the meeting is in the hands of the group. It has been
known for the two groups to get together before the meeting to
agree joint objectives for the meeting – but this has not
happened very often! The activity is ripe for a number of
conflict and confrontation situations – who will chair the
meeting (the tutor always resists attempts to put him in the
chair), how can conflicting objectives be overcome, how can an
aggressive element in the group be overcome, and so on.

The value of this, which is after all an activity in intergroup
relations compared with similar situations in previous versions
of the course, is that on this occasion the members are very
much aware of overall behaviour and are already attempting
modifications. In addition, if things go wrong there is time and
a readiness to resolve the problems as the participants are still
trying to work as one group.

BEHAVIOUR PLANNING

Day 4 starts, following the feedback the previous evening of
individual and group behavioural data, with a much fuller and
more structured approach than previously of what to do with
the new-found awareness.

The general approach taken is a close examination of
behaviour and the likely reactions to different forms of
behaviour. The observed and discussed reactions and interactions experienced on the course are used extensively in this
examination and the various research findings of observers such
as Peter Honey are also included.

The positive approach to modification is presented in the
form of objective setting for interactions. Most people are

aware of the value and techiques of setting objectives for task aspects – production targets, sales targets and so on – but the planning of behaviour for an interaction is much less common. Emphasis is placed on this aspect of planning objectives and practice is given through case studies on the techniques discussed.

'WHERE ARE WE NOW?' ACTIVITY

The principal variation in the use of this activity from previous versions of the course, is that a period of time is given for the course members to consider individually what they want to get out of the activity and to plan how they will achieve both task and behavioural objectives.

The advantage of this approach is that the activity is performed in a much more realistic and productive way, particularly if the individual objectives are disclosed and discussed early in the activity. The behaviours are usually also more appropriate than in the early stages of the course and even in more recent activities. These changes will be referred to later in this chapter.

LEARNING TRANSFER

An important problem encountered in all forms of training, and not least in human relations training, is ensuring that the learning achieved on the training course is transferred to the working environment. Some researchers suggest that no more than 10 or 20% is the maximum amount of the training which will be remembered and hopefully practised back at work. This will of course vary with the complexity of the training content, the range of aspects covered, and to a very large extent, the method of learning and the opportunities to practise. A further major factor, over which the trainer normally has little or no control, is the support and encouragement given to the learner by his boss or colleagues on his return to work.

This latter factor will vary considerably from one organisa-tion to another and one boss to another, and will depend on the attitude taken to staff development in the organisation. In so many cases a learner attends a training event with no preparation in conjunction with his boss and no interest shown or follow-up undertaken on return from the event. For example, if the bosses of learners attending courses perform pre-course briefings and post-course debriefings in only about 50% of cases, this suggests that the organisation itself has little interest in the development of its staff. After all this means that about half the managers who send their staff on courses do so without showing any interest in the results. These are often also the managers who complain bitterly that the training has not benefited their staff.

At the opposite end of the spectrum is the planned approach to an individual's development within an organisation. The typical process in such situations is that, at the time of application or nomination for the training, the need for and the suitability of the training event will have been investigated thoroughly by the learner and his boss. In a positive case, attendance on the course will then have been agreed. Shortly before the training, the learner and manager will have had a further discussion to clarify that the need for the training still exists; to discuss the course objectives and any personal objectives the learner might have; to consider the potential for application of any learning that may be achieved so that the learner might particularly concentrate on that aspect; and to arrange a further meeting following the training.

If the plan is to be effective this subsequent meeting *must* be held, and shortly after the trainee's return to work. The content of this debriefing meeting will usefully include general discussion about the course; the satisfaction of objectives, both course and personal; the level of learning achieved; and, most importantly, what is now to be done. At the end of many courses the learners produce Action Plans which are their statements of intent to introduce or practise certain aspects of their learning. The Action Plan must form a critical part of the discussion during the debriefing meeting and the manager or supervisor must have an unavoidable responsibility to support the operation of the plan.

This support may simply take the form of an active interest in the performance of the plan, or may involve the boss taking steps to ensure that the learner is in a position to put his plan into operation. The interested boss will realise that a training course is only one small step in the development programme of his staff and the course is most unlikely to be able to stand alone. Continuation and development of the learning achieved will require a coaching involvement over the following period. This coaching may involve the boss becoming directly participative in the learning development, his active involvement in bringing in others to support the learner, or his enabling the learner to follow a planned programme of self-development of which the training course would be part.

Apart from a proactive stance of trying to ensure that the learner's manager or organisation take the staff development issue seriously, the trainer has little power. Consequently his responsibility is to ensure that the learner leaves the course with the motivation and the means to continue.

This trainer responsibility is approached on the Mark 3 course by the issue to the learners on the evening of day 4 of a questionnaire which directs them to:

 – consider in specific terms what they have learned
 – identify the helping and hindering factors they will face on
   return to work
 – plan provisionally which aspects they would like to put into
   practice back at work.

During the morning of day 5, the course participants are paired and given time to discuss with their partner their considerations as a result of the learning and the learning transfer audit. They are also invited to produce, as a result of this discussion, and using each other to test out ideas, a realistic Action Plan which they will discuss with their boss on return to work. A copy of this Action Plan is left with the trainer for eventual follow up.

The Mark 3 course has obviously many differences from the versions preceding it and validation of the course suggests that it has been even more successful and satisfying than its predecessors. This appears to be so from the comments of the participants, both immediately at the end of the event and subsequently, and from the subjective assessment of the trainer. Validation and evaluation of human relations training is very difficult, but one quantitative, immediate validation factor is available at the end of the course.

BEHAVIOUR MODIFICATION

I have stated earlier that BAs are completed on every possible occasion during activities on the course and this data is presented to the participants rather more than halfway through the course. The course members use this data on which to base behaviour modification plans which they can attempt to put into practice during the remainder of the course. In order to have some element of objective feedback of their success or otherwise, BAs are completed on any activities or discussions subsequent to the modification decisions. It is accepted that the behaviour and subsequent data will be contaminated by such factors as an over-intent to perform more effectively, considerable awareness for at least part of the time that BAs are being completed, and the unknown factor of how temporary any improvements may be. But at least the opportunity is available to show that, whatever the constraints, behaviour *can* be modified. It is then up to the individual to maintain the improvements and modifications according to the circumstances.

Table 6.1
Behaviour modification data

Category	Pre-modification %	Post-modification %
Proposing	7	13
Building	1	3
Seeking information	16	24
Giving information	43	34
Summarising	1	3
Supporting	6	10
Open	1	1
Disagreeing	2	1
Attacking/blocking	6	2
Bringing in	3	5
Shutting out	14	4

Data records have been maintained of pre- and post-modification behaviours and Table 6.1 summarises these results. The comparative behavioural data shows a general decrease in the usually more unhelpful behaviours of disagreeing (without giving reasons), attacking, blocking and shutting out, and a significant reduction in the simple process of stating views. These reductions are balanced by increases in what can be considered generally as the more helpful aspects of behaviour – building, seeking views, supporting, bringing in and summarising.

7 T-groups, encounter groups and transactional analysis

The kind of training described in Chapters 5 and 6 is obviously not the only effective approach to interactive skills training. It is simply the method that I have found most useful and in step with the philosophy cited earlier. Other trainers and training organisations practise different forms of training courses and ideally the budding human relations trainer should be at least aware of the range of approaches, if not actually testing them out himself as a student or observer. Many of the approaches available are variations on a number of basic themes and the training purchaser should examine the contents closely before making a commitment.

T-GROUPS

T-groups are similar to the interpersonal skills training just described, particularly the Mark 2b version, but with some significant differences. The principal difference is that whereas with the Mark 2b there was a minimum amount of structure, in the T-group there is normally little or no predetermined structure at all.

The word T-group derives from the 'Training Group', an approach to human relations training developed from the small group discussions approach of Kurt Lewin in the 1940s and further developed in a training approach at the National Training Laboratories in the USA. Since those days a number of training organisations have introduced variations of the original T-group, particularly in the United States, but also in

Britain and other European countries. The training approach is also known as Laboratory Training, Encounter Groups or Sensitivity Training, but within the variations the basic approach is the same.

The philosophy of T-group training which differs little from most other interactive skills approaches includes that:

- real learning comes from experiencing real situations, albeit in a training environment, rather than constructed activities
- learning will be achieved by honest feedback among the group
- the 'here and now' of what is happening in the group, particularly in terms of feelings rather than actions is of the highest importance
- learning will be achieved whatever the event occurring provided that the atmosphere is conducive to the learning being sought.

In order to put this philosophy into action, T-groups have objectives which again are hardly removed from those of other interactive training:

- to increase the sensitivity and awareness of the participants to their own feelings and reactions and those of others
- to increase the ability to assess and analyse what is happening within the group and between individuals
- to increase the participants' skill in adopting new behaviours and adapting existing behaviours so that the appropriate behaviour pattern is adopted, feedback can be given and received with sensitivity, and feelings can be controlled.

Within the T-group there is an atmosphere of dual roles for all the group members, in which members are observers of what is happening, but participating fully at the same time. They are encouraged to raise immediately any issue which might arise from the activity of the group – pleasure, concern, anger, sorrow – and have these explored fully within the group.

The trainer or facilitator has a special and different role in the T-group compared with other types of training, particularly those of a structured nature. His fundamental role is that of an encourager and guider, motivating the participants to concentrate on the here and now, to be aware of everything that is happening, and to give and receive feedback related to these events. However, in performing these roles he must be unobtrusive and neutral in his approach, giving feedback himself only whenever absolutely necessary and ensuring that this is non-judgemental. He is not there to impose his own views on the group and rarely presents any input sessions: when he does, these are usually at the invitation of the group when it wishes to understand the 'why' of what is happening. For many trainers these are very difficult roles to enact, particularly if they have previously been accustomed to a more didactic or prescriptive approach. He must be able to sit quietly while the group is taking some action, even though he can see that the group is going badly wrong. Perhaps the ultimate test of an effective T-group facilitator is that he can leave the training room for say, ten minutes or more and his absence not be noticed. He must also have sufficiently strong nerves to leave the group on its own for long periods of time and resist the feeling that he should be sufficiently in control of the situation all the time and is indispensable.

A T-group typically consists of up to twelve members who come together in a residential centre for about two weeks, either as a 'stranger' group, a 'cousin' or a 'family' group. The start of the course can vary considerably. In some events the early stages follow a traditional type of approach in which the facilitator explains his role in the course, his willingness to help the group whenever called up to do so, and that the group would learn from an examination of its own activities and behaviour. However, the facilitator gives no indication of how this should be produced or that the process will be completely in the hands of the group.

An alternative, rather more extreme beginning is that the group convenes in the advised room at the directed day and time, but no trainer appears. Quite often either silence prevails for some time, or desultory side conversations take place, until typically someone breaks the lack of action and says something like: 'It's obvious that we are being left here to get on and do something ourselves. Has anybody any ideas what we should do?'

This contribution can be greeted in a variety of ways ranging from 'Leave it alone!' through 'Why did you feel that you should raise the question of what we should do?' to 'I was expecting somebody to crack and I though it would be you!'.

Whatever the initial stages may be, the course atmosphere is tense and uncomfortable and remains so until the group realises that the progress of the course is very much in its own hands and takes action accordingly. Once the process has got under way, the exchange of feedback on feelings and reactions comes more naturally and freely. It is this feedback which leads to the satisfaction of the course objective of increasing sensitivity and awareness.

The path, of course, is not smooth and on many occasions the process can be traumatic and hurtful. However, it is almost impossible to typify a T-group, as so many different paths can be followed to achieve the objectives, the variations resulting from the natural differences between every group of different individuals. Much will also depend on the degree of guidance and intervention of the trainer, which incidentally is often much more than is reported in descriptions of T-groups, and although the training is regarded as unstructured, this is not necessarily and completely true. Certainly the course is not filled with structured exercises, but more covertly a structure can be seen in the trainer's interventions.

ENCOUNTER GROUPS

Encounter groups can, although will not always, differ quite widely from the basic T-group and in general are characterised by an approach that is directed almost completely to the feelings level. Members of an Encounter group are encouraged in, more often than not, non-verbal activities of a highly experiential nature to display their feelings and emotions. If feelings and emotions can be displayed openly they can be explored and the individuals will learn and be helped by others how to cope with them. The approach certainly takes on the general format of gestalt therapy and the activities often include such 'trust' games as guided walks with one partner blindfolded; internally revealing activities which ask the participant to put himself in the place of an inanimate object and articulate as that object; rejection games where the experiencer has to try to be accepted in something the group is doing. In the hands of a skilled and sincere practitioner these activities can be revealing and valuable, but there is always the danger that the emotions and results go further than a less-skilled facilitator is able to control.

The structure of the membership of T-groups was mentioned earlier in terms of 'stranger', 'cousin', and 'family' groups. Each type of group will have its own advantages and disadvantages. In a 'stranger' group in which participants may come from different companies or organisations, with no pre-knowledge of each other and no contact after the event, once the initial uncertainty is over the members are more likely to be more open with each other than in the other groupings. As a result the learning experiences can become deeper and more illuminating. However, once the course is over, each individual with his new insights will have to return to his own work environment which may be unsupportive and/or even hostile to his new approach.

The 'cousin' group of members usually come from the same organisation, but have little normal contact with each other. Openness may still be relatively easy to encourage and maintain, but there may always be a partial barrier which may not emerge and which will inhibit disclosure to the full extent 'in case it gets around the company'. The problem of free translation of the learning experienced by the 'stranger' group will also be present, unless the company is one in which a large number of individuals have passed through T-groups and can offer support to the fledgeling.

The 'family' group of members who normally work as a team or closely associated group in the workplace, offers many advantages denied to other groups. If the T-group concepts, philosophies and learning are accepted fully by all the group, the end of the course is not the end of the experience as the association, at an enhanced level, can continue and develop within the team. The principal barrier that has to be overcome in this case is found on the course. People who are working so closely and at different hierarchical levels may not be willing for personal or career attitudes to open up and disclose aspects which they normally keep hidden.

VALUES AND DANGERS

A number of investigations have been conducted to assess the value in terms of learning and particularly the dangers associated with T-groups. Perhaps the major study in Britain was led by Cary Cooper in 1979 for the Manpower Services Commission. He looked at particularly the psychological effects on managers who had attended small group training programmes ranging from the unstructured to the structured.

The results of this survey are detailed and in some instances at variance with the findings of other researchers, but can be summarised as:

- roughly 5% could be identified as having a potentially negative experience or a maximum of 10% on more restricted criteria
- 11% were stated by their fellow trainees as having been 'hurt' by the experience (the trainer quoted 19% in this category)
- the trainees were followed up after seven months and it was found that only 1.76% could be identified as having sustained negative effects
- as a positive approach, 67% of the individuals named as having been hurt by the experience, were also named twice as having been helped
- 59% of those cited as having been hurt, showed marked significant improvement seven months after the event.

One conclusion may be that 'in the short term some kind of emotional reaction may be, *for a small number of participants*, a necessary precondition to long term change' (Cary Cooper in *Improving Interpersonal Relations*).

The study also included an examination of the potentially positive effects on managers of this type of training. The overall conclusions were that as a whole the groups involved in the training obtained positive benefits, by becoming 'emotionally more stable', 'trusting and adaptable'. The improvements did not necessarily become evident immediately following the events, being observed at the seven months review.

One factor which emerged from the study was the relationship of 'high' risk and 'low' risk participants to the trainer and the training styles. The greater likelihood of adverse experience to the high risk groups – the taciturn and serious, shy and timid, introverted and self-sufficient – occurred when the training was less structured, relatively intimate, person-centred and focused on the here and now. The risk was increased when the trainer was assertive or aggressive, uninhibited and spontaneous, impulsive and lively, and sensitive and open.

On the other hand, the conditions which contributed to positive outcome required:

- a trainee – self-sufficient, conservative, apprehensive, and somewhat tense and somewhat controlled
- the training – high degree of structure, low intimacy, little confrontation, more remote interactions, little emphasis on the here and now
- the trainer – supportive, low level of anxiety, relaxed and with low involvement.

The final conclusions of this survey and a number of similar surveys, suggest that valuable learning can be achieved in the T-group setting. But careful attention must be paid to the nature of people attending and, above all, to the experience and skill of the trainer in handling critical personal events. There are also some strong feelings that an equal amount, if not more, transferable learning can be achieved by other approaches, usually of a more structured nature. This has certainly been my own experience as a T-group participant and in the comparison of the interpersonal skills training described in previous chapters.

TRANSACTIONAL ANALYSIS

Although Transactional Analysis (TA) is not a complete training approach in itself, it is sufficiently different from other techniques to be used as the basis of human relations training.

TA had its origins in the therapy practice of Dr Eric Berne in the United States. Berne observed that clusters of behaviour could be identified in his patients and he evolved the concept that there were three basic patterns of behaviour controlled by an inner force, the ego. Consequently, the three patterns are identifiable as ego states.

The three ego states can be identified in an individual's behaviour and from this stage the concepts were transferred to the training world as a means not only of analysing behaviour, but also determining the driving forces behind the behaviour. In this way TA extends the boundaries of interactive analysis which looks at the observable behaviour only and, thus additionally, analyses the covert aspects of behaviour and indeed personality.

The origins of personality are often considered to include two elements: an inherited personality element which is supplemented or even subsumed by elements which are learned. The learned aspects of personality, and hence behaviour, can be considered as three internal tape recorders which record the experiences we have, particularly in the early part of our lives, and these recordings are played back throughout the remainder of our lives.

EGO STATES

The three tape recordings, or ego states, are referred to as the Parent, Adult and Child states. The Parent state contains all the emotions, feelings, attitudes and behaviours learned by an individual as an infant, from birth to about the age of 5, principally from parents, but also from other strong parent figures which have an impact on a child. Our parents have attitudes, stances and behaviours which become indelibly stamped on our perceptions and are retained for playing back once we are grown up ourselves. These recalled behavioural aspects become evident in the prejudiced, nurturing or critical approaches we take with others in the same way that our parents reacted. When one acts, thinks, behaves, feels as one's parents used to do, our Parent state is in the act of replaying.

The reactions to events in the Parent state are very evident when we ourselves are parents and it is often so surprising to us when we hear ourselves saying to the children 'Good boys don't behave like that' in exactly the same way one of our parents used to do. But the same reactions and behaviours can be observed in our working lives when we take on illogically prejudiced, critical or nurturing approaches.

Identification of the Parent state is achieved in observation of the behaviours of:

- setting limits and constraints that have no logical base
- disciplining, judging and criticising
- making rules and regulations (The Critical Parent)
- giving advice and guidance
- protecting and nurturing
- keeping traditions (The Nurturing Parent).

Typical Parent words used include: 'do, don't, should, shouldn't, must, ought to, have to, can't'.

A typical conversation ascribed to the Parent mode could go:

A. 'Isn't this awful, the way prices seem to be going up all the time.'
B. 'Yes, I'm sure it's all the fault of these new ways they have of making things.'
A. 'It wasn't like this when I was young. They left things alone to develop naturally.'
B. 'Yes. I remember when . . . .'

The Adult ego state can operate at any age and is based on the learning which develops as we mature, provided we take the opportunity to accept this learning. The Adult collects information in looking at the facts and makes decisions from this stage in a logical manner. The Adult gathers external data from what is going on round about him and internal data from the feelings expressed by the Child and Parent states; approaches the choices in a rational, logical way; and makes decisions based on all the options available and the likely probabilities.

Typical Adult behaviours are sensible and controlled, reasonable and reasoned, logical and rational, and appear in verbal contributions as, for example:

A. 'What information have we so far on this subject?'
B. 'Well, the latest computer data is . . . . . .'
A. 'Are there any factors which will stop us proceeding?'
B. 'No. All the data is in step with the main projections'
B. 'Right. This is how it looks as if . . . .'.

The third ego state is the Child state. The tape which produces the Child behaviour is recorded during infancy, again up to the age of about 5. When we were children we behaved in a variety of ways which can be repeated in an adult form when we grow up. As a child we expressed uninhibited joy, sorrow, anger distress, distaste or behaved compliantly, politely, creatively or were rebellious.

In the grown up state the Child is expressed as having:

- carefree, curious, funloving, adventurous, uninhibited behaviours and attitudes

and using such words as

- 'let's, I want, I feel great, why don't we, come on then.' (The Free Child)

or

- overcompliant, defiant, rebellious, complaining, whining, downcast eyes

with typical words

- 'Please can I, I'll try hard, Please, Thank you and Sorry, all at appropriate times (The Adapted Child).

The three states are usually represented diagramatically as:

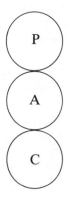

The observation and analysis part of TA is the structural analysis element, but, as with other forms of analysis, it can be extended to actual transactions between people.

TRANSACTIONS

Transactions can be described as complementary, crossed and ulterior.

Complementary transactions take the form of interactions between people when the responses from the other person are the ones that are desired by the initiator of the transaction or interaction.

In Figure 7.1, the Complementary transaction is operating at the Adult level, where the initial contribution is Adult and the response is in the same mode. The result of this interaction is an acceptable event which satisfies both contributors.

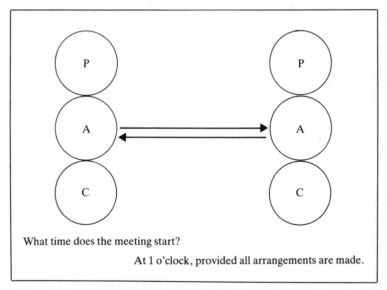

What time does the meeting start?

At 1 o'clock, provided all arrangements are made.

Figure 7.1   Complementary transaction at Adult level

Similar Complementary transactions can occur at the Parent–Parent level and Child–Child level, and although the

resulting transaction does not produce results of earth-shatter-
ing importance, both participants are satisfied.

Complementary transactions can also take place between
different ego states while still retaining harmony while the
transactional lines do not cross: Figure 7.2.

However, all transactions are not harmonious and Crossed
transactions occur when the response received is not the
desired response. If the initial contribution, the Child's cry for
help to the Parent, is not responded to in a complementary
manner, problems will arise. This is shown in Figure 7.3.

Even though a transaction does not seem to be going badly
and at the superficial level appears to be complementary,
everything is not always as it appears to be. On the face of it,
the transaction shown in Figure 7.4 is complementary and
satisfactory.

However, below the surface, a psychological transaction is
taking place at the Child level, as shown in Figure 7.5.

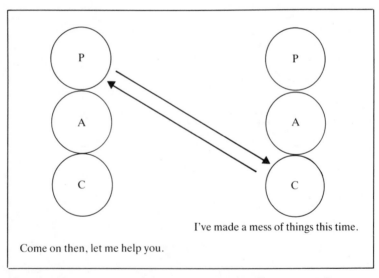

Figure 7.2   Complementary transaction at Parent–Child level

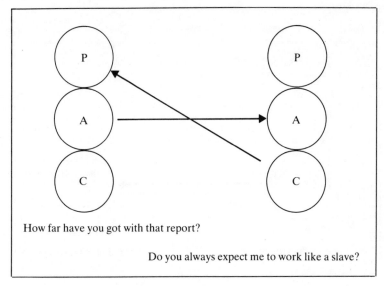

Figure 7.3   Crossed transaction at Parent–Child level

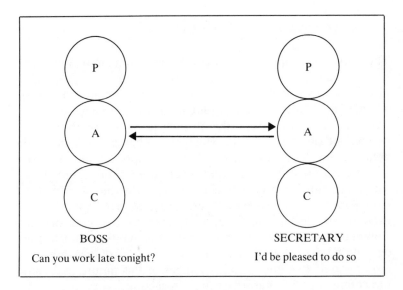

Figure 7.4   Ulterior transaction at Adult level

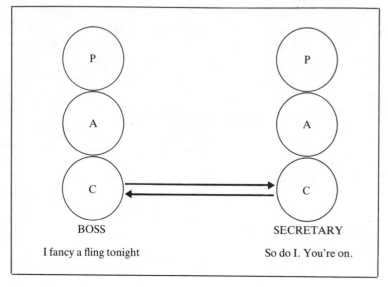

Figure 7.5   Ulterior transaction at Child level

TRANSACTIONAL AWARENESS

The important application of TA in interactions between people is awareness of the state in which you, as perhaps the originator of the discussion, are approaching the other person, and whether this is the appropriate mode of approach. You also have to be aware, from the responses made by the other person, of the ego state in which the other is behaving and hence feeling. Figures 7.1 to 7.5 show simply the initiation of the interaction. What is perhaps even more interesting is how the interaction or transaction progresses. In the cases of the complementary transactions there are few problems as they proceed at the implicitly agreed level to the end of the transaction or until there is mutual agreement to change the ego state level, say from Child–Child to Adult–Adult, or Adult–Adult to Child–Child. Changes of this nature maintain the complementary nature of the transaction.

However, if we consider the transaction initiated in Figure 7.3, in which the originator, quite reasonably as boss to secretary, makes an enquiry about the progress of a report. This transaction is at the Adult–Adult level and the boss is expecting a similar Adult–Adult response giving the information he is seeking. But, for some reason of which we are unaware, the secretary instead of reacting as an Adult, responds from a Child state. Perhaps she has just had an argument with someone and is emotionally still disturbed, or perhaps she is unwell. Whatever the reason it is apparent that she is responding in the rebellious Child state, appealing to the Parent state of the boss.

What does the boss do now? One option he has can be to continue at the Adult–Adult level in the hope that she will see reason and respond in a like manner. If she is, however, firmly locked into the Child state, such an approach would be abortive and might even increase the level of the rebellious response.

A second option that is open to the boss is to switch to a Parent–Child approach, the Parent response being of the Critical Parent nature. This transaction is of course complementary, but many of us have had the experience of what happens when a parent uses the heavy approach on his rebellious child. The situation has every likelihood of being exacerbated.

The third option, although demanding self-discipline and using an amount of time that may not be readily available, may have the best chance of success. If the boss recognises the rebellious Child state, he may then respond as Parent–Child, but this time as the Nurturing Parent in a placatory manner, perhaps acknowledging that 'Yes, we do seem to be exceptionally busy at the present and I know how much work you have to do!' This response will almost certainly produce another Child–Parent reaction and the discussion can be maintained at this level. Eventually the secretary will calm down and the aware boss will recognise the time to try to switch the transaction back to the Adult–Adult level.

The three ego states are considered to exist within us all and none is considered as good or bad, since the balanced person will probably need to use any of them according to the situation. The problems involved include the identification of the ego state of the other person and the decision on which state to use in response. This is all required while the interaction is occurring.

The dangers of operating within ego states are that one might become hooked into a particular state most of the time, particularly when the use of that state is not appropriate. Someone who is strongly hooked into using the Parent state can either be highly autocratic and dominating if the emphasis is on the Critical Parent, or too people-oriented in his job if the balance is strongly biased to the Nurturing Parent. The constant Child can be a pain and will be most unlikely to be a serious, conscientious worker. The permanently logical, rational Adult can be a bore whose staff scream at him, inwardly, to let his hair down once in a while and have some fun.

It follows, therefore, that the balanced person will not allow himself to be hooked into one state above the others. A strong Adult will be able to control the Parent and Child tendencies and bring them into use at the appropriate times. The appropriateness of the time will be determined from the logical and rational approach of the Adult.

But TA is not used only to describe and analyse the ego states which give us analyses of the transactions in which we are involved and consequently direction as to which ego states we should use. Consideration of transactions also leads us to observe and analyse the games we play in life.

GAMES

Games are an important part of TA and demonstrate an additional aspect of behaviour. They are very popular pastimes of people both at work and in the social scene and can be defined as a series of transactions which occupy two or more people, in which the pattern of events results in an outcome of 'bad' feelings on both sides.

Many varieties of game-playing exist, but the outcome is always predictable, and it is predictability which appeals to people as it helps them feel that all their problems are caused by others. Other reasons for playing games can be to receive strokes (see later) or as a way of structuring the time to avoid boredom.

A typical game is NIGYSOB (Now I've got you, you son of a bitch). This game often occurs in the meeting environment when at a particular meeting another person exhibits behaviour and approach in such a way that you are put down, frustrated, or denigrated in some way. This action can make you decide to get your own back at the next meeting, and you approach that meeting with this in mind rather than the task of the meeting. The other person, your persecutor, may encourage the game by resisting your attempts to put him down, and in his turn tries to score further points off you.

Another common game example is 'Yes but'. The initiator of this game approaches, let us say, a group of colleagues and describes a problem with which he is having difficulties in providing solutions. He gives the impression that he would welcome suggestions. However, when suggestions are made he will invariably respond to the 'Why don't you . . .' with 'Yes but . . .' until the well of suggestions dries up. He then walks away saying something like 'Well, I suppose I'll just have to find my own solution as I thought I would!'.

In both these cases there are dangers and risks to all, with emotions and attitudes reacting to being put down. It is, however, relatively simple to avoid being made to participate in the games of others by, in the two situations cited,

- not reacting when someone tries to score points off you in the meeting
- refusing to give suggestions when 'Yes, but' arises.

RITUALS AND PASTIMES

Rituals and pastimes can be considered as safer forms of game-playing as their intent is more in terms of passing time than scoring points. However, there is always the possibility that a pastime can develop into a dangerous game.

A frequent ritual in which we engage is the morning greeting to another person, asking 'How are you?' The initiator of this ritual certainly has little or no interest in the state of health or well-being of the person greeted, and that person, knowing this absence of real interest, gives the ritualistic response 'Fine, thanks'.

The ritual can be broken by a newcomer to the ritual who answers with a statement of how unwell he feels. The initiator of the ritual cannot understand this reaction, is not interested in the response, and is irritated by the breaking of the ritualistic predictability of response. The other person feels bewildered by the apparent lack of interest in his answer and this bewilderment can produce even worse feelings which can produce a long-term breakdown of relationship.

A long standing ritual can be broken one morning because the person greeted really does feel down, and instead of giving the expected response, states his feelings. This has the effect on the other person similar to the earlier instance cited with a possible breakdown in the relationship.

Pastimes and rituals occur frequently on social occasions or quasi-social occasions at work. Gatherings of married couples are often characterised by the men grouping to discuss 'My car . . .', 'My DIY activities . . .' and so on, while the wives discuss 'Did you see in x shop . . .', 'Did you hear about . . .'. Superficial discussions of this nature can often be essential before more serious turns of talk are realised. The boss in the office often goes out from his own office for a typical walkabout and stops to chat with some of his staff with whom he knows he can start the conversation with 'Did you see the match last night?'.

These activities can often be valuable when there has to be an exchange of members between groups. The approach to another group can be initiated by 'We have just been talking about X. What do you think?', X being one of the accepted pastime subjects. In this way, the superficial approach of a pastime can be used particularly to ease the movement or take the interaction to a deeper level.

STROKES

One of the basic concepts of TA is that people require strokes to maintain their needs for recognition, affection and attention, as identified earlier by Maslow. Children are the prime example of this need, but adults have an equal need, although this need is generally well concealed except perhaps in the case of adults with a dominant Child ego state.

The importance of strokes is such that people will prefer having negative strokes to receiving no strokes at all. This is evidenced when people who have suffered their annual appraisal interview and, having had neither good nor bad news from the boss, comment 'I wouldn't have minded if he had bawled me out for something – at least I would know how he felt!' People need to know, but want the bouquets as well as the brickbats.

One of the problems of human nature is that although most of us are looking for strokes, particularly positive ones of praise and compliments, there is the danger of not being able to give overt signals of acceptance. Let the husband beware of not noticing and commenting on his wife's new hair-do, dress or whatever, but he must be prepared to accept a response of 'Oh, this old thing' or 'Oh, I've just tried something different' rather than a direct response of gratitude for the stroke.

If strokes, either positive or negative, are not given many problems can arise including the greater likelihood of games being played so that at least negative strokes are received. However, depending on the culture, too many positive strokes can be as dangerous as negative ones, and one result can be the initiation of the game of stroke collecting for collecting's sake.

TRADING STAMPS

In addition to collecting strokes, a TA concept is that people also collect what are known as trading stamps which represent feelings and which are discharged at a later stage. As in the real world of trading stamps, so in TA there are different kinds of stamps denoted by their colours.

Gold stamps represent good feelings which are collected when praise, recognition or justification is given, and redeemed when the collector has a 'full book'. The redemption may vary in degree from sitting back at work for 10 minutes – 'I've earned the rest', to taking longer periods of time off.

The opposite to the gold are the brown stamps which are the products of bad feelings in terms of repressed anger, frustration, depression. Redemption of brown stamps is again delayed until the collector can take no more of unjustified criticism etc., i.e. the book is full. This is quite a common occurrence with non-assertive individuals who are subdued by their boss on every possible occasion. Eventually even the quietest mouse can take no more and at some point in time, when the brown stamp book is full, often when the other person is not expecting such a reaction, an explosion occurs. However, different people react in different ways and the release of the accumulated bad feelings can be nothing more than throwing an innocent, inanimate object across the room or going to a colleague's room and having a good grumble.

Stamp collecting is a dangerous occupation as there can be nothing worse than the forced containment of feelings, particularly bad ones. Most people need praise, but an unhealthy situation arises when the search for gold stamps becomes the pre-occupation. The determined brown stamp collector would not need to discover traumatic ways of releasing his frustration by, for example, expressing his feelings at the time of the downputting event. Unfortunately, this is not always possible, perhaps if immediate release of feelings may result in something worse. However, the agony of frustration can be reduced by an awareness and acceptance of the situation.

LIFE SCRIPTS

Life scripts are a powerful part of TA in which an individual determines his personal plan for life at an early age. Berne suggested this occurs at about the age of 4 to 7 or so, as the result of the external influences of parents or other parental figures. The script produced at this age can be so strong that the adult life can be dominated by this, even if it is found that progress and relationships are affected by what is happening.

A common example of a destructive life script is the effect on a child of 'dominant' parents in terms of always being told what, how and when to do something, to accept authority and not to question decisions or prescriptions. If these effects are sufficiently strong, an attitude or life script can be established in the child so that he can adapt to make life acceptable. As he grows up he accepts that the role, which has become normal to him, is the one which will give him success in the remainder of his life. Perhaps the commonest form of life scripting is based on a childhood injunction that 'Big boys don't cry'. There are many occasions on which a grown-up male could benefit from a cry, but because of his adherence to his life script, a stiff upper lip is maintained and extreme pressure and frustration are hidden, sometimes with extreme results.

TA TRAINING

The factors described by TA in terms of ego states, transactions, games, strokes and so on are used as a basis for training in life and social skills. Training is aimed at modifying the main constituents of TA, such as:

- reducing the inappropriate outbalance of the use of the Parent and Child states, but increasing where necessary access to the Free Child
- bringing strokes into a degree of relevance with the greater ability to control negative strokes
- increasing the awareness of the use of ego states in transactions and the ability to control these states
- reducing game playing or at least minimising their effects
- bringing the effects of stamp collecting into perspective and offering ways of reducing the related attitudes
- giving the opportunity to re-assess a restrictive life script and produce a new design for life.

Training, using TA as its base, can range from a simple introduction, with a view to greater awareness, to ego states and the variety of transactions, to full training in life modification. I have used the simpler approach quite effectively within a course concerned with a range of one-to-one interactions. Although on these occasions there was little opportunity to modify behaviour within TA terms, a common language was introduced and the course participants were able to assess their performances in a more analytical way.

A typical fuller course includes full descriptions and analytical discussions of the TA theories described earlier, and also considerable opportunity to engage in activities designed to:

- assist a greater awareness of the incidence of TA behaviours
- practise modification of unwanted behaviours and attitudes
- develop the use of TA concepts in real life situations.

Although TA has been on the training scene for a considerable time, it cannot be claimed that it is accepted universally as a responsible approach.

It has, however, advantages in its flexibility in looking at not only overt behaviour but also the covert reasons for these behaviours in terms of attitudes, motives and feelings. This flexibility is evidenced in the range of training approaches in which it can be used. As mentioned earlier, it can be used as a simple input of theory and concepts, or in interactive skills, team building, interviewing skills, group leadership and membership skills, and even in application to complete organisations in organisation development.

Few of the 'accepted' theories of management and human relations development are incompatible with TA and consequently TA can be integrated with training involving these models and theories.

TA gives participants and adherents to the approach a common language for both analysing behaviour and describing it. The concept is optimistic in that it approaches behaviour as having the capability of change.

However, TA is considered by many as having insufficient research bases and there is natural suspicion as a result of its development from therapy. To many people the advantage of the TA language can become a disadvantage and be regarded as jargonistic, and to British audiences too American. Those who are adherents and devotees of TA use the language as part of their normal communication and can appear to those who are unaware of TA as being an 'in-club'. In fact, some TA users have been accused of using this language facility to put down others who were unaware of what was being done to them. This type of action, of course, tends to devalue the technique.

A final disadvantage can be that because the TA approach attempts to bring to the surface psychological elements of an individual's personality, points arise which the individual might not wish to be exposed or of which he has been aware and which could produce unproductive feelings. If the trainer is not skilled, some participants could find themselves in, or be forced into, a psychological state with which the trainer is unable to cope.

REFERENCES AND RECOMMENDED READING

Barker, D. (1980): *TA and Training*. Aldershot: Gower.

Berger, M.L. and Berger, P.J. (1972): *Group Training Techniques*. Aldershot: Gower.

Berne, E. (1980): *Games People Play*. London: Penguin.

Berne, E. (1975): *What do You Say after You've Said Hello?* London: Corgi.

Bradford, L.P., Gibb, J.R. and Benne, K.D. (1964): *T-group Theory and Laboratory Method*. Chichester: Wiley.

Cooper, C.L. and Bowles, D. (1977): 'Hurt or Helped', *Training Information Paper* No. 10. London: HMSO.

Cooper, C.L. (Ed.) (1981): *Improving Interpersonal Relations*. Aldershot: Gower.

Hanson, P.G. (1981): *Learning Through Groups*. University Associates.

Harris, T.A. (1973): *I'm OK You're OK*. London: Pan.

James and Jongeward, D. (1971): *Born to Win*. London: Addison-Wesley.

Jongeward, D. (1973): *Everybody Wins: TA Applied to Organisations*. London: Addison-Wesley.

Lakin, M. (1972): *Interpersonal Encounter: Theory and Practice in Sensitivity Training*. Maidenhead: McGraw-Hill.

Novey, T.B. (1976): *TA for Management*. Bradford: MCB.

Smith, P.B. (1969): 'Improving Skills in Working with People: the T-group', *Training Information Paper* No. 4. London: HMSO.

8 Other approaches to interactive skills training

The approaches and methods in interactive skills training described so far have been ones which have followed to a large extent either unstructured or strongly psychologically based models. But other training techniques utilise structured models or are even more firmly based in therapy approaches. Many of these human relations approaches are concerned with leadership and management styles training.

THE MANAGERIAL GRID

Typical of the leadership style of human relations training is the approach based on the Managerial Grid of Blake and Mouton. Blake and Mouton identified and labelled a number of management styles across a spectrum with two axes – concern for people and concern for production or tasks. Grid training considers that both concern-elements can be contained in a management style and the level of each concern determines this style.

The level of each concern is rated on a scale of 1 (low) to 9 (high) and is plotted on the two-axis grid, the verticle axis relating to the concern for people and the horizontal one to the concern for production or the task (Figure 8.1). Five basic styles are identified in this way.

A 1,1 style manager is described by Blake and Mouton as 'Impoverished management' where concern is low for both people and production. In this style the manager, although wanting to remain within the organisation, makes no effort to

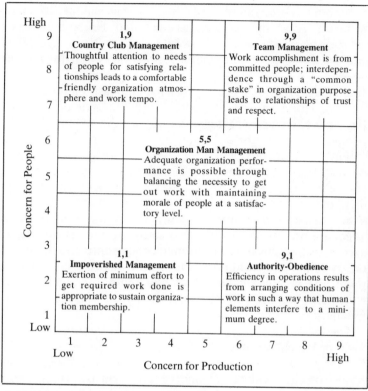

Figure 8.1   The Managerial Grid ®*

become committed either to straining to excel in producing or building good relationships with his staff. He is usually a non-directive person who will not take sides in a disagreement, not became he wants to take a neutral stance, but because he does not wish to be involved in conflict. This attitude does not encourage loyalty and although his staff do not know where he stands, they do not care.

On the other hand a 1,9 manager goes out of his way to have warm friendly relationships with his staff and defers to this at the expense of having minimum concern for the task. Conflict is something to be avoided at all costs, but if he cannot avoid it he will try to sooth the bad feelings generated. His reaction when his staff do not behave as he would wish, is that he has failed and needs to do something to restore the warm feelings he needs.

Similar to the 1,9 style, but with the emphasis on the concern for production rather than people, is the 9,1 style of manager. His characteristics are tight control to the extent that the people performing the task come into the equation to a minimal extent. He demands obedience to his authority and will press his own views and ideas even though this action may produce conflict. This is, of course, the description of the autocrat or dictator.

5.5 management is that in which the manager balances an adequate production level with a satisfactory level of morale, accomplishing this balance through compromise and a reliance on systems and tradition. He rarely takes the initiative, preferring others to take the lead or find a safe approach: he will then go along with the view so that he can maintain his popularity.

The fifth major style, 9,9 is characterised by commitment to high task achievement, but not at the expense of people. Rather the 9,9 manager succeeds through the consultation, participation, involvement and commitment of his staff with whom he works hard to develop into a team. He uses the team approach effectively to obtain productive ideas and, although he will have ideas and convictions of his own he does not force these, being willing to change his view if the idea of another member is sounder. Conflict is treated as a natural event in the team, but it is brought into the open and resolved.

The Grid approach has been used extensively in the training of managers in their attitudes to management and leadership and with a corporate emphasis can be applied to the cultural style of the organisation.

Courses with the Grid base commonly follow a pattern in which the participants are helped to identify their preferred and actual leadership styles and obtain a complete understanding of the nature and effects of the disparate styles. A number of personal audit instruments are available for this process and substantial input will explain the model.

Activities can then follow, a process which by now should be familiar to the reader, which will demonstrate in practice the use of the various styles by the participants, feedback being given by Grid scoring and from the group members. Opportunities are then available for the participants to modify their styles, practise these modifications and experiment with different styles in a variety of situations.

The Grid approach which has obvious similarities with other human relations training events can be used similarly with stranger, cousin and family groups, either on discrete training courses or in-company as a longer-term approach.

THE JOHARI WINDOW

Training which uses the Johari Window as its basis has many similarities to the Grid approach, but in this case the concentration of attention is on the personal and internal aspects of people and their observed behaviour.

The Johari Window model of perception and awareness of behaviour originated with Joseph Luft, a psychologist, and Harry Ingram a psychiatrist. These two names explain the unusual title – the forenames of the two originators, Jo(e) and Hari(ry). The basis of the model is that of a window which reflects the various aspects of our behaviour, a two-way window in which information flows out from us to others, and in, as feedback, to us from others. Because of this movement, we can increase our awareness of the reaction of others to our behaviour and benefit ourselves from this knowledge.

The Window has four panes, shown in Figure 8.2, each pane representing knowledge at the various levels. The panes will not be of equal size from one individual to another and each individual's Window is capable of being modified, either as a result of the increase of trust within a group or from the feedback exchanged between individuals.

One pane is designated the Arena and represents what is known about oneself and which is also know by others. It is the area of open and public knowledge, knowledge which an individual is quite happy to share. The size of this pane can vary considerably according to the openness of the individual and his willingness to expose information about himself.

Another pane which is related to the Arena and which is capable of being modified in a similar way, is the Facade or Hidden area. This section of the awareness model represents things known about oneself, but unknown by others. The Facade is clearly related to the various acts or roles we perform in public, roles we want other people to consider as the real us.

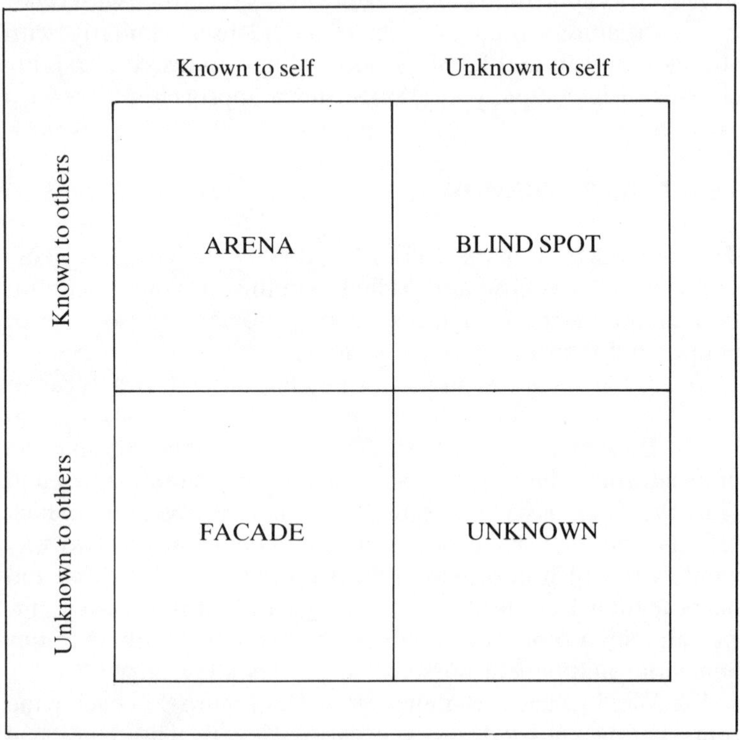

	Known to self	Unknown to self
Known to others	ARENA	BLIND SPOT
Unknown to others	FACADE	UNKNOWN

Figure 8.2   The Johari Window

The ability we have in acting roles determines whether the Facade is maintained or whether our act is discerned and the Arena area takes its place. Often our Facade is maintained from what may be a false sense of security. An individual may be afraid to reveal his true self because of fear that if he does so, he will suffer emotionally. The use of the Facade can often be related to the Child ego state as expressed in Transactional Analysis.

The third pane, the Blind Spot, has a direct relationship with the giving of feedback. It is a common experience for others to be aware of aspects about us of which we are unaware. If the level of openness between individuals or in a group is such that realistic feedback can be given, the individual will learn more about himself. Consequently the Blind Spot area will reduce and the Arena will increase, since the knowledge will be on a shared basis.

The final window pane is the most difficult one as far as movement is concerned, for this is the Unknown area which contains information about us of which neither ourselves nor others are aware. Some of these aspects may be so deeply hidden that they may never surface, but others may be lurking just under the psychological surface and, with the right stimulus, may come to light. Such Unknown aspects may be skills which have never emerged, childhood memories, feelings or skills and other unrecognised resources. Obviously the Unknown aspects may never emerge, or may require considerable pressure, trauma or solicitation to bring them out. If, however, other parts of the Window are modified through feedback, openness and trust, this is the environment in which material has the opportunity to emerge.

Movement of the panes of the Johari Window can demonstrate either the development of a group or an individual. At the beginning of a group's life the Arena pane will be small as few members will be willing to disclose personal facts about themselves or try to seek in-depth information about others in the group. To counterbalance the size of the Arena, the Facade will be large allowing each member to hide under either a neutral image or a completely false image. The Blind Spot will be stable, probably large, since if no real feedback is given, no new information will emerge. No estimate can be given of the relative size of the Unknown area because at this stage this area must be completely unknown. Figure 8.3 demonstrates the image of the group at this stage of its life.

During a human relations course the developmental norm would be expected to follow a path of increasing disclosure of personal information, increasing group cohesion, increasing

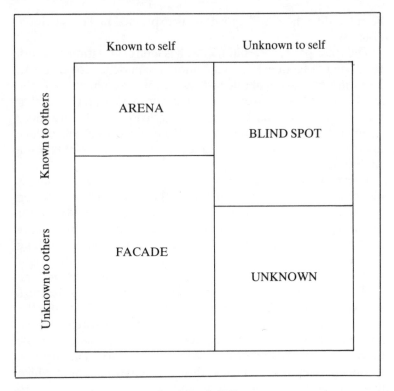

Figure 8.3 Beginning of a group's life

openness and consequently an increase in meaningful feed-back. In terms of the Johari Window representation, these movements produce the changes shown in Figure 8.4.

Because the group members are behaving openly and naturally, the Facade areas must reduce – not disappear completely since few of us will divulge everything about oneself to everybody. A considerable amount of feedback will be given in this atmosphere – some of it will be new to individuals, but much of it will be new as far as the developing group is concerned. Consequently information about the group will open the Arenas of the group to its own development, that is to say a decrease of the Blind Spot aspects.

As stated earlier, the stages of development in Johari terms can also be applied to individuals. At the start of a human

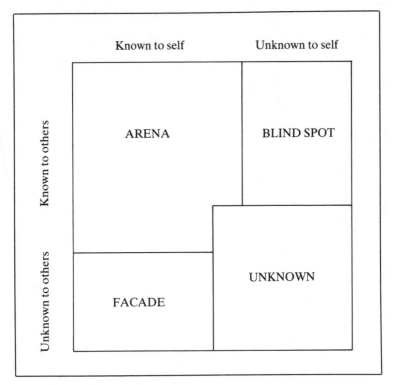

Figure 8.4   The developing group

relations training event, different individuals can be identified in terms of their relationship with the Johari aspects.

Figure 8.5 can be the profile of the poseur who has decided that nobody should find out what he is really like. Consequently he has a welded-on image which he has built up over a period of time. In the case of feedback, if this role is maintained, this type of person neither gives any (he is not sufficiently interested in others to offer this) nor receives any (as he is not interested in others, others will show no interest in him). When he does try to relate to others, he will be seeking views on what they are thinking, what they are doing, what they are feeling – a very strong questioning role. So questioning in fact that eventually the other members of the team will turn on him and demand information on what *he* feels, thinks and so

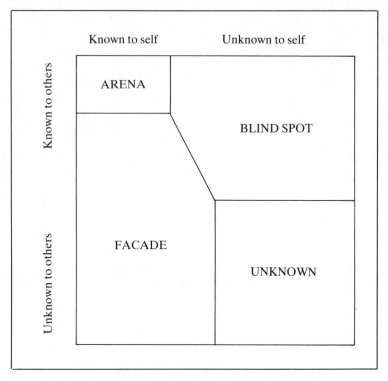

Figure 8.5   Individual in a questioning role

on. The apparent interest in others has been seen for what it probably is and has hindered rather than helped any development of relationships.

Unfortunately, the trainer has to present a profile similar to the one just described, although his questioning should be for sincere helping reasons, and consequently is in danger in an open group of losing empathy and credibility. The challenge of 'What do *you* think?' will inevitably come and must be faced.

The individual with the large Blind Spot area can be a 'lovely' person or a pain in the neck (Figure 8.6). He is likely to be so insensitive to the feelings of people that he will shower feedback, comments, advice to everybody irrespective of whether these are solicited or not. He is so insensitive to the results of his actions that he is unaware of any reactions. Or the

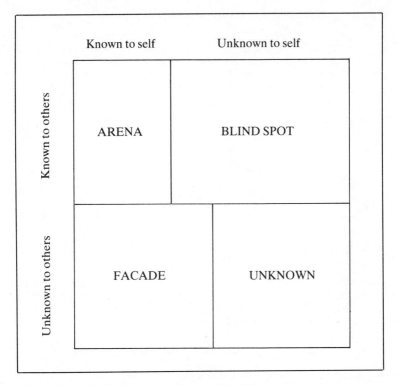

Figure 8.6   Individual with large Blind Spot

reactions can be so violent that they will be difficult to describe as real and meaningful feedback.

Conversely, the individual with the large Arena is very likely to give valuable feedback to others and receive and accept it from others. If the large Arena is an honest and sincere one and is seen and accepted as such, similar movements will be more likely to take place in others.

The final type of Johari individual is difficult to identify by virtue of the almost complete absence of behavioural messages.

The individual shown in Figure 8.7 is likely to be the quiet member of the group, perhaps even completely silent and apparently acting as an observer. Such individuals sit during the group activities, neither contributing nor gaining much, although normally they are likely to disagree with the latter

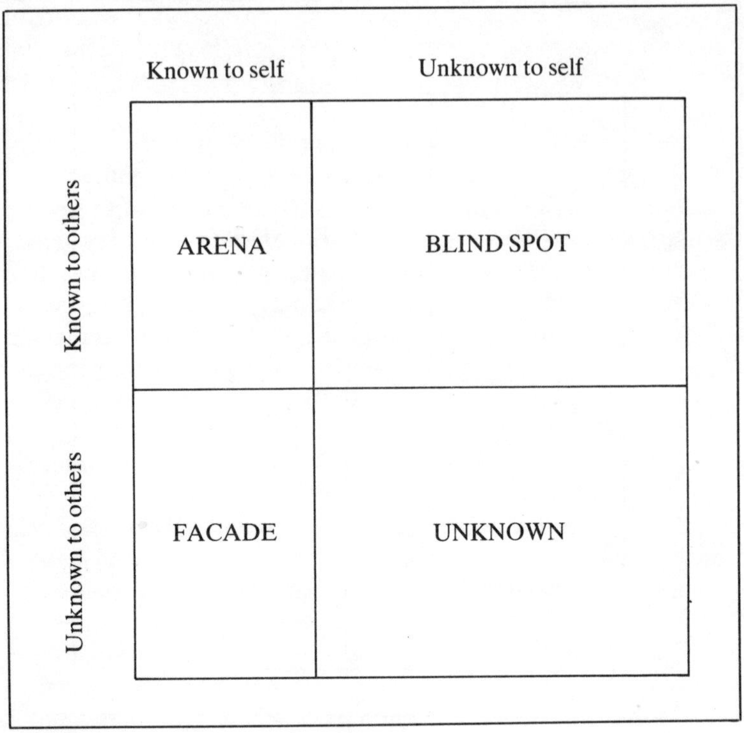

	Known to self	Unknown to self
Known to others	ARENA	BLIND SPOT
Unknown to others	FACADE	UNKNOWN

Figure 8.7   The quiet individual

assessment. They usually defend their position by saying that although they are not saying anything, they are learning more by listening. This may indeed be so when they are taking part in a very functional type of training course where the information is so well presented that clarification questioning is. not necessary and understanding is possible by the course members being simply information receptacles. But this will not work in human relations training where most of the learning is the result of positive interactions between people. The silent member is most unlikely to take definite steps to give feedback to others and as a result is unlikely to receive much feedback from others. Without feedback the Blind Spot area is not likely to decrease and, without a wide range of feedback, any unknown factors are not likely to emerge.

The Johari Window approach to the modification of human behaviour can take a variety of forms, either as a training approach in its own right or incorporated in other learning events.

If the concept is used as the basis for training, the theory of the Window and its feedback facilities are introduced and discussed. Self-rating questionnaires which will identify for the participants their positions and styles can then lead to role and behaviour modification through experimentation and practice in activities. Monitoring of any changes which may occur is built into the training which in principle is aimed at increasing the Arena of both the group and the individual, decreasing the Facade and Blind Spot areas, and as an added bonus, having some emergence of the Unknown factors. In this way, use of the Johari Window and its concepts is very similar to training using the Blake and Mouton Grid as the building brick of the event. As with the Grid and other similar approaches, the learners must accept completely the theoretical model before practice becomes real and the approach can be transferred to real life.

The approach can also be included as part of a course, at a stage when feedback or perceptual awareness of others is being introduced. For example, when the stage is reached on the interpersonal skills course when it is desirable to try to force the pace of the exchange of feedback, the subject can be introduced by a presentational input on the theory and model in terms of self and group awareness and the value of giving and receiving feedback. The input can then be followed by an activity which allows this exchange of feedback. As described in Chapter 5, this type of activity is used on my interpersonal skills training with course members rating each other on a number of behavioural aspects and exchanging this information freely with each other. The particular way in which this is done encourages openness and an increasing amount of feedback and should certainly help towards reducing the Blind Spot area and perhaps a small section of the Unknown area in addition to increasing the Arena by giving the opportunity to offer feedback.

Information about the course participants in Johari terms can be useful in mixing course members when this becomes necessary. If, for example, a course of twelve members has to be divided into two sub-groups of six, this information can be one method of deciding how to select the groups. It is quite possible that a group of twelve will contain representatives of the large-Arena, Facade, Blind Spot and Unknown types. As discussed earlier, mixing could be purely random, but it may be more useful to mix according to types. For example, we might put a number of large-Facade members together with the anticipation of their modification of behaviour in order to progress. The silent, Unknown members together would need to change their quiet ways to produce realistic and effective discussion of the task given.

ACTION CENTRED LEADERSHIP

A more structured approach to human relations training, with an emphasis on the approach to improving the leadership elements, is Action Centred Leadership (ACL). This approach was devised by John Adair and introduced widely in conjunction with the Industrial Society.

A model which every leader should bear in mind is the model of interlocking circles at the heart of every ACL training. The model represents the needs with which a leader has to juggle to maintain complete equilibrium throughout his team.

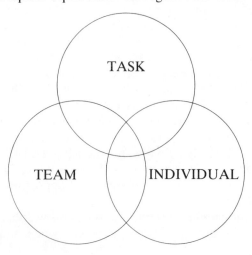

The leader must ensure that the task is performed effectively through the logical and rational steps of planning, organising, operating and monitoring. The individuals in the team or group performing the task all have needs as individuals and the effective leader must be aware of and reactive to these needs, in addition to making use of the abilities of his team members. Finally, the third element, the group or team itself and its needs as a cohesive whole must be recognised and taken care of.

All these three functions must be balanced by the leader. If he pays too much attention to the task, he is doing so at the expense of the other two aspects and although with luck the task will be performed to some extent, that is all that will occur. At worst the members will feel that their needs are being ignored and the task will suffer by being performed ineffectively or even not at all. If too much emphasis is placed on either of the other two aspects, there is the strong risk that the task will not be performed effectively.

The training approach based on the ACL model uses a number of activities in which the leaders are encouraged to consider the three functions in the performance of the task. A leader is appointed for an activity and observers are also selected from within the group. The purpose of these observers is to observe particularly the leader and his skill in balancing the three aspects and to report back after the activity. In this way, the leaders on whom comments are made learn from their practice and can also learn from comments made on other leaders when they are either members of a group or are themselves observers.

GESTALT

At the other end of the spectrum from the highly structured, formal type of training epitomised by ACL which uses 'artificial' activities with, for example, Lego bricks, is the Gestalt approach. Gestalt is a German word for which there is no direct English language equivalent: it translates approximately to 'the whole' and training associated with it attempts to treat the whole person in some way rather than just one aspect. The use of Gestalt as a training method has developed from its origins in psychotherapy, a field in which Dr Frederick Perls was pre-eminent.

In the same way that other training approaches can be used as complete training events or as parts of other training, so with the Gestalt approach. In addition to forming training in its own right, it has been associated with transactional analysis, counselling, team building, sensitivity training, assertiveness training and trainer development. Its use as a complete training approach has many similarities with T-group training or other forms of sensitivity training. The principal base is an emphasis on the 'here and now' and activities arise from the needs which emerge during the training. However, these needs and activities are not restricted to verbal activities or action associated with feelings – smell, touch, trust, emotion are all grist for the Gestalt mill.

Many of the activities used in Gestalt training can be quite traumatic for the participants, necessarily so if deep feelings or emotions are to emerge. Some of the less disturbing and uncomfortable approaches are quite frequently used in one-to-one interactions training and are described later (psychodrama, empty chair etc.).

One of the less threatening activities involves a relationship with an inanimate object, although even this apparently harmless approach can trigger deep emotions and feelings which need to be handled expertly. A willing volunteer is asked to select from within the training room or perhaps the area visible through the window, an inanimate object. Such an object could be a picture on the wall, a piano, an overhead projector etc. The volunteer is then asked to put himself in the place of the object and to describe himself as the object. Usually the description starts quite superficially with a factual description of the object, but if the atmosphere is conducive or encouragement is given, the monologue takes on a different form.

For example, if a piano is selected, after the physical description the speaker might continue with 'I sit here in the corner and most of the time I am ignored. Occasionally people are condescending enough to play me and when they do so I come to life – that's what I'm for. But it doesn't happen enough and I cannot take any initiative. What I would really like to do is . . . . . .'. It soon becomes obvious that the speaker is no longer describing the object as such, but is now using the object's inanimity to allow him to disclose his own feelings in an indirect way. Usually the observers, if any, identify this process before the individual, but when the speaker himself realises he generally feels there is now no need to stop. The atmosphere, the stage of the training and the strength of the feelings aroused will decide how far the speaker will go in his disclosures and how emotionally involved he will become in these disclosures.

An approach to trust is another activity often experienced in the Gestalt approach. Course members pair off, one of whom is blindfolded. The 'sighted' partner then takes the 'blind' partner for a walk in the grounds, but without the use of verbal signals. Guidance is developed through touch and a process of signalling is usually developed. For people who normally rely on their own sight or, at least verbal signals, considerable trust in the 'sighted' partner is necessary and can develop as the walk continues.

Gestalt application to training is very close to the psychotherapy borderline and trainers, unless they are skilled and experienced Gestalt practitioners should approach the techniques with extreme caution. In, for example, the description of the inanimate object, not only the speaker can go through an emotional event. I have seen such an event when after about 15 minutes during which the speaker was disclosing some deep-rooted fears, an observer became so involved with what was occurring and became so upset that he had to leave. He was unable to handle the emotions which were being stirred within himself as a result of the emotional experience of the speaker.

TEAM BUILDING

The most effective form of human relations training takes place where training or development really belongs – the workplace. The workplace in this context can be understood rather loosely to include anywhere – at work or elsewhere – a group of co-workers congregates to continue its work requirements. Consequently I include as workplace anywhere that a team has been brought as a single unit for developmental purposes.

The common ground is particularly valuable when it becomes necessary to build or develop a team of individuals who have to work together to a common objective. In so many working situations the group of people working together remains only a group and does not progress to become a strongly welded team in which the individuals retain their individuality but act as a corporate whole. In order for a group to develop into a team in this way it has to undergo the process of team building or development. Obviously if the whole team is together for this developmental event much faster and further progress will be made than if the individuals had to be helped in ones or twos. In this way a 'family' group is formed, all its members having the same objectives and tasks and the paramount need to work closely and effectively with each other. As the development of the team is so strongly related to the work the team has to do, apart perhaps from the initial stages, the development of the team can progress so much more easily in the working environment, using work events and problems as the tools of development. This in situ training obviates the difficulty found in most training events of ensuring an effective translation of the learning back to work: if the learning is at work and of work, the problem is resolved.

The practical approaches to team building can vary according to the circumstances of the team and the needs of the organisation. An initial decision must be taken whether the team is capable of operating its own processes in helping itself to develop or whether an external agent should be introduced to act as a catalyst or facilitator. The major problem in this decision exists when a completely new team is being considered. It may be that the leader of the team has the skills and abilities to initiate the team processes, or he may be able to do so with the partial or temporary help of a facilitator. On the other hand, the leader may be as unaware of the skills necessary as the rest of his team and he will need considerable help. In many ways, if the process can be facilitated from within, this is the best, certainly a more natural approach which takes away any obvious training element from what becomes a very natural process. However, if the leader is very unsure of his skills, he will be best advised to bring in external help. An unskilled and unaware dabbler in team building is likely to do much more damage than good and the likely result is the loss of the leader's credibility. An 'outsider' can often take a neutral and unbiased view of a situation and can certainly introduce aspects, topics and activities for which the internal leader might not have the confidence.

The introduction of an external consultant or facilitator in any case can be useful when a completely new team is being brought together and needs to develop. However, it would be unwise for the facilitator to stay too long with the team otherwise a strong measure of dependency on his skills and knowledge might develop. The ideal situation would be that while the team is welding together in its early stages, the leader, in addition to taking his part in the development, would be coached by the facilitator in further developmental action to take once the facilitator had stepped down.

The actual process of team building can vary considerably from a straightforward team-building training event held by an outside facilitator away from the workplace, but with the whole team taking part, to a series of events taking place wholly at the workplace.

A team-building event of the first kind is very little different from an interactive skills course similar to the one described earlier, except that the course participants produce a complete family group. At some stages of the event interactions have to be handled very carefully and sensitively by the facilitator, usually because the members already know each other quite well, perhaps both in a work and a non-work situation. Activities, however, can be much more realistic and can be taken from the work in which the team is or will be engaged. Problems which are common to that individual team are likely to emerge and can be dealt with on the course in a practical problem-solving way.

Usually this type of team building course is only part of a total process, the initial stage which is followed up on a regular basis with team building activities at work. It is likely that the original facilitator would be brought in to work with the team on the early follow-up events, but soon the team would take over ownership of its own development.

The work-based approach, with or without an external facilitator is not too dissimilar to the approach just described.

Perhaps the major difference is that the earlier stages can be taken at a slower pace and without the substantial period away from work needed by the initial course approach.

One approach with which I was involved as team leader seemed to be a reasonably acceptable one and certainly produced the required results. The situation was that I was the team leader of a team of five trainers, three of whom were relatively new to the team. The previous team, before the members were replaced, had been a good, close working team, but with the change, and accepting the differences that would make, the new team did not appear to be developing as well as it should/could have done.

At one of our fairly regular meetings the question of team development was raised and (an important factor) it was agreed by the whole team that we would involve ourselves in some activities to this end. We also decided that as there was a fair range of training expertise spread among us and we felt at that stage we could be reasonably open with each other, we could process the operation ourselves without an external agent. Other decisions made at this initial meeting were that we should meet at frequent and regular intervals, and that, between that present time and the next meeting, we should all research and consider ways we could progress and also identify problems which seemed to be relevant to the team's development.

The first meeting was taken up with a discussion of the views we had all formed about how we wanted to progress and what our problems were. Eventually however, we all came round to the view that we needed to look at our problems in a much more disciplined manner – the first learning point resulting from our new team approach! One of us had come across a questionnaire which was intended to help to identify a team's problem areas, so we agreed to try this.

The questionnaire used was the Building Brick approach to team building devised by Mike Woodcock. Woodcock considered that there was a number of essential building blocks for effective teamwork:

- clear objectives and agreed goals
- openness and confrontation of disagreements

- support and trust
- co-operation and resolved conflict
- sound working and decision-making procedures
- appropriate leadership
- regular reviews
- individual development
- sound intergroup relations.

The Building Block questionnaire was completed by all the members of the team and the responses were given to a neutral – a member of another team – to collate. The results of the questionnaire demonstrated the barriers existing within the team, barriers identified by the lower scores. The team was surprised when the results were presented as we all had considered that the team was developing well, within the initial constraints: the questionnaire results showed that a number of problems existed of which no one had been aware.

Once the barriers had been presented, the team discussed the results and decided which ones were the priority barriers for early consideration. These decisions were made using two basic criteria – low scores demonstrating particular problems and the answer by the team to the question 'Where do you want the team to be in a year's time?'.

Four priority areas were determined and over the series of meetings we held various activities and discussions aimed at clarifying our views and trying to rectify the problems. As time went by and we pursued our activities, we found that in addition to solving our major problems, a number of minor problems were alleviated and even aspects which we had not found to be problems as such were improved.

ROLE NEGOTIATION

Once the development of the team was well under way and real openness was emerging in the team, we decided that further progress would be made with an attempt at even greater openness of how we reacted to each other. One complete meeting was devoted to this activity, but the results had ramifications which continued well beyond that occasion.

The activity used was Role Negotiation in which the objectives are to give positive feedback to each other and negotiate contracts with each other.

In order to carry out the activity, each member has a number of sheets of paper, each containing the headings:

It would help me if you were to do less ....

It would help me if you were to do more ....

It would help me if you were to continue..

Each individual of the team identifies behaviours under one or more of these headings with one or more other members of the team. For example, John wants Jim to stop interrupting him quite so much and to bring him in more by asking for his views on the proposals that John wants Jim to continue to make. Fred wants Mary, Bill and Ken to listen more to him when he explains his views, and so on.

In order to make the contracts John will give Jim a sheet completed in accordance with what he wants him to do. Fred does the same with Mary, Bill and Ken and all the other members who wish to do so, send role requests.

At this stage negotiation commences. The role requests are not simply one way communications and if a contract is to be agreed a bargain must be made. Jim on receiving John's requests may agree with them, but simply to agree is making the interaction one-sided and too easy to ensure maintenance. Jim must negotiate with John that if he is to agree to John's requests, John must in return agree not to talk so much, so that Jim does not have to interrupt him. Or Mary, Bill and Ken might require Fred to be more concise and clear in his statements if they are to agree to listen more to him. And so the horse-trading continues until all the possible bargains have been struck and contracts made.

The final part of the negotiation was that once all contracts had been discussed openly and agreed, the contracts were written down as a statement of the team's agreement. In fact we posted the contracts on the walls of the team room and as further meetings were held we monitored how successful the contracts had been.

By this stage the planned team development had progressed

well, but the level we had attained had to be maintained. The regular meetings were continued, albeit with rather longer intervals between them, and from time to time the blockages questionnaire was repeated to ensure that no problems had been ignored or new ones had not developed.

There are obviously a number of ways to approach team building and development and fortunately a start can be made at whatever stage a potential team has reached. The principal factor, one over which so many attempts at team building fail, is to ensure that there is full agreement by the team itself that the activity is necessary and should take place.

ACTION LEARNING

Another approach to human relations training, combining training and real life practice in a similar way to team building, is Action Learning. It also follows the same concept as most effective human relations training approaches – that people learn best by doing.

The approach, whose essence is real life problem solving, was introduced by Reg Revans with a group of coal mine managers. These initial events were soon followed by similar approaches with hospital administrators and Action Learning has now spread throughout the world. With this spread and development, a number of variations have sprung from the original approach, but all have as their base the approach to problem solving using real life problems as the vehicle: the aim is to provide solutions to the problems, not just to produce yet another form of training exercise.

The original concept of Action Learning envisaged the formation of a group of people brought together, from different places, to use its differing experiences to solve the problems of each.

One approach is to form the group from individuals from different companies and organisations. Each individual brings from his establishment a problem and the problem is taken over by another member of the group. This second member then goes on full- or part-time attachment to the establishment to work on the problem. Although a large amount of the work on the problem solving is done away from the Action Learning group, or 'set', there is still a strong group influence. The set holds regular meetings during which the set members discuss the problems they are approaching, ideas they are having, difficulties they are encountering. A set facilitator is usually available to help with the discussion, provide or obtain special inputs on techniques etc. and the individuals benefit in many ways from his support and that of the other members of the set.

Whatever form the Action Learning set may take, the regular meetings (a day each fortnight or month is typical) are a common feature which extends the approach from a simple individual problem-solving activity to a developmental exercise. The set meetings give the members the opportunity to:

- discuss the problems and seek and test out ideas
- give mutual support
- review progress in a structured manner
- have formal sessions on techniques, methods, approaches applicable to the processes they are undergoing
- increase their skills in working with groups
- release their feelings.

The approach described has a number of advantages and disadvantages. As the problem is not owned by the set member who is looking at it, a neutral and objective approach can be made, rather than a biased and subjective attitude born of being too close to the problem. An additional advantage can be that someone external to the problem and its environment may have a greater likelihood of acceptance by the personnel of the organisation. A major disadvantage can be the long period of time necessary for a stranger to familiarise himself with the company organisation and all the other environmental factors in which the problem exists. Within this 'stranger' approach there are two variations possible. One requires that, although the problem solver is foreign to the company, the problem is of the type with which he has had previous experience. For example, an engineer from one industry will approach an engineering problem in another type of industry. The environment will be different, but the problem will be similar to the ones with which he normally deals. This approach will obviously reduce the amount of research time necessary. The other variation is rather more extreme and requires the problem solver to take on a problem with which he is unfamilar in his specialism or experience, looking at a problem connected with the personnel function. In this type of case there will also be a time factor involved in researching the problem itself from a fundamental level, in addition to any company background research. There is of course an additional advantage in that the problem solver is approaching the problem from a position of ignorance, and the resultant completely fresh approach may sweep away any traditional barriers which may have been hiding potential solutions.

Two other variations are possible and are frequently used. In one case the individuals bring with them to the Action Learning set a problem which is owned by them, a problem with which they are completely familiar and which they have to solve themselves. Frequently the set in this type of case will consist of members from the same company or organisation, but this is not essential and a heterogeneous composition can be useful in illuminating the problems from other angles. In this approach the set is used as the vehicle to help the members to analyse their problems fully, produce or obtain possible solutions, check these out against other people and rehearse final actions or presentations. The problem solvers in this situation are approaching problems they would have had to solve in any case, but are learning many more aspects by coming to the solution within and with the help of the set.

The other variation is rather similar in that it will normally include managers from the same company or organisation who, instead of looking at their own problems, will look at problems in parts of their own company with which they are not familar. A personnel man would look at a sales problem in his own company, a sales man would look at a production problem, and so on. This interchange has the added advantage of giving company members a detailed insight into the work and problems of different disciplines within the company.

The final version of Action Learning would be to use the set in a group process approach by having all set members look at one problem. Even within this version there are variations. The members could be a stranger group or a family group and the problem could be one with which they may or may not be familiar.

The value of Action Learning is now beyond doubt, although there is some opposition to its practice in that it is suggested that:

- the problems can be solved in more efficient ways
- the other learning achieved can be achieved in more effective ways
- the process requires the expenditure of considerable amounts of time = money.

Whatever the weight of argument against the approach, there is no doubt that, like many other human relations approaches, it is being used successfully in many places. But, as with the other human relations approaches, it is not the *only* approach.

QUALITY CIRCLES

A consideration of the Quality Circles concept and its relationship to human relations development follows quite naturally from Action Learning. Duncan Smith (*Industrial and Commercial Training*, 15 (1), January 1983) considers that Action Learning could be 'the British answer to Quality Circles' and Reg Revans claims that much of his earlier work with Action Learning was in fact Quality Circles work by a different name.

This comparison is not difficult to understand as both Quality Circles and Action Learning have an identical aim, namely the solving of real life problems in a working group atmosphere. There are, however, a number of differences, but whether these may be only a shade of grey rather than black or white is for the potential user to judge.

Quality Circles as such were introduced as practical events in Japan in the 1960s and their use is now spreading rapidly throughout the world. The basis of a Quality Circle is the meeting together on a regular basis – say one hour weekly – of a group of *volunteers* in-company who work for the same manager, foreman or supervisor. During these meetings, job-related problems are identified, analysed and have solutions proposed. The group then has the task of presenting and selling the proposed solution to the appropriate level of management and, if it is accepted, implementing it and monitoring its progress. The principal benefits are that the group learns how to work closely together on problems which affect its members directly and that they have a strong sense of ownership of the resulting solution. A strong commitment must result from this ownership of the solution as it is put into operation, and as the employees can see ideas of their own put into practice, there will be a greater degree of commitment to the work of the company.

For Quality Circles to succeed there must be full support from senior management, not only in accepting the require-ment to look at proposals made by the Circle, but also to make the time and training available. Training in the techniques of a Circle is essential as one of the reasons for possible failure of a Circle is that it is regarded as just another discussion group or talking shop. It is normal for the company to appoint a facilitator – often a member of the company's training department – whose responsibility it is for introducing Quality Circles into the organisation and for ensuring that Circle leaders and members have the necessary training. The facili-tator will also be very much in evidence in the early days of the life of a Circle to assist or advise on any process problems and provide any additional training necessary.

The actual training for Circle leaders and members can vary considerably, depending on the existing skills and knowledge, but commonly includes such aspects as meeting skills, problem analysis and solving skills, and presentational skills. There will be spin-offs during the life of the Circle in the form of increased team building and interactive skills, group techniques and leadership qualities. But the emphasis must be on the self-generative process of the Circle itself, its developing skills in problem solving, and a demonstration to the world outside the Circle that products of sufficient and acceptable quality and quantity can emerge from the Circle.

Mike Robson, who has had considerable influence on the introduction of Quality Circles into Britain, gives a number of examples of problems tackled by Quality Circles in the UK (*The Training Officer,* 18 (4), April 1982). These range from a group of cleaners in the shipbuilding industry who saved their company £25,000 per annum by solving a problem of waste disposal, to a group of draughtsmen who saved £5,000 per annum by solving a simple problem of the distribution of drawings which had not been considered previously. Most applications of Quality Circles have been in the manufacturing industries, but Circles exist in banking, insurance, hospitals and public administration and there seems to be no reason why they should not succeed in any setting where the organisational atmosphere is right and more than lip service is paid by senior management.

THE VERTEAM

The basic structure of a Quality Circle is horizontal and fits naturally into an organisation's hierarchy. Normally the members of a Circle are from one section of a work force with little grade or responsibility level differences except perhaps for the Circle leader who is the manager, foreman or supervisor of the group. Edmund Metz considers that the Quality Circle is highly effective in solving what he calls Type I problems – those over which the Circle has control, and some Type II problems – those over which the Circle has limited control only. However, he feels that the Circle is in difficulty when faced with Type III problems – those over which Circle members have neither control nor influence. Metz suggests that to solve Type III problems a completely different form of Circle is needed, one which has a vertical structure – the Verteam Circle. This different type of Circle is considered to be necessary for many major problems which require a wider knowledge of the background and constraints than would be available to the normal shop floor Quality Circle. The members of the Verteam would be drawn from all levels and departments of the organisation including senior officers who would bring greater knowledge and greater implementation authority with them. Normally the problem to be solved would be selected by top management.

In other ways the Verteam would operate like any other Quality Circle – solving real problems, meeting regularly (or as necessary), volunteer members, trained in Circle methods, services of a facilitator, working as a team and making management presentations on proposed solutions.

The Verteam approach confirms the problems of discussing the group approaches to human relations training: either a particular approach is a combination of two or more techniques, or the differences are so slight that it is difficult to separate two approaches. As human relations training is a relative newcomer to the training scene and is still in the process of developing and stabilising, innovations or apparent innovations are inevitable. The training scene is prone to 'flavours of the month' and human relations training is susceptible to these vagaries. So the principle of *caveat emptor* must apply when a company is looking for an effective human relations approach and even previous success of a programme is no guarantee: the success would have been with a group of people different from the one currently in mind. Purchasers of training or training methods must study the aims and objectives, content and methods, philosophies and controls before committing themselves. I have tried to present in some detail some of the current approaches – there are others which may be more relevant to your requirements. All you can do now is to read the brochures, talk with companies and individuals who have participated, and ask many questions.

REFERENCES AND RECOMMENDED READING

Adair, J. (1978): *Training for Leadership*. Aldershot: Gower.
Adair, J. (1979): *Action-Centred Leadership*. Aldershot: Gower.
Berger, M.L. and Berger, P.J. (1978): *Group Training Techniques*. Aldershot: Gower.
Blake, R. and Mouton, J. (1978): *The New Managerial Grid*. Gulf.
James and Jongeward, D. (1971): *Born to Win*. London: Addison-Wesley.
Luft, J. (1970): *Group Processes: An Introduction to Group Dynamics*. Mayfield.

Metz, E.J. (1981): 'The Verteam', *Training and Development Journal,* December.

Passons, W. (1975): *Gestalt Approaches in Counselling.* New York: Holt, Rinehart and Winston.

Perls, F. (1973): *Gestalt Therapy. Excitement and Growth in the Human Personality.* London: Penguin.

Revans, R. (1982): *The Origins and Growth of Action Learning.* Chartwell-Bratt.

Revans, R. (1983): *The ABC of Action Learning.* Chartwell-Bratt.

Revans, R. (1981): 'Action Learning: its Terms and Character', *Management Decision,* 21 (1).

Revans, R. (1983): 'Action Learning: the Skills of Diagnosis', *Management Decision,* 21 (2).

Revans, R. (1983): 'Action Learning: the Forces of Achievement or Getting it Done', *Management Decision,* 21 (3).

Revans, R. (1983): 'Action Learning: the Cure is Started', *Management Decision,* 21 (4).

Revans, R. (1983): 'Action Learning: Kindling the Touch Paper', *Management Decision,* 21 (6).

Revans, R. (1984): 'Action Learning: Are We Getting There?', *Management Decision,* 22 (1).

Robson, M. (1982): *Quality Circles: A Practical Guide.* Aldershot: Gower.

Woodcock, M. (1979): *Team Development Manual.* Aldershot: Gower.

Woodcock, M. and Francis, D. (1981): *Organisation Development through Team Building.* Aldershot: Gower.

9 Activities and interventions

These topics relate both to group human relations training and to the one-to-one interactions, so it will be useful to consider them as a bridge between the group and individual approaches. Activities are certainly used in one-to-one interaction training, but they are more commonly found in group training. My definition of an activity in human relations training is wide, ranging from an individual having to introduce himself in a particular way, through structured activities which have no direct relationship to the work, or fully job related (usually a case study), to 'here and now' unstructured activities which have arisen naturally in the group process.

UNSTRUCTURED ACTIVITIES

The unstructured activity is in one respect the easiest and in another the most difficult. There are none of the selection problems that one finds with structured activities, which have to be chosen carefully. However, reliance on an emerging, unstructured event demands that the tutor is listening very carefully to the group all the time, understanding everything that is happening and assessing the most appropriate time to pick up the point and feed it back to the group. Perhaps the understanding of what is happening is the most difficult area as the overt and covert aspects of communication may not be in step, or, in the terms of the Transactional Analysis we considered earlier, the transactions are really at the psychological level although appearing complementary. However, this is a risk that the tutor has to take and he must make his suggestion for action in such terms that he can react to subsequent indications of covert transactions.

A fairly typical unstructured activity in a group training event might arise from an incident occurring in another activity and this aspect might be picked up by either the tutor or the group itself. One such event comes readily to mind and I have observed it being processed in both these ways. During an interpersonal skills course while the group was performing the structured activity of considering the elements which produce effective team working, some discussion on the election of a leader arose, but was only settled in the terms of the activity. As this activity took place early in the course and the group would be performing a number of other activities during the course, it seemed reasonable to assume that this topic would have to be clarified by the group sooner or later. Why not sooner? In fact, on a number of occasions on which I have seen this subject arise in this way, the group has decided, or has asked the tutor if it could follow the structured activity with a decision-making activity to clarify this matter for the group. On occasions, when the group has not come forward with the idea, I have suggested that this would be a topic which they would have to come to terms with eventually. Invariably they have accepted this comment and immediately launched into the decision-making activity. Quite often, a follow on, unstructured activity of this nature can lead to the raising of other spontaneous relevant topics which can be the useful bases for discussion and action if the structure of the course permits.

Much will depend on the nature and constraints of the course as to how far these naturally occurring incidents can and should be taken up. On courses which themselves have little formal structure and which are concerned with the here and now of interactions, they can be vital to the event. For example, if a group is highly and interactively discussing something and one person opts out, the tutor (who may be the only one who has observed this) has to decide on his intervention strategy. He may feel that the group is not going to comment: consequently the trainer may intervene in the discussion and suggest that the group might wish to look at an inappropriate incident which is occurring and the effect and possible consequences of this.

Unstructured activities can also be used in training events of a one-to-one interaction nature. During a training event on counselling techniques, for example, when the learners are practising the techniques, it is quite common to use constructed role plays or case studies as the bases of the interviews. But the trainer should always be listening for such comments as 'This case is similar to one I have back at the office' or 'A real problem I have back home is better than this case study'. If such comments are made, it is often useful to take the opportunity and build the practice interview around the real situation rather than the artificial case study.

CASE STUDIES

Many activities on training courses are based on case studies which are directly related to the job being performed at work by the learner. These activities can be quite simple in character and can form a series of activities to cover a range of learning points. Activities of this nature can be concerned with, for example, the manager's role in delegation. The individual learner or group of learners are given a description of a singular situation with which they would be familiar at work and are asked to provide a solution or an indication of what they would do or say. In the delegation example, the information which might be given is that because of certain time constraints two tasks from a list of six tasks must be delegated. The decision must be made on which tasks, how they should be delegated, to whom and so on. The activity can in fact satisfy several training objectives – problem solving, decision making, task delegation, communication etc.

Or in more directly human relations related activities, the exercise could be concerned with the action to be taken on a problem produced by a member of staff. Such a problem could be one of discipline, interpersonal relationships, work methods or any of the many human relations problems which so commonly occur at work.

One of the complaints frequently raised against activities of this nature is that the information given about the incident or task is scant. However, if the information is extended the simple activity becomes a case study.

ACTION MAZES AND IN-TRAYS

Between the simple activity and the full blown case study lie such learning events as the action maze and the in-tray exercise.

In the action maze, the task is approached by individuals who are given an information sheet which gives the basic details of a working situation with either a technical problem or, more usually, an interactive problem. The individual is required, having read the information, to make a decision from a set of multi-choice answers. Whichever choice is made the learner is then directed to another stage of the situation, the stage depending on the answer given to the question on the first sheet. At the second stage a further decision is again required and the learner moves on to yet another stage. Progress continues through the maze until the final, 'correct' decision is made.

The advantage of this type of activity is that each learner can proceed at his own pace and the amount of skill possessed or developed determines how long it takes to work through the maze. The skilled participant can reach the final decision quickly, having made the correct choices throughout the maze in the least number of moves. The unskilled individual is likely to make a number of inappropriate choices and at worst could move around in a number of circles before eventually making the correct final decision.

One of the disadvantages with the action maze in training is that the learner who has read extensively before taking part in the activity, could give all the right answers whether or not the real basis for the moves is understood. Also, although it is stated that the learner can proceed at his own pace, pressure is put on the slower members if the activity is performed in a visible group.

In-tray exercises, or as they are sometimes called in-baskets, also provide the learner with decision choices, but on this occasion from a much wider range than the action maze.

A typical in-tray exercise provides the learner with a basket of letters, minutes, reports, internal memos and notes. He is told that he has only a certain amount of time available – too little to deal with all the material – before he leaves on holiday, on a course or to a different post. This type of activity extends the simple activity described earlier by providing a more difficult task to accomplish, but requires the learner to perform effective problem solving, decision making, delegating and organisation.

MAJOR CASE STUDIES

A case study is more or less the same as the simple job-related activity, but more complex and complicated. For example, a human relations activity might be concerned with the need for a manager to conduct a discipline interview with a member of his staff. Information about the member of staff and the problem is given and provided the interview process is appropriate the complete study can be terminated by action agreed at the interview. On the other hand, the case study might be concerned with the relationships of all the staff in the office, and information is given not only about the inter-relationships but also about the task of the office, successful performance of which depends on satisfactory relationships.

In such a case study a maximum of information is given, perhaps even a surplus, so that the group has everything with which to solve the problems. On occasions, less information than is necessary is provided so that the group needs to seek further information, either from the tutor or by practical research methods which are readily available. If the learners are from an organisation or part of an organisation in which computers are everyday vehicles of data collection and retrieval, computers and the type of information normally available are made available to help in the solution of the case study problems.

A complex and extensive case study can be given to a group in a more personalised way than simply giving the information and requiring the solution of the problem. The group can be formed into a pseudo-company which has to solve the problem relating to the company. Individuals are given roles of MD,

Sales Director, Production Director, Personnel Director and so on and the constituted group attempts to function as if it were a real company. If the problem presented is very complicated and may have to extend over several days or even weeks, the activity can be presented as a Business Game. If the course is sufficiently large, it can be divided into smaller groups who in addition to trying to solve the problem, are in competition with each other thus simulating the real life competition of companies. Or at least as far as it is possible in the artificial environment of a training event.

STRUCTURED ACTIVITIES

The widest definition of a structured activity includes the more complex case studies, business games, simulations, in-trays and action mazes, in addition to less formal and complicated exercises. They can be job-related or completely general in their application, but whatever the basis the trainer must be absolutely sure of his objectives and reasons for having the group perform the activity.

A typical structured activity is one in which the building of a structure is involved – a mast, a bridge or similar structure – with pieces of Lego or similar children's building materials. This is the task aspect of the activity, but much more can be included in the objectives.

The activity starts with the selection of a leader, or a leader for each group taking part in the activity, and the issue of the activity brief to these leaders. Time is given to the group(s) to plan and organise their activity and the opportunity is also given to practise whatever construction is necessary. Constraints are usually built into the operation with financial sanctions being imposed on the number of pieces used in the construction, the time taken to complete the task and other physical attributes of the structure such as the height of a mast. The group must, during the planning period, try to aim for maximum profit by avoiding the possible sanctions or at least minimising their effects.

Once the planning period has been used and the group has made its plans on how it is to proceed with construction and for what profit it is aiming, the actual construction phase commences. In this phase the group(s) put their plans into operation and the success or otherwise of the plan and objectives is seen – with measurement against the sanctions, how long did the group take, how high (long) did the group build the mast (bridge), using how many pieces of building materials? The actual results are compared with the planned results and discussion can take place on the difference between these and why they occurred, in addition to the comparison of the results of each group.

An activity of this nature can be used simply as described – to give practice in the leadership practices of planning organising, operation and control, and also the elements of profit forecasting against calculated risks. These are all principally task oriented approaches and can be highly satisfactory in this respect.

However, emphasis can be placed instead of or in addition to the task orientation, on the people aspect of the operation and it is in this aspect that the activity will be used more in human relations training. Normally the group will be observed during the planning phase particularly, the observations being made either by direct observers – fellow trainees or tutors – or by indirect recordings with audio or video equipment. The observers will be looking for the use of people resources by the leader and the interactions between the members. I can recall one occasion on which I acted as observer for this activity, the leader became so actively involved himself in the task that he completely forgot about using and leading the group. After quickly reading the brief he extracted the building pieces and with three of the five members started experimenting with various constructions. No attempt was made to use the graphs which gave information on the various sanctions, but worse, the information was virtually disregarded and one of the group did not become aware that the information was available. Ideas were not sought and the four experimenters worked as individuals, monopolising the building pieces to such an extent that the remaining two members opted out to all intents and purposes – this was not even noticed! However, just before the end of the planning period one of these members had a look at the graphical information and made a comment which showed that he had grasped the implications of the information contained in the graphs. This comment was ignored!

The construction phase for this group resulted in the operation of a plan to break even, rather than make a profit, and in fact a loss was made. In the discussion which followed, the leader was crucified by his own group, particularly by those members who had been ignored and the leader learned a lot!

What is the place for structured activities such as that just described, in human relations training? Obviously they can be used in looking at the role and activities of the leader of a group or meeting; the reactions and interactions of the group, team or meeting members can be observed and analysed; and the relationship between the task and people contents of an activity can be consolidated.

One of the arguments raised against activities concerns whether the activity should be job specific or general in its format. The argument for a job related activity is that participants will be able to relate to a situation with which they will be familiar. Because of this it is considered that the participants will more easily relate the lessons of the activity to their real working life. Consequently the group will take more interest in the activity and be more committed to succeeding in the activity – particularly if they are pragmatists! On the other hand the arguments for a general type of activity are that it can be constructed to ensure that the objectives are attained, that any type of mixture of participants can take part in the same activity, and that a wider, more interesting type of activity can be introduced.

There are of course arguments against both approaches. One can say that a job related activity although having a relationship to work can never completely relate to that work. Even though it is real-life based, it will be looked upon as artificial as it has been transferred to a training course. Participants can and do complain that they do not like this type of activity as they like to get away from work aspects when they attend a course. There is always the problem that if the activity is job related and the training objectives are wider than the completion of the task alone, the members can become too involved and interested in the task to take any notice of other factors – the process, behaviours, group and individual needs.

The general activity can be looked upon as unrealistic, 'mickey mouse' and gimmicky and too far from the real world of work. But the major criticism is that it puts too much demand on the trainees to accept the lessons and then relate from the general to the specific of real life work.

Which is the strongest argument? My experience has been with both types of activity and I have received all the arguments cited above from the same types of groups – whether the activity was job- or non-job related. To give you some indication and help the type of comments I have received are that:

- they preferred job-related activities to which they could relate easily
- they preferred non-job related activities as they found them more interesting and could easily relate the lessons to their work problems.

One answer is to mix different types of activity in a course, perhaps retaining the job related ones to later in the course when you are sure the group has the skill to consider all aspects of an activity.

ACTIVITY OBJECTIVES

There can be a tendency for trainers, when they are not quite sure what to include in their training event, to say 'Oh let's put an activity in here. It will break up those two long sessions.'. The same comment is used for the use of a film or a guest speaker, or some other different form of learning. There is nothing wrong in using the activity with an objective of relieving an otherwise boring training day if:

- it has been determined logically and realistically that an activity was the most appropriate event at that stage
- the other elements of the course have been considered and found to be completely appropriate themselves
- another important element is not being displaced through lack of thought.

However, there are many more reasons or objectives for including activities in our training events. The principal justification must be linked with the way people learn. In the majority of cases the practical application of a technique or method has considerably more value than reading or being told about it or even being shown how it works. This is evident in the success of the Tell, Show, Do method of instruction. The practical evidence is borne out by the many surveys into people's preferred styles of learning when the practical approach is invariably a high ranker. But the trainer can have important subsidiary objectives within the basic reasoning.

COMMUNICATION

One of the main problems encountered in the operation of an organisation is the deficiency in its communications systems. Consequently a large proportion of emphasis in training is towards attempting to ease this problem. If a group is formed to perform an activity, it must perforce communicate within itself and thus satisfy what may be the principal objective of the trainer.

The objective may be as simple as getting the members to talk to each other and on many training events this approach is disguised within an activity which may have the task achievement as its overt objective. I described earlier the activity used in the Mark 3 Interpersonal Skills course to produce introductions. In order to reach any stage in this activity the members, who are strangers to each other, have to talk to each other and discover factual information so that the task might be achieved.

INTRODUCTION ACTIVITIES

There are quite a number of 'getting to know you' exercises which can be used at the introduction stage. The 'creeping death' approach or one of its variants certainly do not come under this heading, but similar, simple methods do. The group can be paired off and invited to interview each other with the intention of then introducing the person interviewed to the remainder of the group. This method allows each member to talk in depth with one other person and also share the obtained information with the rest of the group. If the participants have any difficulties in the content of the interview, they can always be given such guidance as 'Determine the three best (most likeable/favourite/strongest) attributes and the three worst (least likeable/abhorred/weakest) attributes of the other person'. This approach can introduce some problems of listening as we found in the case of the 'creeping death' as inevitably some internal rehearsing of a future contribution will occur.

The introductory activity, particularly in human relations training, need not be as relatively passive as the interviewing techniques and many varied approaches are described in the literature on exercises and activities. One method I have used quite successfully has been to give each member a sheet of newsprint and asked them to write on this paper six adjectives describing their best attributes and six describing their worst. Many variations and additions to this basic approach can be evolved. The information can be posted on the walls of the training room and the group encouraged to question the individuals to clarify and extend the information. Or the information can be posted anonymously and the group is invited to match a description with an individual. Another approach can be for members to select from their handbags or wallets an object which represents their personal communication or interactive style and then describe to the group why this object was chosen. Or the same can be done with an object in the training room.

One very active method that I have seen used effectively is to have all the participants mill about the room talking to each other. Each starts off with a blank sheet of paper pinned to them and as a new item of relevant information is discovered about them it is entered on their 'label'. A considerable amount of fun can occur with this approach when the activity is finished and each member can read his own 'label'. Most people are surprised at how much information about themselves they have disclosed and many at *what* they have disclosed. The varieties of this type of activity are endless.

TRIADS

When people talk to each other there is no guarantee that the receiver is doing anything more than hearing the words which have been spoken. Unless some specific action is necessary or feedback is required, much of what we say is in danger of being heard but not listened to, or even not being heard. An activity to demonstrate this and train the participants to listen is known as 'Triads', an activity which has been in training use for a considerable time.

The requirements, as the term 'triad' suggests, are three people. Two of the three are required to take an initially active part in the exercise, while the third acts in an observational/judgemental role. A subject for discussion, preferably one which is capable of producing heated discussion or disagreement, is chosen by the two active participants and one starts off the discussion by making an opening statement. When the contribution has been made the other person will reply. But before doing so that person must summarise what the speaker has said. The third person acting as judge will assess whether the summary was correct. The reply can then be given and the new receiver has to go through the same process. And so the activity continues for as long as it has been decided that each discussion should last. The 'judge' then takes the place of one of the participants in the previous discussion and the whole process is repeated with a different subject and then again until a discussion has taken place between each 'pair' in the triad.

DISCUSSION GROUPS

The principle of putting the learning group into an activity simply to have them talk to one another can be extended to introduce a specific purpose into the discussion. The group can be given the task of discussing and coming to a conclusion on a particular topic whether this is a job related topic or one which has no direct relationship to work. In the former case, the purpose of the discussion might be to produce agreement on a particular work action or support for that action and, in the latter case, the objective might be simply 'to have the group discuss'. There are obviously other objectives possible in situations such as this, the most prominent of which would be found on a training event concerned with training discussion group leaders.

OBSERVATION

Whatever the primary objective might be in bringing the group together and to communicate in some way within the group, these events can also be used for a purpose external to the group. A group which is participating in an activity can be used as a vehicle for observation whether to train observers in such techniques as the identification of critical incidents or as interaction analysts, or to provide observers practising Behaviour Analysis so that the data can be fed back to the group.

RELEASE

A much wider objective for producing a 'talking' group may be to allow the release of emotions, feelings, activity or feedback. In the area of emotions and feelings, a stage may be reached during a training event when the tutor realises that emotions or feelings have reached a certain stage and may need to offer the group an activity in which these attitudes might either be released or subjugated. The specific objective and activity will depend on the group need and the principal danger will be in the trainer's assessment of whether he should help the feelings to be released or contained at that time. It may be, of course, that an appropriate way of absorbing the feelings might be to introduce an active activity in which the physical processes would ease the mental tension. This type of activity can be the equivalent of the individual jumping up and down on a cardboard box to release his feelings in a non-harmful way.

DEPLOYMENT OF SKILLS

Perhaps the most frequent use of activities on training courses is in connection with the skills and techniques being presented on the course. The request for these may come from the tutor who may need to supplement some of the training or from the learners for the same purpose.

A course which is intended to teach a number of skills based on models, techniques and methods will not achieve success if they are only talked about. In fact, the greater likelihood of success will be achieved if the practical applications on the course far outweigh the theoretical inputs. The practical activity can thus be used:

- to demonstrate a model, theory or technique
- to give practice in the skills presented
- to utilise the model and the skills in a practical situation.

As far as the last named use is concerned, it may be that on a course which might contain skills training in problem solving, a real problem with the group might emerge. This is an ideal opportunity to put the problem solving model(s) into effective use on a real 'here and now' problem. This is a much more effective learning vehicle than practice on constructed case studies, although one cannot always depend upon a catastrophe occurring on a course to provide a real problem!

ASSISTING GROUP DEVELOPMENT

Whatever the nature of the training event, learning is supported when the group is working as a reasonably cohesive whole rather than as the group of strangers or relative strangers it was at the beginning of the course. The vast majority of groups progress through the cycle described earlier and much of this development is achieved by the group working together on a common activity. The nature of the activity for this purpose alone is not critical and this objective can often be linked with others. A typical example of an activity designed for this purpose is the 'Where are we now?' activity described in the Interpersonal Skills course.

ACTIVITY CONTENT

The content of any activity will naturally be related to the objectives of the activity and the group which will be participating. The principal activity contents in human relations training will include:

1) *Openers.* Getting to know each other, self-introduction, introduction of others, stating first impressions, stating personal objectives.
2) *Dyads.* One-to-one interaction role plays and interviews, communication between two people.
3) *Triads.* Listening, summarising, discussing.
4) *Interactive improvement.* Increasing self-awareness, operating as a group, building relationships, developing the group, team building.
5) *Interactive awareness.* Increasing self-awareness, practising analysis, excluding behaviours, practising behaviour modification.
6) *Group skills.* Problem solving, decision making, problem analysis.
7) *Feedback.* Sharing feedback verbally, exchanging questionnaires, co-counselling.
8) *Intergroup activities.* Competition, conflict, co-operation, hierarchical differences, win/lose – win/win strategies.
9) *Leader skills.* Interventions, strategies, styles, types.

The specific content of any of these activities can be as wide as the imagination of the group or the facilitator and as extensive as the resources available. The activities could include practical approaches in which items are constructed or destroyed; words are used to complete puzzles, construct new languages or produce poems or stories; media instruments used to produce cameos, advertisements or speeches; questionnaires and other instruments used to test and demonstrate; and so on.

OBSERVING ACTIVITIES

A number of approaches to observing activities in a meaningful way exist and several have already been mentioned briefly. The apparently simplest and most obvious approach is to have the participants themselves take note of what they are doing while it is happening so that the process can be discussed subsequently. The advantages of this approach are that there is no need for onlookers, either course colleagues or trainers, and so the group will have no external distractions. This atmosphere is most conducive to free operation and duplicates as nearly as possible the real life situation at work when it is rare that we have people observing our work. On the other hand the likelihood that any deep observation will be performed is remote, as people are remarkably myopic particularly when they are involved and absorbed in a task. People who are untrained are equally unaware of actions and emotions existing around them and when this is pointed out to them subsequently, a most common comment is 'Good Heavens, was that happening. I saw nothing.' So if we require an objective and full observation, it is necessary to look wider than the participating group.

The next stage in effective observation must be for the trainer to act as observer. He will probably be doing this in any case for his own purposes and a skilled trainer should be capable of effective observation on behalf of the group. But his presence may be a distraction or even a deterrent when the group is performing a task. The purpose of observation must be so that feedback can be given; it may be that the group will not accept any feedback given by the trainer.

If the observational feedback by the trainer is not acceptable to the group, there is a chance that it will be if delivered by colleagues. Using part of the group as observers is probably the most common approach to observation in training. The advantages are that the rest of the group is likely to accept their presence more than that of the trainer and in the feedback session the peer observers are likely to give hard feedback, perhaps harder than the trainer would give. However, there is no guarantee that these comments would be accepted, and they may be rejected as the performing part of the group will not consider the observational skills of their colleagues sufficient to guarantee effective feedback. An additional disadvantage to using the part of the group as observer means that some members of the group will not have the opportunity of taking part in the activity. Of course, if there is more than one activity, the observational roles can be rotated; if there are sufficient activities each member will have the opportunity to act as both participant and observer.

An extension of the use of part of the group in an observational role is known as the 'fishbowl'. A number of variations in the operation of the fishbowl exist, but the basis is that part of the group performs a task while the remainder sits round the circle observing the action. The variations will be seen in the methods and amount of the observations. The observers can be allocated different observation tasks – planning, leader effectiveness, group participation and so on. Or, if Behaviour Analysis is used, the observing group can be allocated an individual performer to observe and BA. Or each observer can analyse the performance using different forms of interaction analysis – simple contribution scoring, directional sociograms, duration of contribution and Behaviour Analysis both verbal and non-verbal. The use of these observational instruments can be for pure observation – that is in order to give feedback to the observed. Or they can be used to give the observers practice in the use of the instruments. For example, each observer can produce a BA of the complete group and the results can be compared with each other and possibly with the trainer's analysis to check on accuracy.

Once the activity is complete and the appraisal has been given, the roles are reversed and the participators become the observers, and the observers the participators.

PREPARATION

One essential element in the observational process which must not be omitted by the trainer is the extensive preparation of the observers. Observation has a number of specific techniques and for the observers to perform effectively they should be skilled in these approaches. A useful method I have used successfully is, perhaps while the participants are preparing for the activity, for the observers to meet and decide as a group such aspects as how they are going to observe, what they are going to observe, what aids they are going to use, how the feedback will be given and so on.

When people are involved in observation, subjectivity or the risk of this is always present and subjectivity produces the risk of the rejection of the observational feedback. One way round this problem is to introduce mechanical observational aids rather than humans. An audio recorder can be used to record the verbal content of the activity, or better still closed circuit television linked with a video cassette recorder will record both the verbal and visual contents. Feedback using these means is non-judgemental and as the group listens to or watches the playback it can make its own judgements on its performance.

Human observers and modern technology can be combined to try to make effective observations and give realistic feedback. The closed circuit television camera moves the observers out of the room in which the group is performing to the other end of the circuit where they can observe the group on the TV monitor while recording is also taking place. The feedback can be multi-based and if the participating group disagrees with what it considers to be incorrect subjective comments by the observers, visible proof can be provided from the video recording.

A significant problem encountered in the successful use of such aids as CCTV in observation and feedback is the factor of the additional time involved. There is very little use in recording an activity if the recording is not to be used. Obviously it is usually not necessary to replay the whole of the recording, but selecting scenes and events of a critical nature, showing and discussing these events, takes a considerable amount of time which must be taken into account when planning the training. Sometimes the additional time cannot be made available in a constrained course and although the trainer may wish to use CCTV, this may not be possible.

Preparation for the observers is not the only preparation the trainer must make when involving the group in activities. Simply because the trainer does not have to prepare a complex and complete brief for an input session, this does not mean that he does not have to prepare for an activity. In fact, many activities fail in operation and the principal reason for the failure, as with failures in many areas, is the lack of reasonable preparation.

The first stage of preparing for an activity is for the trainer to know the activity as thoroughly as possible. Thoroughness is much easier if the trainer has constructed the activity himself, but most activities used by trainers have been produced elsewhere. Available activities must be read through thoroughly and completely understood so that the trainer has no need to refer to the activity notes while the activity is being performed. However, even though the details have been understood and memorised, it is a safe move for the trainer to prepare a detailed flow chart showing the stages of the activity and the needs at each stage. But the best preparation must be for the trainer actually to participate in the activity himself in the role of student before he includes it in his own training. In this way he can, at first hand, discover any problems of operation or difficulties of interpretation of the instructions. With this acquaintance with the activity, everything should run smoothly provided the participants are briefed thoroughly on what is required of them.

But the problems for the trainer in running an activity occur not only before the activity, but also when the activity has been completed. Most of the value of an activity is in the appraisal and analysis of the event after it has taken place – how successful was the event, who helped and hindered the process, how appropriate was the leader's style and so on. There are obviously a number of ways in which this post-activity appraisal can be conducted – by the group from a discussion guidelines instrument; free discussion by the group; or discussion led by the tutor. If the latter is to be the method, the trainer must be completely prepared for this event, this preparation easing the flexibility of the event as the trainer must also be ready to play by ear variations of the appraisal. In such a case the trainer will have a number of post-activity questions ready to at least start the appraisal session, and also a number of questions to use when perhaps the appraisal has strayed from the plan and needs to be brought back into line.

The alternative approach of allowing the group to conduct its own appraisal has been mentioned. I have found this approach to be particularly valuable as it offers the group ownership of the progress of the learning event. There are of course risks that the group will not conduct the appraisal in a way which increases the group's learning, and this risk is higher earlier in the course. One approach can be to have the appraisal of the first activity tutor-led and subsequent ones more and more student-led with advice as necessary from the tutor. The later ones would be completely student-led. At the intermediate stage I have found it useful to give the participants, immediately following the event, a questionnaire with the questions based on the objectives of the activity. In a typical questionnaire I use in general group situations, the questions include:

– to what extent did the group meet its objectives?
– how systematic was the activity/meeting?
– what were the three best features of the activity?
– what were the three worst features of the activity?
– who helped the process most?
– who helped the process least?
– how appropriate was the leadership style?
– what have you learned from the activity?

The individual participants were asked to complete the questionnaire and then the group uses the information in an appraisal of the activity. In such events it is rare for the trainer to have to intervene once the process has started.

ACTIVITY BRIEFING

Perhaps the most common reason for failure or poor operation of an activity is inadequate briefing of the group. Obviously if the activity is particularly complex, a clear written brief is essential and it may be desirable for a brief to be issued for any activity. But a written brief may not be the only guidance which is desirable to be given to the group. Sometimes some elements of the brief need verbal explanation because of complexity or because it is sometimes not desirable to write down every item of information or instruction. Whatever the written form of the brief, some verbal instruction will be desirable in most cases or even essential.

The activity, particularly if it is not job-related, may benefit from some comments by the trainer on the reasons for the activity, although it is usually not desirable to be too detailed in this respect. After all, most trainees accept the decision of the trainer that if he gives them something to do, it is relevant to the training process. However, this acceptance is not *always* present. If it is felt that full disclosure would diminish the value of the experience for the participants, it is often valuable to make a simple announcement to satisfy the participants. Such an announcement could be 'I need you to trust me for this activity, as if I tell you too much about it the necessary surprise element will be absent'. The brief should then be issued and the trainer should ensure that the instructions are understood, at least as far as the basic process information is concerned. Once the brief has been issued and cleared, the trainer should then withdraw. It is often a matter of personal judgement or a decision related to the training objectives whether the trainer should intervene on any occasion while the activity is progressing. The temptation to do so can be very strong, particularly when it becomes obvious that the group is going badly awry, but in most cases to intervene is probably the wrong decision to take. Certainly when the process of the group's approach to tasks is the problem, in most cases it is desirable to have the group dig itself out of any hole into which it may have fallen. In general terms, more learning results from a group going wrong and realising this than for an erring group to be helped back to the right path. But the trainer must be prepared for eventual rationalising by the group when the activity is being discussed, and the trainer is likely to be accused of hindering the group by not intervening.

WHEN THE ACTIVITY GOES WRONG

The worst moments for the trainer can be in circumstances such as those just described, that is when either the activity itself has gone seriously wrong or the participating group has taken a wrong track and is in difficulties.

If the crisis is because of the performance of the group, as suggested above, in most cases it will be appropriate to hold back and let the group work its own way out of the problem. The remedial process can be a strong aspect of the subsequent appraisal of the activity, and even more so if the group does not solve the problem it has created for itself. But if the failure is obviously because of the activity itself, other action may be necessary.

No general advice to the trainer in this situation can be a universal solution for the failure may be due to many reasons. But some safety preparations can be made for instances in which failure may be a possibility: this action at least prepares the trainer for such an eventuality. Some of the possible actions may be to have a supplementary input session ready; to go straight into feedback and appraisal on what had preceded the failure; or perhaps to introduce another activity. There may be, of course, occasions when it may be necessary to admit immediately that the activity has collapsed.

Whatever the immediate remedial action taken, the trainer must assess as soon as possible the reason for the failure. These reasons may include:

- the activity may have been set up wrongly
- the group had been exposed to an excess of activities
- the activity was too unrelated to the training for the group to accept its credibility
- the activity was too complicated
- the activity was seen as a threat to the group
- the activity is one used too frequently and has become too well known.

AVAILABILITY

Trainers who wish to use activities have three main options:

- to construct one's own activity
- to adapt an existing activity
- to use directly an existing activity.

Many of the published activities have been used on a large number of occasions and provided they are used for the purposes for which they were constructed, most have been well validated. The main problem is that if the trainer has not previously experienced the activity, it has to be decided whether the particular activity is relevant to the group and the training objectives. However, most publishers of structured activities also suggest or recommend the range of usages. A selection of publications offering a range of structured activities is given at the end of this chapter.

In many cases, activities produced for particular purposes can be modified to satisfy other objectives. This is particularly so in the case of activities requiring the performance of role plays. Usually such activities have a specific setting – say for example the engineering workshop, with the participating characters taking the roles of foreman, shop steward, senior machine man, chargehand etc. It takes little imagination in most cases to transfer the physical setting to, for example, the sales office, with the participants' roles translated to the sales manager, senior salesman, salesman, chief clerk etc. If the engineering shop foreman needs to be an activist, the role of the sales manager can be similar in that respect and so on.

Construction of one's own activity can be much more difficult, but much more satisfying than buying 'off the peg'. However, considerable skill is necessary in the construction, but it should certainly be within the skill level of an experienced trainer.

Of prime importance is the need to determine the objectives for the activity: from this determination the content can be constructed in general terms. If, for example, the objectives are concerned with the planning and effective use of time, the activity would be constructed to include the need to plan, and time constraints would be imposed so that time would be used effectively.

Other factors which may have an effect on the activity can include the size of the group, the established relationships of the members, the time available and so on. If the trainer has a large group which he requires to perform the activity, he must decide whether the activity should be undertaken as one large group or in several smaller groups in competition with each other. The stage of development of the group must be an important factor if the activity is to be acceptable. The receptive attitude of a group at the start of a course is usually quite different from that when they have spent ten days together. And what the trainer can ask them to do can be quite different. The size of the activity will depend on the time available or the time necessary to achieve the objective. The majority of activities used on training events are of short duration – from 15 minutes to an hour or so, but they can also last for several days or even several weeks when they become the complex case studies known as business games.

Once these factors have been considered, the trainer can settle down to writing the activity – one brief for the participants and one, more detailed, for the trainer. The wise trainer when he has produced a redraft of the redraft of the draft, will test it out for comprehension with either a fellow trainer or preferably someone who represents the potential trainee. Once any snags have been ironed out, a second test is preferable, using if possible a group as similar as possible to the training group to test the activity from the practical point of view and to give some indication of how long will be necessary for the activity.

The final main area of the activity which the trainer should ensure that he has covered sufficiently has been mentioned earlier – the questions the trainer will be asking during the appraisal of the activity or the areas which will need to be otherwise covered in the appraisal.

There can be little doubt that an appropriate series of activities can make a training event not only enjoyable but a meaningful learning experience. But the trainer must not develop the feeling that a training course will be easier for him with activities rather than input sessions. Rather it is the reverse. The trainer must present the activity in the best manner possible, remain alert and observant while the activity is being performed, and control the appraisal in the most appropriate manner. All of these are so much more difficult than the relatively simple and straightforward presentation of an organised input session. Many trainers have made this mistake and regretted it.

INTERVENTIONS

One important problem for the trainer when he is controlling an experiential training event is his role while the activity is progressing. His role is clear when he is presenting a formal input session – he is virtually in complete control of the situation. But when the group is performing an activity, the trainer has effectively handed over control to the group and if he intervenes he must have complete justification for so doing. Particularly in an interactive skills training event when most of the activity is experiential, the facilitator is in a quandary at times not only whether to intervene, but when, how often and with what kind of intervention. There can be few trainers who have not at some time expressed concern at their skills in this area and even experienced trainers find difficulties in ensuring that they say the right thing at the right time in the right way, or alternatively, appropriately make no intervention at all.

The style of intervention can vary, but three main appropriate forms can be recognised – the helping, the guiding and the informing interventions.

HELPING INTERVENTIONS

A typical example of the helping intervention when a group is in the process of giving and receiving feedback, but is not progressing well because of the methods used. One member might be telling another that he is 'a nuisance' and naturally this type of feedback is not being accepted. At this point the trainer could usefully intervene in a helping way by suggesting that he might put forward some methods of giving feedback in an acceptable way. However, to intervene in this way is not so simple since the trainer has to ensure that the group is prepared to accept the proposed intervention and listen to the description. It is also essential that an intervention of this nature must be clear and concise or the group will regret accepting the intervention and may react differently on the next occasion.

Even more effective as a helping intervention is to make it even more related to what is happening within the group. During a recent interactive skills course I made an intervention with an individual member and some minutes later noticed from his non-verbal signals that he was under some tension. I raised this with him and he immediately disclosed that he was resenting me because he felt I had unfairly 'picked on' him. We talked this out between us and obtained some reactions from the rest of the group, and the conflict was completely resolved. After this incident, with the member's agreement, I explained to the group how I saw the incident, what action I had taken and particularly my recognition of the non-verbal signals and the value of this.

GUIDING INTERVENTIONS

This type of intervention is much more difficult to make and has a much higher risk factor attached to it than the helping approach. The trainer must be able to assess whether the intervention he has started is progressing slowly because of the difficulty of the interaction, rather than because the other individual does not want the intervention to continue.

One example which happened to me recently came about because a member who was feeling very tense in the group had refused an invitation by the group to discuss his problem. Although the rest of the group appeared unhappy about this refusal, no further approach was made to him. I assessed that the situation could become critical if the problem was not resolved and consequently I started my intervention by clarifying that the group was unhappy by the lack of resolution of the problem. This was confirmed as the case so I described the problems which might ensue from a lack of resolution and suggested to the problem individual that he might benefit from talking through the problem. This was the high risk period for if he had again refused he might have retired even further into his shell as a reaction against what he would see as my pressurising him to discuss. He eventually agreed, however, but was very reluctant to disclose his feelings. I guided him into a more articulate state by using open questioning, testing understanding and reflecting techniques. This approach was particularly relevant as the group had recently been looking at techniques of this nature and my actions served two purposes. Fortunately the approach to the individual worked well and fortunately the group recognised the use of the techniques. As soon as he was talking freely and the problem was coming out, I tended to withdraw and in fact some of the other members of the group recognised this tactic and came in themselves to finish the interaction and bring the problem resolution to an eventual conclusion.

INFORMING INTERVENTIONS

This type of intervention might be relevant when a group is appraising its progress during a recently completed activity, but are becoming hopelessly confused because of the many issues being raised. The assessment is in danger of failing owing to this confusion. The trainer can intervene usefully at this stage by producing a summary of what they have raised in discussion and suggesting that they might take these events one at a time. Or he can suggest that the group might find it useful if he summarised the process as he had seen it and that the group could use that summary as its basis for the discussion from that point.

In this type of intervention the trainer must be very careful not to give any indication that he is taking over the group or offering himself to the group as a crutch. His intervention must be clearly only a statement of information which will be of use to the group.

CONFLICT INTERVENTION

If the interventions described are introduced effectively they will be welcomed by the group and will be recognised as helping contributions containing no challenge to the group. However, trainer interventions can be seen as a challenge to the group, either because of an inept intervention or a deliberate move by the trainer. The latter approach must be regarded as of very high risk and must be used with considerable skill and judgement. Obviously such challenges can vary considerably in character and severity and will depend on the circumstances leading to the intervention.

One of the less traumatic challenge interventions is when the trainer questions a member who insists on using 'we' all the time and is obviously not accepting ownership for any individual personal actions. Similarly the use of 'one' where the individual is hiding behind generalities. If the trainer intervenes when this pattern is establishing, the true feelings or views can emerge. It is also interesting that on most occasions the rest of the group has taken note of the comment and all stop using 'we' and 'one' and themselves challenge members of the group who continue to use them.

Much more direct and emotive challenges can be made, but the trainer must be certain that he has the techniques, skill, expertise and credibility to deal with the, often, explosive reactions to his approach. Many trainers feel that there is no justification for such approaches, the same results being achieved by less aggressive means. The approach has its roots in the methods employed by some schools of thought in psychology and therapy. Perhaps that is where it could profitably remain.

Whether to intervene in a group process can present a delicate decision for the trainer to take, and the results of any intervention can never be safely predicted. It may be that there is a golden rule for trainers which states that the last thing a trainer should do is to intervene and, if in any doubt, to keep quiet. After all, the less the trainer intervenes, the more the group is encouraged to work out its own salvation and learn in the process.

So if in doubt – don't.

REFERENCES AND RECOMMENDED READING

Adair, J. and Despress, D. (1978-1980): *A Handbook of Management Training Exercises*. BACIE. Volume 1, 1978. Volume 2, 1980.

Cinnamon, K.M. and Matulef, N.J. (1979): *Human Relations Development: Applied Skills Training Series*. Volume 3. Applied Skills Press.

Elgood, C. (1984): *Handbook of Management Games*. 3rd edition. Aldershot: Gower.

Francis, D. and Woodcock, M. (1975): *People at Work.* University Associates.

Goodstein, L.D. and Pfeiffer, J.W. (From 1982): *The [Year] Annual for Facilitators, Trainers and Consultants.* University Associates.

Heron, J. (1975): *Six-Category Intervention Analysis.* Guildford: University of Surrey.

Jones, J.E. and Pfeiffer, J.W. *The Annual Handbook for Group Facilitators.* University Associates. Annually from 1972.

Mill, C.R. (1980): *Activities for Trainers: 50 Useful Designs.* University Associates.

Morris, K.T. and Cinnamon, K.M. (1975): *A Handbook of Non-Verbal Group Exercises.* Applied Skills Press.

Morris, K.T. and Cinnamon, K.M. (1979): *A Handbook of Verbal Group Exercises.* Applied Skills Press.

Pfeiffer, J.W. and Jones, J.E. (1974-81): *A Handbook of Structured Experiences for Human Relations Training.* Volumes 1-8. University Associates.

Suessmith, P. (1978): *Ideas for Training Managers and Supervisors.* University Associates.

10 One-to-one interaction training

So far the approaches to human relations training which have been discussed have been concerned principally with either the relationships of groups or the interactive skills of an individual in general terms, e.g. a style of leadership. However, the majority of our interactions with other people occurs in a one-to-one interaction when we are conversing, discussing, influencing, consulting, negotiating or interviewing one other person. The interactive skills lessons learned in the group training activities are little different from those necessary in face to face interactions and in most cases the skills can be transferred without any problem. If, for example, it has been seen that a particular individual talks too much in a group, there is every likelihood that he will do so in other situations. If this is so, his behaviour modification plans produced for the group are easily transferable to his one-to-one interactions. The principal difference between group and singular inter-actions is that when we are relating directly to one person we have to be even more aware of how we are behaving, how we are being received and how we are reacting to the other person. In the group, events can be and often are ignored; in a direct interaction with one other person, the searchlight beam is concentrated so that every part of the interaction is fully illuminated.

There are also some differences in feedback. When feedback is being given in a group, to a group, by a group, problems can be avoided by other members who see things differently or say things in a different manner. In this way the individual can hide within the anonymity of the group. But feedback between individuals offers no such escape and so demands a higher degree of care and sensitivity.

TYPES OF ONE-TO-ONE INTERACTION TRAINING

One-to-one interaction training can take on a variety of forms and be for a variety of purposes, but paradoxically occurs mainly in a group. There are exceptions to this paradox and these other approaches will be discussed later. Most of the training is concerned with interviewing in some form or other and much of the variation is related to the techniques involved rather than the behavioural skills. One-to-one interaction training commonly includes:

- interviewing: discipline, correction, grievance, selection, promotion, dismissal, appraisal
- counselling
- influencing
- consulting
- assertiveness
- coaching
- negotiating.

TRAINING APPROACHES

There are many similarities in this list of approaches and the techniques too can have many similarities, not only to each other but also to the group training activities which have been described. For example, training in counselling can follow a pattern of didactic teaching, experiential learning, deduced learning, discovery learning etc.: the techniques employed could involve Behaviour Analysis, Transactional Analysis, Gestalt and so on.

Perhaps the most common approach is a fairly traditional, but a well tried and tested one and involves bringing together a group of people who have a common training need in the techniques and skills of interviewing. The range of interviews about which they can be concerned can be quite extensive and would include most of the events mentioned earlier. In order to satisfy these needs a course has been designed and it is in the basic approach that the trainer has his first choice.

The traditional approach to learning can be described as deduced learning. On a course operating in this manner the initial step is the presentation by the tutor of the behavioural skills necessary in interview situations. A teaching input of this type would probably include a discussion of the types and application of the different forms of questioning – closed, open, leading, multiple and multiple choice. Some time might be given to the technique of reflecting, a technique very useful in the counselling interview where direct questioning could have an adverse effect on the responses of the interviewee. These opening sessions might be completed by a discussion of the aids and barriers to listening, probably the most important skill in any form of interviewing.

Following the well established practice, practical activities would follow the input sessions so that the trainees could consolidate and reinforce the learning of actual experience. Quite simple situations can be produced in which the trainees can interview each other and practise the use of the techniques. The group would be divided into pairs or threes and asked to interview each other with such simple briefs as 'What do you dislike most about yourself?', 'What would you do to contain football violence?', any subject in fact on which the interviewee might have an opinion or view to express and which will give the interviewer the opportunity to bring out these views, using the 'new' techniques. If the group is divided into threes, the role of the third person is usually to control and assist in the evaluation of the interview. The roles are then reversed until everybody has had the opportunity to be the interviewer.

The skills of listening are usually reinforced separately and may be practised effectively by the Triad activity described earlier.

The trainees are by this stage expected to have a reasonable grasp of the general behaviours of interviewing. The scene can now change so that specific interview approaches can be considered. Let us say that the course objectives include discipline, grievance, selection and counselling interviews. Such a course could be divided into four sections, following the general introductory stage, each section considering in depth one interview type. The practice in each section would be similar. First would come an input session describing the special techniques and structuring relating to the particular interview. This would be followed up with a period of practical activity during which the trainees would have the opportunity in small groups of three or four to practise the techniques and structure which had been presented. Appraisal of the interviews would take place within the small groups, with or without the aid of the trainer or any other appraisal aids. Following the practical activity the course would move on to consider another type of interview and the process would be repeated.

I have been involved in courses of this nature and there can be no doubt that they can achieve a good measure of success. But there is a considerable risk that by the time the group has reached the third type of interview, they (and the trainer) may be becoming bored with the repetitive process. One way of avoiding this is to vary the approach for some of the interview stages. If the first interview type is approached in a way similar to that just described, the next type would warrant the variation, then a return to the original approach and so on. One variation used has been to divide the group into small groups and ask them to look at a possible structure for the interview. The variations between the answers given by the different groups at feedback time can promote considerable discussion and from the agreed answers an appropriate structure can be formulated. The groups can then go ahead and practise using *their* structure. A modification of this approach for the small group stage can be to have each group look at one stage of the interview – preparation and opening; main body of the interview; closure and subsequent action. From the report back of each group a combined structure is produced which can be tested in the subsequent practical activity.

This compromise approach includes both the deduced-learning and the discovery-learning methods and there is some risk that the two approaches can be compared by the learners, to the unfavourable reaction to one and some rejection of learning because of this. Although mixing of learning approaches can prevent boredom arising, the rejection danger is always present.

One way of avoiding the problems of mixing may be to concentrate on one approach. We have seen how the solely deduced-learning approach can become boring for both the learner and the tutor. The other extreme is to utilise only the discovery-learning approach. In such a situation there are no inputs given by the tutor, rather the trainees are invited to try out various interviews and, from these experiments and the discussions following the attempts, the trainees discover experientially the problems of an unstructured, unskilled approach. Consequently they determine for themselves a more effective approach, try it out and discover any bugs, and, having re-assessed the approach, try out a revised edition. The theory behind this approach is that if the groups have sweated blood over producing a satisfactory technique for itself, it is much more likely to recall and use this approach than a technique suggested by the trainer (even though they may both turn out to be the same!).

It has been written and said so often that a training course is probably the least effective way of encouraging learning. If this is so, individual tutorial help is the most effective. The problems in this approach are many and if a large number of people are to receive training in the same topic, to do this on an individual basis may be expensive in resource terms. Hopefully this task would not fall on the training faculty alone, but where it rightly belongs, on the shoulders of the line manager. Unfortunately not every line manager is sufficiently motivated or skilled to carry out this task and some of the work at least would fall on the trainer.

One example of this consultative approach in which I became involved concerned the training of managers in the leadership of meetings. There were problems of putting this out to the line managers as these were principally the ones who required the training. Obviously as a number of managers were involved a training course seemed to be the answer. However, this did not work out completely in practice in view of the very wide range of training needs among the managers concerned and the artificial nature of a training course. The individual members of the group requiring training were analysed and for some it was decided that a more individual approach was possible and desirable.

The approach was of a three-stage nature, the first stage of which involved the trainer/consultant meeting with the learner-manager to determine as far as possible his training needs, his attitudes to the leadership of meetings and to start the process of learning. The second stage occurred with the trainer attending at least one meeting led by the manager, to observe such aspects as the behaviours exhibited by the leader in relationship to the members, the structure of the meeting, its effectiveness and any other observable, relevant elements. In addition to the meeting observation, soundings were also taken of the views of the meeting participants, including those of the leader himself. These views were obtained with the use of a post-meeting questionnaire, an example of which is shown in Figure 3.1 in Chapter 3 (see p. 34).

Once the questionnaires have been completed, the answers are collated and analysed by the trainer. This information is used for the third stage, a final discussion between the trainer and the manager. There can be no particular, pre-arranged pattern for this final discussion at which a number of the problems can be resolved or even a recommendation for fuller training might be made. The meeting observation from stage 2 acts as the basis for this discussion and particularly the feedback from the meeting participants. This approach has been found to be very helpful to both the learner and the trainer, and particularly satisfying to the latter, especially when he was invited to attend a further live meeting to see the fruits of his intervention.

Whether the training is concerned with the skills of interviewing in discipline, counselling etc.; in influencing other people; in developing assertiveness or improving negotiating skills, the training approach is very much the same. It can involve the deduced-learning approach of input followed by practice, or the discovery-learning method, or the compromise approach of using the group to determine the structure of at least some of the situations. Whatever the approach, one can be assured that some form of experiential activity will be involved if any real learning is to be achieved.

ROLE PLAYS

In many respects, the safest role play is the formal, artificially constructed situation. Usually this is the safest approach when the trainer is relatively inexperienced or the trainees are in an early stage of their interactions with each other.

The reasons for these safety aspects are, in the first case, the process is known and to a large extent predictable, and secondly the case study is known to be artificial and therefore neither participant can feel particularly threatened.

The structure of this type of case study is an artificial, constructed situation in which there are roles for each of the participants. Each participant learns his role, whatever the extent of this may be, and acts out the role with some form of observation being performed.

Immediately one can determine some basic variations in this approach to role plays. The roles in the simplest forms are far from complex, being simply an indication of the position and the attitudes within a described situation. Evolvement of the roles within the situation is left to the participants as they react to each other and develop the roles within the natural extension of the basic information. One advantage of this approach is that it helps towards a more natural expression of an artificial situation as the roles develop naturally. But this approach requires role players who have the ability to enter into the roles and, in effect, to have some acting ability in their skills and make-up. The need to develop the roles can be a considerable disadvantage for those without the acting ability and the minimum information can be used as a rationalisation for any lack of success.

The natural solution to this criticism is to build up the role and give more information to each of the role players. Consequently there is little, or less, need for the role player to rely on imagination to perform the role in the interaction. But even in such a case rationalisation by a poor performer is possible with the accusation that there was too much material for the role player to assimilate. The case study writer can never win!

ROLE DOUBLING

Doubling or ghosting is the term used when participants other than the original role players take part in the interaction, but do not necessarily take over the interaction. The switch of players has to be made skilfully and if occurring on more than one occasion, must not upset the basic role player. If the participants are not too experienced in the technique, it will be safer for the trainer to demonstrate the method himself initially when a natural occasion arises.

One occasion for doubling occurred when I was the trainer looking after a practice appraisal interview. The interviewer had admitted before the interaction that, although she had prepared thoroughly for the interview, she was very nervous. Some five minutes after the interview had started she dried up completely. The interview could have been terminated there and then or I could have made an intervention from the sidelines, an obviously artificial one. Instead I went and stood behind her, said to the interviewee 'Now tell me about any problems you are experiencing'. The interviewee looked a little surprised but started describing his problems. He needed a little prompting so I stayed in this position long enough to ask a clarification question and reflect one of his feelings: then I quietly returned to my seat. The interviewer gave me a glance then took up the interview from that point with obviously renewed confidence.

A little later in the interview, the interviewer stumbled and looked as if she was going to lose her way again. From the corner of my eye I noticed one of the observers moving a little agitatedly, so I motioned her to stand behind the interviewer as I had done. She did so and asked a question as the interviewer, then seeing that the original interviewer had recovered, resumed her place and the interview continued smoothly.

At the end of the interview one observer expressed concern at the two doubling interventions saying that he would have resented them as intrusions if he had been the interviewer. However, the interviewer responded that at both stages she had been completely lost, had welcomed the interventions and had learned a lot from the way the interview had continued – otherwise the interview would have collapsed and she would have learned nothing.

Once a pattern of doubling interventions has been achieved, an open invitation to double can be extended, but with the warning that if it is overdone, the value will be diluted.

This can be a typical pattern of doubling progress. The doubling can not only help the interviewer along, but it can allow a wider sharing of the interview experience than by restricting the interaction to the two original participants alone. Once the group is accustomed to the technique of doubling and are able to use it skilfully, an open invitation can be given to the observers to double whenever they see the need to do so, provided the interviewer is willing, or if the interviewer requests it. If some of the members are too shy to intervene in this way, they can be encouraged to do so by an arrangement of the doubling on a rota basis, entry probably being controlled by the trainer.

ROLE REVERSAL

If a real life case is introduced, role reversal can be a technique to increase the amount of learning in a novel way. Normally when one has a real problem one is too involved to look at the problem rationally and consequently the role play can be fraught with barriers which hinder the problem owner from seeing the problem clearly. How often have we heard people say 'If he could only see that problem from my point of view'? Role reversal is one way of attempting to do just that.

The role play starts off normally with the problem owner taking his real life part, but at a critical stage of the interview the trainer requires the two participants to switch roles. If the problem owner has been taking the part of the interviewer, roles are switched so that the interviewer becomes the interviewee. Being forced to take the other person's part, and therefore attitude, the problem owner has to argue from a completely different viewpoint and begins to see the problem from the other's point of view. On so many occasions one can see realisation dawn on the problem owner's face as he starts to accept that there is another, perhaps more appropriate, viewpoint.

The role reversal can progress as described with the reversing occurring at a stage during the interaction. The trainer has to be very sensitive to the event so that he can assess the most appropriate time to effect the switching. This possible problem can be avoided by reversing the roles from the start of the interaction. This approach, however, is much more difficult to achieve in terms of realism and ease of the interaction: the problem owner, acting an unusual role, can find the very early stages of the interaction difficult. If this problem is to be overcome, perhaps with the support of the trainer, the interaction can develop into a really meaningful event.

In addition to the advantage of demonstrating practically that there are other points of view in a problem and giving the problem owner the opportunity to see the problem in the way that others may see it, other advantages include:

– an increase in spontaneity
– an increase in insight and awareness.

In the first case the role reversal moves the problem owner out of his stereotyped stance and in the second there is an increase of insight into the views of others – even for some people that there are views other than their own!

THE EMPTY CHAIR

One-to-one interaction training owes many of its techniques to psychology and therapeutic approaches. The 'empty chair' is one of these and is often used to take the pressure off someone who wants to release the feelings produced by a problem. One of the difficulties about traditional role playing in interactions is that there is a requirement for either two role players or one problem owner plus one role player. Even when a real life problem is being used, there is still the need for a supporting role player who has to learn the situation and the role. Obviously, where roles are involved there must be some element of artificiality which can get in the way of the interaction.

The 'empty chair' technique or monodrama can only be

attempted at a stage in the training event when the atmosphere among the participants is open and trustful and is conducive to the exposure of deep feelings. Two chairs are positioned facing each other: the problem owner sits in one and the other remains empty.

In one variation of the technique, when the problem owner feels ready to do so, he starts to describe the problem to the 'person' in the empty chair. Because there is no possibility of unsettlement by another person, interruptions or failure of another to grasp the problem, the problem owner can develop his argument or case, and usually becomes so involved in the monologue that he forgets he hasn't a live partner. Possible solutions can be put forward and discussed and even conclusions can be reached. At the very least an opportunity has been given for the problem owner to verbalise his problem without any added complications of other people and roles.

Another variation, which demands rather more activity, involves the movement between the chairs by the problem owner. The event progresses with the participant, having developed the initial phases of the problem, moving over to the empty chair and asking questions, raising objections or making comments as if he were a permanent participant of the interaction. The alternate switching of chairs continues until the problem has been talked through.

PSYCHODRAMA

The psychodrama approach to problems in one-to-one interactions is an extension of the 'empty chair' technique and the real life approach where the problem is producing highly emotional feelings which need to be released. The empty chair or a fellow participant can be used in the progression of the interaction, but the fundamental process is to relive the bad experience.

A skilled facilitator can help in guiding the problem owner through the process by moving him into a state of reliving the experience as realistically as possible. As the facilitator, who normally acts out the relived problem with the problem owner, leads the other into a highly emotive state, the facilitator must be skilled not only in training techniques but also in therapeutic counselling skills, skills which a trainer does not usually possess. Without these skills the emotional strains may prove too much for the problem owner and the facilitator must be capable of dealing with the worst that can happen. As in so many areas of human relations training, the line between training and therapy is very thin.

HOT ROLE PLAYS

Perhaps the most natural role play is when an issue arises naturally in the 'here and now' of the training event and the issue is used as a basis for an interaction. Commonly this comes about from a problem arising between two people on the course and the event is acted out within the group in order to (a) solve the problem and (b) give the participants the opportunity to practise real interactive skills. The 'here and now' aspect of the event gives it the title 'hot'. The hot role play normally requires little setting up. The subject for the inter-action is already there. All the facilitator needs to do is to invite the participants to sit down and talk through, having agreed with them that the interaction would be played out in front of the rest of the group or alone.

A recent event in which I was involved as facilitator was typical of this type of interaction. During a feedback session one afternoon of this course, one member disclosed that he was having bad feelings about another member as a result of something which had occurred earlier in the day, and these feelings were interfering with the current interaction. I sug-gested that he might wish to talk the problem through with the other member and after some consideration both agreed. They also agreed to do this in front of the remainder of the group. The group had asked if this could be done as (a) they wanted to experience the interaction and (b) they wanted to observe how the situation would be handled. The presence of the group made the start-up of the interaction slower than would normally have been the case, but with my (helpful) inter-ventions it soon started to develop and the feelings emerged. It was obviously painful for the member who had initiated the opening up of the problem, but he persevered and when difficulties arose during the interaction allowed the group to participate in the interaction. The event almost became a 'family' counselling session but the end result was that the problem was talked through and the real difficulties resolved.

OBSERVATION AND FEEDBACK

Valuable though interaction practice may be in one-to-one interaction training, the practice is not complete without some form of appraisal of the event.

The first step in this action is the decision whether the interaction should be observed directly or not. Without observation there is little opportunity for feedback and the interaction will lose much of its learning value in consequence. The major options for observation include:

- observation by the tutor alone
- observation by the fellow course members.

The other options for both these approaches are:

- direct observation in the room with the interaction participants
- indirect observation by means of closed circuit television.

Although the tutor is probably the most skilled and experienced observer, he is only one voice and his non-member position may not allow his views complete acceptability. I have seen a group combine against the trainer and his views because, although he was right, they were not then prepared to accept these views from someone who was not one of 'them'. Fellow course members have a greater likelihood of having their views taken into account and the use of more than one ensures that major incidents are noted by at least one.

Of course, there is no reason why the tutor should not supplement the 'lay' observers, but it can often happen that the appraisal will proceed quite smoothly without the official tutor present. However, before the appraisal, while the interaction is taking place, even the presence of fellow course members, let alone the tutor, can restrict the naturalness of an interview. One way of avoiding this problem is to remove the observers to another room where they will be able to see and hear the interview over a closed circuit television link. Unfortunately the presence of a TV camera can itself produce new problems – the participants become so aware of the camera that they behave unnaturally. However, in most cases the camera syndrome soon disappears and the interviewer and interviewee settle down to a more natural approach. In fact, once the participants have become used to the camera's presence, the interview can progress even more easily than if other people were present in the room.

Whichever method of using observers is chosen, a considerable amount of preparation is necessary. The observers must be well drilled in what they are to look for and how to do this. It is normal when a number of observers are available, to divide the observational tasks between them. One (or more) observers can be detailed to look at the structure of the interview, other(s) to observe the specific techniques used, and others to observe and record the behaviours used. The tutor must ensure that the observers are fully aware of these structures, techniques and behaviours so that their observations are realistic and meaningful. There is little value in an observer commenting on an event only to have it contradicted by fellow observers or the participants. This preparation may be quite extensive depending on the complexity of the type of interaction. A useful venture, while the participants are reading their roles and preparing for the interview, is for the observers to be studying their roles and agreeing among themselves who will observe which particular aspect. Perhaps it may also be useful for them to design their own observational sheets or, at the least, decide which ones from the range available they are going to use. Such a sheet might be one of the special Behaviour Analysis interview sheets as described in Chapter 4 (Figure 4.2, p. 67).

If CCTV is relied upon as the principal observational instrument, a recording being made of the interview, the tutor will be wise to make notes of critical incidents and their recorded position on the tape. After the interview, when the interviewer is watching the recording replay, he can take particular notice of these parts of the recording. Otherwise the feedback can be left to the recording playback alone.

When live observation is used, either through the CCTV link or by direct observation in the interview room, a full range of feedback is available. The order of observer comment is capable of variation and the order can be varied even from one feedback to the next. A pattern which I have found to be useful starts with the interviewer himself. In this approach the interviewer is asked what he felt himself about his own performance. Most people will quite readily comment openly on their performance and commonly will be more critical of themselves than others would be (or would dare to be). However, it would be asking too much to expect a complete appraisal from the individual and in fact a highly critical self-appraisal can help other appraisers who can be in a very desirable position to reduce the critical nature of the inter-viewer's self-appraisal. Whether this is possible or not, the observers would be asked to comment next and add their views of the interview. Finally the views of the interviewee are sought as the receiver of the techniques, methods and interview structure. Then and only then does the trainer make any comments – if there is anything left to say. If everybody has been too kind to a poor interviewer, the trainer must make some critical comments, but he should be able to make these in such a way that they are constructive. If he does not do this, he is in danger of losing his credibility as the poor performer will know that he has been let off too lightly and the observers will feel that if the trainer does not comment he has failed to observe the poor performance. If the others have been too critical, the trainer can at least put the interviewer's feelings together again by commenting on the better parts of the interview – there are always some!

It will be seen that the approaches to virtually any human relations interaction, whether in group relationships or one-to-one interactions are basically similar, requiring an open approach to the behaviour of the event. Full appraisal of what has happened and is happening is essential and, although the trainer has a critical part to play, the event is made or broken by the participants who *must* participate. For the participants, the adjectives they use to describe the event include traumatic, disturbing and hurtful, but also caring, enlightening and helpful. For the trainer, the experience, whichever way the event progresses is memorable, traumatic and nerve-shattering. In the case of the latter member, the reactions will always be different from the traditional approach to training or the provision of technical training. When he enters the training room each morning, the trainer will never be certain what will happen during the day, whether in fact he will still have a group of course members at the start or at the end of the day. But, if the event has been successful, the participants have grown as a result of the experiences provided, and awareness, skill, behaviour and interpersonal competence have increased, the trainer's reward is a warm inner glow of having given and helped others improve their place in life. This sounds very trite, but I have felt this so strongly on many occasions. But if the event does not progress in this way, there are no words to express the contrition and other negative feelings of the human relations trainer.

REFERENCES AND RECOMMENDED READING

Atkinson, G.G.M. (1980): *The Effective Negotiator.* Quest.

Back, K. and Back, K. (1982): *Assertiveness at Work.* Maidenhead: McGraw-Hill.

Fletcher, J. (1973): *The Interview at Work.* London: Duckworth.

Fraser, J.M. (1966): *Employment Interviewing.* London: Methuen.

Honey, P. (1978): *Face to Face.* New Jersey: Prentice-Hall. (Also published 1976 by Institute of Personnel Management.)

Kelley, C. (1979): *Assertion Training.* University Associates.

Maier, N.R.F., Solem, A.R. and Maier, A.A. (1975): *The Role Play Technique.* University Associates.

Scott, W. (1981): *The Skills of Negotiating.* Aldershot: Gower.

Shaw, M.E., Corsini, R.J., Blake, R.R. and Mouton, J.S. (1980): *Role Playing: A Practical Manual for Group Facilitators*. University Associates.

Stewart, V. and Stewart, A. (1977): *Practical Performance Appraisal*. Aldershot: Gower.

Williams, M.R. (1971): *Performance Appraisal in Management*. London: Heinemann.

11   On-the-job problem solving

If the reader has been sufficiently interested to reach this point in the book he will have realised that in human relations training, although there is a high possibility of a rewarding outcome for both trainer and trainee, the risks and dangers are equally high and often more so. The trainer's skills must be good and he must have knowledge and ability in a very wide range of techniques and methods. Although he does not have to be a psychologist, his skill must be close to that required in that discipline, yet have sufficient insight to know when he is approaching dangerous ground which is beyond his capabilities – not only recognising the situations but also having the skill to circumvent the problem.

These reflections suggest that unlike many forms of technical or job-specific training, the human relations trainer must be a 'professional', full-time, experienced trainer rather than the part-time trainer or the manager-trainer. This is certainly the case with training which is of a sensitivity or pure interactive skills nature, but less so in some forms of one-to-one interaction training – some interviews where the emphasis is on techniques and structures; or negotiation training where again there is strong emphasis on technique and method.

But there is one part of human relations development in which the manager is king and the trainer has little influence – coaching on the job.

COACHING

It has been stated earlier in this book, and the statement is well supported by a considerable amount of research, that maximum learning occurs when it is related directly to the job. We learn best by doing the job itself. However, some qualifications must be made on this bare statement. There are some subjects where this approach must be the most appropriate one, but others where it is equally inappropriate. The basic requirement for learning on the job is that there is someone available to assist in the process. Certainly many jobs could be learned to a certain level by a trial and error approach, but these are strictly limited in scale and there would also be a prohibitive time factor. Similarly, many people performing at a particular level need an additional hand to help them to develop. If they have the innate skill and ability to develop without the external influences then there are numerous self-learning and self-developmental processes they can follow. But if help is needed this is best delivered in what is described as coaching.

Coaching has as many definitions as there are ways of approaching the method, but generally it can be described as on the job training or development using real work as the controlled vehicle to achieve the aims. Also to facilitate the process a skilled coach, who preferably and normally will be the learner's immediate boss, is required. Without the coach, learning on the job is reduced to the parallel of throwing a child into the deep end of the swimming pool and telling him to learn to swim! Some will learn to swim after a fashion; others will drown. I can speak from personal experience of the inefficiency of that method, although obviously I didn't drown!

Apart from the fact that most people will learn best from actually doing the job there are a number of other reasons why coaching should be considered. We have looked earlier at the different styles of learning preferred by people: some people simply cannot learn if they are sent on a training course; others through various constraints may not be able to travel to a training course. For others the learning need may be so complex that a long gestation period may be necessary and this would not be available on a training course. There may not be a

training course for the subject in question – not all requirements are met by courses, particularly when the demand for
such training is small. Also some people have an inbuilt
antagonism to courses and would not learn if forced to attend.

In instances such as those just cited, the home-brewed
variety of training will have an obvious appeal *where the boss
wants training and development to occur.* It may be that the
course avenue is not available or appropriate. In such a case the
boss may simply accept the fact and do nothing more. A lot of
words are written or spoken about the value of coaching as a
vehicle for learning and few people will deny the rectitude of
these statements. Trainers and researchers are certainly aware
of its value from the surveys of learning approaches and
assessments of the amount of learning transfer following a
training course. Senior management supports the coaching
approach since it appears to offer value for time and resource,
it obviates the need for workers to absent themselves to attend
a course and it appears to be an effective method of learning.
Line managers, the level where one would expect the majority
of coaching projects to take place have, or express, similar
views to those of senior management. But as it is they who have
to coach, they say:

- much as they would like to, they haven't time to coach
- they haven't the skills of coaching
- their type of work doesn't lend itself to coaching
- what is the training department for anyway?

Naturally, much of what happens will depend on senior
management. If it expresses the lip service only referred to
earlier, the more junior managers will not accept that it is they
who are the coaches of the organisation. The approach must
work and be seen to work throughout the organisation and
throughout the hierarchy, for, if senior managers coach their
juniors, a natural chain reaction will be produced.

TYPES OF COACHING

A further decision must be made once the basic agreement on
coaching has been reached. This decision will link very closely

with any management or organisational development policy operating within the organisation. If positive approaches of this nature are not in operation, one type of coaching is still relevant, but if full organisational enlightenment exists, two approaches are possible. The two approaches to coaching can be described as:

- remedial
- developmental.

Remedial coaching is necessary when individual employees have specific training needs in their existing work, the operation of which is suffering because of the need to improve their level of performance. This is the classical training need which traditionally is satisfied by the individual's attendance on a training course, but which, as we have seen, may be better obtained through coaching. Probably the greater number of coaching assignments fall into this category.

Where the atmosphere in an organisation is more conducive to the real development of staff rather than firefighting activities only, coaching can be approached from the point of view of the development of the individual. In such cases, the coach is not concerned with bringing the individual up to a satisfactory level of performance, but with developing that person *from* a satisfactory level to an even higher level with a view to possible career advancement or, at the least, increased job satisfaction.

COACHING TECHNIQUES

The techniques and approaches to either of the two forms of coaching – remedial and developmental – are basically the same and follow a pattern of:

- initial discussion
- activity
- review.

When it has been raised between the boss and the individual that coaching is not only necessary but that it should take place, the action to process the event can proceed. Either the boss can raise the subject as something he sees as necessary or the individual can raise it as necessary or desirable from his point of view. But whatever the avenue along which it is raised, it is essential that agreement to proceed is reached at an early stage between both the boss (coach) and the worker (learner). Often this can happen quite naturally during a discussion which was not initiated for coaching purposes. The more natural, so much the better. Once the subject has been raised a logical process can be initiated with the relatively clearly defined steps.

THE INITIAL DISCUSSION

The first stage must be a full discussion between the coach and the learner. At this meeting the initial subject for agreement is the identification of the training or development need, or clarification and confirmation of this if there has been previous discussion. The identification must be as clear as possible so that both parties are fully aware of what they are setting out to achieve and why. It may be that in this clarification and consolidation process a number of training needs are identified. In such a case it must be clear which one or ones the coaching assignment will be seeking to solve. Sometimes the needs may overlap with each other to the extent that all may be taken together, but as a general rule it is usually easier and more effective to deal with one aspect at a time. At the conclusion of this stage of the discussion the coach and learner will have agreement that:

- either a training need exists or development is desirable
- the training or development needs have been clearly identified or specified
- a contract exists between the two people to move forward by means of a coaching assignment.

With this agreement, progress can now be made to produce an Action Plan. This plan will obviously vary from instance to instance, but common factors will include a full description of the steps proposed; who will be responsible for whatever is agreed; what will be required of the learner and the coach; when the various steps will be taken and how long will be allowed for each step, and so on. This Action Plan must be written down and copies held by both so that there can be no misunderstanding of what was agreed. Everything which was agreed must be entered in the plan and a desirable aim is to have the plan at least in draft form before both participants leave the meeting. This saves subsequent disagreement on possible errors or omissions and also saves the need for further organisational meetings.

An absolutely essential entry in the Action Plan is an arrangement for the holding of future meetings – dates and times as far as possible. These arrangements should be realistic so that, as far as possible, they can be adhered to.

It may be that more than one initial meeting may need to be held, depending on the complexity of the coaching requirement and often, as a result of points raised at a meeting, it is necessary for both parties to have some time to consider what has been discussed or to consider possible further action for discussion at another meeting.

The style of this initial discussion will obviously be very important and the coach will be well advised to follow counselling guidelines in terms of:

- listen rather than talk
- listen actively
- ask open questions
- seek views, ideas and proposals rather than state own views or prescribe own solutions
- seek agreement rather than prescription.

ACTIVITY AND REVIEW

Once the plan of action has been agreed, whatever is to be done should proceed immediately. If the plan includes delegation, the coach must ensure that he is in fact delegating work and not abdicating. If a coaching assignment is to start, it demands the interest as well as the involvement of the boss-coach and this combined interest and involvement must be continued throughout the assignment. The activities themselves will have been agreed during the initial discussions and most effectively will be normal aspects of the learner's work, or if the coaching is in a developmental mode, other real work with which the learner would not otherwise have become involved.

Reviews will have been built into the Action Plan and are a most important aspect of the coaching assignment, demonstrating the continuing interest of the coach. The aspects which will normally be included at the review meetings will be:

- an assessment of how the Action Plan is working
- an assessment of the stage reached in the plan
- a discussion and resolution of any problems arising
- agreement on progress to the next stage

or, if the initial coaching assignment has been completed

- agreement on further learning targets
- construction of a further Action Plan.

A COACHING ASSIGNMENT

If we follow the plan just described, we can trace the development of a hypothetical coaching assignment.

Fred is a young, alert supervisor who is exhibiting every indication that he is capable of progressing well. He is a good organiser of his staff who respect him and work well for him. A lot of his work requires considerable forward planning and it is rare for anything to go wrong with his arrangements or unsuspected problems to appear out of the blue – he has always anticipated these and made the necessary contingency plans. At his recent annual appraisal interview with his manager he was congratulated on these aspects, and many others, of his work. However, two aspects of his performance needed to be discussed as they were not up to (a) the standard of the other aspects and (b) a level which would be expected. These aspects were in oral communication and written communication. Orally, Fred had valuable things to say, but was hesitant and convoluted in his presentation and consequently he made little mark on the poeple he was trying to influence or inform. Similarly in his writing, all the essentials were there, but his structure left much to be desired and he had a style which, being kind, could only be described as his own.

Both these aspects were openly discussed during the appraisal interview and it was agreed that the top priority as far as Fred's present job was concerned was to do something about his written work. A coaching approach was agreed and both Fred and his manager, having decided on a date when they might get together, agreed possible approaches during the interim period.

Several days later when they met as agreed, an initial discussion meeting took place as outlined earlier and the Action Plan produced included:

1) That Fred would attend the effective writing course run by X.

2) That prior to attending the course Fred and his boss would meet to discuss the course and Fred's personal aims and objectives.

3) That immediately following the course Fred and his boss would meet to discuss Fred's reaction to the course, what he had learned and what he intended to put into operation.

4) That on X date, Fred and his boss would meet to have a discussion on the company's house-style of writing reports.

5) That Fred would continue drafting reports, but at the drafting stage he and his boss would meet to discuss the draft. (As Fred normally had to produce at least two draft reports a week, it was agreed that under normal circumstances these meetings, of approximately half an hour duration, would be held on Wednesday and Friday mornings at 10.30 am.)

6) That the drafting review meetings would continue for two months at the end of which a full review meeting would be held.

The Action Plan for a purely developmental coaching assignment would be very similar with the possible exclusion of the training course. The work used in the assignment in this case would be written work for which the boss would normally be responsible, rather than the learner's own work. This work would be given to the learner initially as drafting work which would then be discussed fully, but eventually when the learner had mastered the work, certain items could be delegated on a permanent basis.

WHO IS TO DO THE COACHING?

The principal complaint aimed at coaching is that it involves the expenditure of a manager's time. No one can disagree with this, but it must be insisted that it can only be time well spent. In the remedial coaching assignment on Fred's written work a time log would show for the manager

– initial meeting	1½ hours
– pre-course briefing	½ hour
– post-course briefing	½ hour
– eight twice-weekly drafting review meetings	8 hours
– final review meeting	1½ hours.

This represents a total of 12 hours or so over a period of something like thirteen or fourteen weeks, by the end of which Fred could be well on the way to producing written work of a much more acceptable, perhaps well acceptable, standard.

Some organisations approach the responsibility for coaching rather differently. The basis for this approach is that their managers do not have sufficient time to devote to *effective* coaching nor do their managers have or are expected to have *effective* coaching skills. The answer in these situations is to have 'professional' coaches or management advisers who take over these functions. There may be substantial argument for this approach, but I see two main disadvantages:

1) The external coach must himself have limited time which will be a constraint on the number of learners he can coach.
2) The introduction of an external coach is removing the prime responsibility for training and development of staff from where it belongs – with the line manager.

The second argument I feel is sufficiently strong to avoid in most cases the introduction of the external coach who would also logically have to be responsible for all pre- and post-course briefing meetings, and have the oversight of the operation of all Action Plans produced by learners at the end of courses. An impossible task. But apart from this, the value of management is being reduced by removing responsibilities which are an essential part of that task.

INDIVIDUAL PROBLEMS

Sometimes the problems of the individual can be solved by coaching, sometimes by some other form of training, sometimes by the exertion of discipline and sometimes by even more extreme measures. In general terms, all these approaches are simple as they represent the practical action in the problem process. Perhaps the stage prior to this action is the more difficult one: the decision about what type of action to take. When we are presented with a technical problem, although the action itself may be difficult, the decision on what to do can be straightforward. A machine breaks down – decision: strip the machine down to find the faulty part. A nuclear power station shows every urgent indication that the atomic pile is getting out of hand – decision: take certain logical counter-atomic action or shut down the pile – and so on. When we have to consider human relations problems, the decisions are rarely as straightforward, as so many variables can get in the way, variables which we may not be able to uncover as we can in a machine.

The description of Transactional Analysis in Chapter 7 suggested one approach to the reasons for these variables, but one has to accept the concept of TA to accept that this is the basis for the variable. Such acceptance may be a big step as we are stating what is going on in someone's mind. Can we be as sure as this? Behaviourists such as Peter Honey do not believe that we can, and in fact suggest that it is dangerous at worst, or time consuming and open to error at best, if we do so. The attitudes of this school of thought are that:

1) Behaviour, that is the overt factor in our relationships

with others, is the part of our being which has the most impact on others and consequently on their reactions to us.

2) Concentrating on overt behaviour saves a lot of hard, and probably inaccurate work of trying to interpret or determine the covert aspects of why someone is doing something.

3) People's covert attitudes, motives and feelings are secret and may or may not be affecting their behaviour (what they do) – we simply do not know. Probably the most graphic effect of this is the guy who punches you on the nose, but is smiling as he does so. Why is he smiling? I don't know, but I know he has hit me and I'm going to hit him in return!

Taking account of the overt behaviour alone may not give us all the answers, but it will give us answers of which we can be reasonably confident. It is obvious, for example, from what I have written in this book (my behaviour) about my inter-personal skills training that I am a behaviourist. I may or may not agree within me with what I do, but the behavioural evidence is that I do – and that is the only evidence you have and must accept.

SOLVING PEOPLE PROBLEMS

Peter Honey has developed an approach for solving human relations problems, both for another person and yourself. He claims it to be a simple but effective approach and having used it myself for both personal problem solving and for presenting to other managers for their use, I can support his claim.

His approach involves what he describes as BMod and FMod, standing for behaviour modification and feelings modification respectively. BMod, as it deals exclusively with overt behaviour, is the part of the technique which is applied to the solving of the problems of others. FMod, which is concerned with the modification of feelings, can only be applied to one's own problems.

BMOD

Honey explains his BMod approach by means of a simple model:

$$\boxed{\text{CUE}} \;\; \text{which triggers} \;\; \boxed{\text{BEHAVIOUR}}$$

$$\text{which leads to} \;\; \boxed{\text{PAY OFFS}}$$

The cue is normally the behaviour of someone else to which the problem individual reacts and produces the problem behaviour. If one is considering a recurring problem there should be the opportunity to observe repeating behaviours which may be acting as the cues. For example, Ted always loses his temper whenever Bill makes a suggestion which impinges on Ted's work (but never when Mary or Sam or Fred make similar suggestions). It would seem that this is the cue for him to lose his temper which is exhibited by his shouting and disagreeing with Bill or otherwise attacking him verbally. Finally one asks 'What is Ted getting out of behaving in this way?'. Here one has to be very careful that assumptions about covert, internal feelings are not made and one must therefore rely on the observable activities. After all, the behaviour may be because he wants Bill to like/hate/attack etc. him – or perhaps none of these – we do not know. What we do observe is that *after* Ted has behaved in this way

- Bill stops talking
- people ask Ted what he would do
- his subordinates rally round and actively support him.

We can interpret this situation as his seeking attention and support, but we cannot be sure about this interpretation. What we can be sure of is that this happens when he behaves in this way, otherwise he would not repeat the behaviour.

This is only half the approach, the diagnostic stage, since having identified and analysed the problem, it is necessary to do something to modify the problem behaviour. Consequently the second part of the model suggests:

| NEW CUES | which will lead to | NEW BEHAVIOUR |

which will give | NEW PAY OFFS |

In the first instance we have to determine the new behaviour which will be appropriate and which is our objective. In this case we can say that we want Ted:

- to make the initial proposals for work in his own section
- not to lose his temper with Bill.

Note that our objectives are not simply the reverse of the original unwanted behaviour, but a positive approach.

The new cues will relate to the circumstances we can change to produce the new behaviour. These could include:

- a quiet talk with Bill to wait for Ted to make his own proposals
- have Bill build on Ted's proposals
- have Bill make suggestions rather than proposals and to direct the question to Ted
- to seek agreement for Bill to discuss suggestions with Ted prior to the meeting
- the chairman to bring Ted in and ask him if he has any ideas or proposals to make.

Ted will still need pay offs for his new behaviour to satisfy his needs and if he behaves in the new way:

- his relationship with Bill can become closer
- he will not need to be defensive about his own section
- he will be given every opportunity to speak
- he can still disagree with a suggestion made by Bill, but as it is not in the form of a proposal he will not need to react violently
- life will be more peaceful for him.

The BMod approach can be applied to most human relations problems and problem situations but will be most appropriate when:

- the problem behaviour is that of someone other than yourself
- the problem is significant
- you are in frequent, regular contact with the problem person
- the problem is persistent.

FMOD

FMod is the extension of BMod to looking at problems of your own and particularly when your bad feelings are the problem. Although the BMod approach ignores covert feelings since they are internal to others, FMod can accept these attitudes as we are looking at our own feelings and attitudes. The FMod approach is similar to, but rather more complex than that of BMod, although again it can be expressed in the progressive stages of a model.

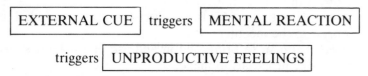

Although there is some controversy about whether feelings are inherited or learned, the active response of these feelings whether expressed internally or externally is usually the result of an external trigger or cue. Even the person who is described universally as 'bad-tempered' is not so *all* the time and with *everybody*. There will be particular people, events, situations which will ensure that his unproductive feelings show in the form of his bad-tempered behaviour, but there will also be occasions when his behaviour will be quite different. So, generally, as the model shows, some incident will trigger a mental reaction in the individual who will have bad or unproductive feelings.

| HINDERED BEHAVIOUR |

leads to | EXTERNAL PAY OFF |

leads to | INTERNAL PAY OFF |

The unproductive feelings will in many cases be evident in overt behaviour of an undesirable nature which, as in the case of BMod, will give pay offs both of an external behavioural nature and also in terms of internal feelings. The burst of bad temper referred to earlier may have an external pay off in silencing the other participant(s) and will give the bad-tempered person the internal pay off feeling 'That showed them who's boss around here! – even though at that stage he is alone because everybody has walked away (literally or figuratively) and left him!

An attempt to modify this chain of reactions *should* be easier to perform than in the case of BMod where we are attempting to change another person who may have no motivation to change. In FMod, as we are dealing with our own feelings, as we have decided to consider the problem, it is reasonable to assume that we shall also attempt to do something about it.

It may be impossible to avoid the external triggers as they may be outside our control, so although they occur and generate our unproductive feelings, there are options open to us which can include

– ignoring the cues, if this is possible
– suppressing the unproductive feelings
– releasing the feelings harmlessly.

The first option has obvious difficulties, particularly if the cue is of a practical nature which demands that we take action. If, however, the cue is of a more emotive nature we may be able to ignore the debasing remark, the comment intended to act as bait and so on.

The problem with the second option is that the unproductive feelings, though actively suppressed will still exist, and being suppressed may produce an unhealthy state, at best equivalent to the collection of brown TA trading stamps.

Release can take many forms, either simply by expressing and bringing out the feelings into the open and talking them through, or by using some form of relaxation or release techniques, or by replacing the thoughts or feelings with new ones. Any of these possibilities can take a variety of approaches, particularly the release feelings in a harmless way: a common example of this is to cry when you are not accustomed to this process, or, more physically, to jump up and down on and destroy a cardboard box!

Honey claims, and my own personal experiences support him strongly, that many problems of a long-standing nature and for which solutions have previousl/ been sought in vain, have been solved by the BMod/FMod approaches.

Human relations training and approaches have an obvious application in the group environment whether in a training event or in a real life team; in the one-to-one interview interaction, again either in the training or real life environments; and in the practical approach to individual problems or development. Wherever there are people there will be people problems and developmental needs. Even a future of increasing technological involvement, unless carried to the science fiction ultimate of a totally robotic world, will include people and hence the need to balance human inter-relationships.

THE APPLICATION OF COMPUTERS

So far very little mention has been made of the use of computers in human relations training. Programs are available for the analysis of constructs produced by Repertory Grid interviews and it is not too difficult to arrange direct input of the Grid constructs as they are elicited from the person being interviewed. We have seen that much more analysis can be obtained from behaviour analysis data than by manual methods once the data have been fed into the computer. Other advantages are the ability to store large amounts compactly instead of on a collection of data sheets and the ease of retrieval of both the data and the analyses.

Other more direct uses of the computer include the storing and analysis of validation and evaluation data, and of course, the speed and storage facilities of the computer are invaluable in the management and administration of training – allocation of trainees and accommodation, control of training supplies, training statistics and so on.

But what about the direct use of the computer in human relations training itself? The computer is being applied in a number of training areas and terms such as Computer Based Learning (CBL), Computer Based Training (CBT), Computer Assisted or Aided Learning (CAL), Computer Assisted Training (CAT) and Computer Managed Training (CMT) are becoming more common in the vocabulary of trainers. Certainly in training for such activities as fault finding, logical decision making, statistics and accounting, the computer with its logical approach has made a strong impact. The impact has been less in human relations training. Perhaps this is necessarily so in an area of training where, in so many cases, the logical approach does not achieve the required objectives since we are dealing with the emotional, irrational and illogical liabilities of people. Until the full development of Artificial Intelligence, the computer will have difficulty in assessing, for example, 'I hate you' as anything other than a simple expression of hate. The human 'computer' will, rightly or wrongly, interpret or attempt to interpret this statement in a number of ways based on inflection, tone of voice, non-verbal signals, the mood of the receiver, the environment and so on. It is often said that the computer has no real place in human relations training. This may be true, but we must remember that it is not long ago that trainers were saying

- 'closed-circuit television can't help in interview training'
- 'videos are a luxury in training'

and even further back

- 'why show a film? The trainer can explain it all'.

There are a number of factors which tend to discourage, or at least do not encourage, the human relations trainer to consider computer application.

Although computers have been around for some time, they are becoming more and more common in schools and their application, or application of parts of them, are becoming part of our life – cheques, credit cards, calculators, watches, washing machines, etc. but to many people – including some in the world of training – computers remain a mystery. This mystery, as so often, is based on ignorance or lack of knowledge about computers; the why, how and what of their construction and operation; and the new language which flows so easily off the tongues of the computer experts, particularly when computer language words for actions or items which have immediate parallels in the non-computer world are used. Perhaps the simple answer to this problem is education. Many parents feel threatened by or certainly inferior to their children who talk and act very knowledgeably and naturally in the world of computers, a world which is alien to the parent. But this is the result of the children developing in an environment of computers and taking them in their stride.

The sense of mystery is probably the underlying cause of the other inhibiting factors also. Because they are not very knowledgeable about computers and their applications, trainers with this barrier will do nothing to increase their skills or even knowledge in the computer field. The effect of the mystique is to produce such thoughts as 'It's all too complicated for me so I shan't even try to learn about them [in case I fail and make a fool of myself]'. I can remember that I used to say similar things and for the same reason about driving a car, before I took the plunge and had my first lesson.

As a direct result of not learning about computers and their application, the trainer will naturally be unconvinced of the value of using them. Until he has had 'hands-on' experience in a practical situation, this attitude is likely to persist. The inhibitions will make him avoid experience or he will erect barriers even when the application is seen to work.

A rather different inhibitor is related to the trainer's fears for his job. He has heard many stories, right or wrong, about the introduction of computers making trainers redundant: 'If I use a computer in my training, I might not be needed!'. Very few trainers should have this fear since the computer will rarely be capable of taking over *all* the training and skilled people will be needed to produce programs for the computer. But perhaps more importantly the trainer will be released from the restrictions of the training room and can then take on a wider role of initiator, interventionist, adviser, consultant and evaluator – all the activities which have been so difficult to perform owing to lack of resource time but which are as essential as the training itself.

HUMAN RELATIONS APPLICATION

The use of the computer in training is bounded by the limitations of the computer and the imagination of the user. Some training can be completely computer based whereas in other forms of training the ideal is a multi-partnership of trainer, traditional visual aids, film projector, audio and video recording and/or playback, and computer, each part of the partnership performing in the area for which it is best fitted.

Most aspects of human relations training rely on direct interaction between people, whether in the field of inter-personal skills, negotiating skills, interviewing skills or something else. But unless the learning event is entirely without structure and format (a T-Group, for example), there is a very definite place for the computer. Before people can interact more effectively and in a different way from that in which they normally perform, they must be given the opportunity to consider new models on which to base their behaviour. Such models abound and are the subjects of input sessions by trainers, or in the form of film presentations or discussion group sessions. For example, there are Maslow's Hierarchy of Needs, the Johari Window Perception model, Behaviour Analysis, Transactional Analysis, etc. All these models can be converted into computer programs which can either

- teach the subject in a straightforward manner
- teach the subject in modules and test after each module
- adopt a programmed text learning approach
- provide a question and answer 'discussion' with the learner, requiring either standard or 'free' answers.

For instance, a teaching program for learners new to the behaviour analysis which is to be used during the learning event might describe the categories used in the analysis. After each category and block of categories, the learner's understanding would be tested by requiring the learner to key-in answers to either multi-choice questions or, in the more advanced interactive programs, to provide answers in the learner's own words. If the learner has progressed satisfactorily he can move on to the next stage, but if the correct responses are not given the learning path has to be retraced until the learner has achieved the necessary learning. At the end of this stage, when all the categories have been covered, the learner can be questioned by the computer over the whole range of the learning provided by the module. The trainer can then step in and arrange live practice in analysis, or practice utilising audio or video equipment. Subsequently the learner returns to the computer to correlate the practice results with a master analysis which has been programmed into the computer. So that realistic correlation comparisons can be made, the feedback data are produced for each participant on individual, and if relevant, group printouts.

In a more interactive mode the computer can be used to present an action maze which might involve, for example, the pre- or post-testing of learners on staff relations courses. Or the program might stand on its own so that an individual learner might assess his skill in handling personnel.

An action maze starts by giving the learner an incident with a worker, either as a practical incident or some other interactive situation. A number of optional responses is then offered to the learner and, following the response selection, the learner is referred to the relevant next stage. There are a number of possible 'next stages', each offering a different incident to which the learner is required to react. Again for each incident there are a number of optional responses. The learner follows the maze from stage to stage, optional response to response, until the end of the maze when the final solution is reached. There are a number of paths of different length through the maze, the paths with the smaller number of responses being followed by the learners who chose the more correct responses.

The main problem with a manually activated action maze is

the number of sheets of paper in use as a result of the number of stages and the number of optional responses. A maze based on three optional responses at each stage could appear schematically as Figure 11.1 overleaf. In this maze there are 19 possible stages and as each stage has 3 options there will be 54 pieces of paper plus the initial incodent sheet and the final solution sheet. The actual number of sheets used will depend on the path followed. Participant A completed the maze by the most direct route and thus used 7 pieces; B took 9 moves with 10 pieces and C had 11 moves requiring 12 pieces, two of which were from the same set as he visited stage 5 twice. The more stages and the more options available at each stage, the more the pieces of paper necessary; with 5-options at the 19 stages we are talking about a minimum of 92 pieces per set.

This approach can be simplified by having the maze on the computer and if desired, the number of stages and options can be increased considerably, and in the more advanced programs a free choice of response can be given. In the computer mode, after the initial question has been posed and the learner has keyed-in the response, the process is repeated with the computer asking the questions and giving the options, the learner keying-in his chosen responses.

So, in the field of human relations training, the non-human computer has a definite place, a place which is growing in stature as the implications of computer technology and the capabilities of the computer are recognised by human relations trainers.

REFERENCES AND RECOMMENDED READING

Dean, C. and Whitlock, Q. (1983): *A Handbook of Computer-based Training*. London: Kogan, Page and Nichols: New York.

Honey, P. (1980): *Solving People Problems*. Maidenhead: McGraw-Hill.

Megginson, D. and Boydell, T. (1979): *A Manager's Guide to Coaching*. London: BACIE.

Singer, E.J. (1979): *Effective Management Coaching*. IPM Publishing.

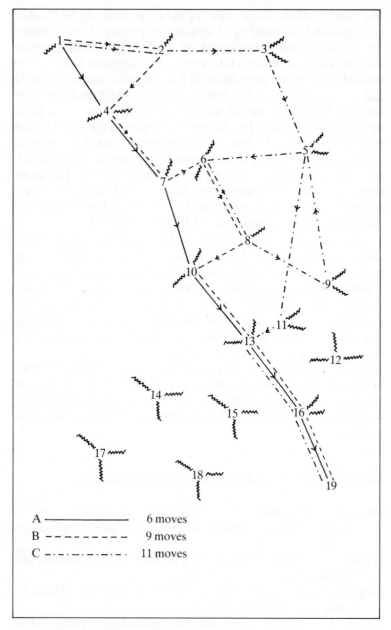

Figure 11.1   3-option action maze

12 Assessing the effectiveness of training

No book on training can be complete without some comments on the methods of assessment of that training, and human relations training cannot be exempt from this requirement. It is often said about some forms of training that full assessment is difficult, if not impossible: human relations training is one which falls into this category. If the learning is concerned with the acquisition of a 'technical' skill, then validation and evaluation are relatively simple processes. Let us take the example of an electricity meter reader. If at the end of the period of training he can read meters correctly 100% of the time, the validity of that training process is beyond question and full evaluation must show that as the result of the acquired skill in reading meters, the organisation for which he has been trained is not losing money through inaccurate readings. The learning can be assessed at the end of the training by simple tests of accuracy. The position will be similar in respect of many other manual, clerical or technical skills where it is usually quite simple to assess the impact and value of the training. It is much more diifficult to do so when we are considering the more subjective areas of human relations training where testing may be difficult or impossible and can be generally only subjective.

The example of the meter reader raises the question of the use of terms. The two most commonly applied to training are evaluation and validation. Evaluation seems to be the one most used even when the users really mean validation.

Validation has been defined, for internal validation, as a series of tests and assessments designed to ascertain whether a training prograamme has achieved the behavioural objectives specified. As external validation, it is defined as ascertaining whether the behavioural objectives of an internally valid training programme were realistically based on an accurate identification of training needs (Department of Employment *Glossary of Training Terms,* 1971, HMSO). In other words, validation is a test of whether the training achieves what it set out to do and whether the objectives were the appropriate ones.

Evaluation is defined in the same publication as 'the assessment of the total value of a training system, training course or programme in social as well as financial terms'. Evaluation is shown to differ from validation 'in that it attempts to measure the overall cost benefit of the course or programme, and not just the achievement of its laid down objectives. The term is also used in the general judgemental sense of the continuous monitoring of a programme or of the training function as a whole.' From this description it is obvious that evaluation uses much wider brush strokes in the assessment of training than validation, and looks not only at the training itself, but the learning achieved, its transference to the work and the value to organisation of the learner's increased skills.

Hamblin takes a more simplistic view of the definition of evaluation saying that it is 'any attempt to obtain information (feedback) on the effects of a training programme, and to assess the value of training in the light of that information'.

Whichever definition is taken, there can be no doubt that evaluation in most senses is not always a meaningful or feasible exercise. In most cases we can appraise, assess or test the learning achieved at the end of the training event, but to extend that appraisal requires us to:

- determine whether and to what extent the learning is translated to the working environment
- determine whether the learner, as a result of the training, is operating at a more effective level than prior to the training
- determine whether the organisation has benefited from the training in terms of efficiency and actual financial value.

It can, therefore, be seen that the greater part of evaluation takes place away from the training event and requires the expenditure of considerable time and resource in its execution. There is a decision of principle and practice that must be taken by the trainer if he is to take account of evaluation in training. The onus for the validation of training must certainly be on the shoulders of the trainer – even if he does not feel obliged to or is obliged to by his employer, he should be questioning, for his own peace of mind, whether the training is effective. Beyond this the question is raised whether the trainer should be involved at all in evaluation.

A parallel can be made with other sectors of industry by considering the sale of a washing machine by the manufacturers to a sales outlet. The manufacturer is obliged to ensure that the machine is constructed in such a way that it can perform the range of functions that its researchers have shown is required or desired by the client. He is also obliged to ensure that the machine is in good working order. As a result he has reacted to the clients' needs by producing a working machine which includes the features stated in the specification, based on the needs of the clients. The parallel with training is clear in that the trainer, having identified or having had identified for him the training needs of his clients, provides training relevant to those needs and satisfies himself that the training is satisfying the objectives.

In the washing machine analogy, which I must admit is not an absolute analogy, the manufacturer does not go out to his clients to ensure that they are displaying the machine in a way that will ensure its sale, nor to confirm that the clients' clients (the customers) are using the machine properly, or that the machine suits the requirements of a particular customer. This evaluation, to a greater or lesser extent, must be the responsibility of the client. The trainer performs his training in a manner as effective as possible, attempting to ensure that the participants extract the maximum amount of learning and that the training is in step with the identified training needs. Beyond this, apart from a subjective interest and perhaps from vanity, the trainer has no real responsibility. The clients, that is the learners and their managers, are the ones who are responsible for evaluating the training once this has been delivered. The trainer is in no position to assess the extent to which the learner puts his learning into practice and how effectively, nor can he assess the value of the performance of this learning to the organisation's functioning. These assessments are the responsibility of the learners' manager who should, if they find that the training is no longer satisfying the training needs, inform the training department and agree new training standards. Of course, the caring trainer will from time to time initiate enquiries to the line managers seeking information on the clients' satisfaction or otherwise – but that is all.

There is a movement at the present time which is suggesting that the role of the trainer should be much more outward looking than hitherto, and he should develop more of a consultancy approach, being more responsible for initiatives and approaches. There must be no lack of support for this natural extension of the trainer's restricted role, but care must be taken that the responsibility is not taken away from the line management either in development or the assessment of the value of the trainer's intervention.

Research into what can be described as an ideal evaluation approach can show that to operate the approach more resources are required than are available to actually perform the training. The practical ideal is a marriage between training and line management who between them can contract to train, validate and evaluate as far as is practicable. This approach involves the extraction of elements which are realistic from the total list of elements in the impracticable ideal system.

Various levels in the evaluation process can be identified and described as:

- the immediate reaction level
- the immediate outcome level
- the intermediate or moderate-term level outcome
- the ultimate or long-term outcome level.

In the restrictive view of the trainer's responsibility in this scheme, validation is involved in the first two levels, and pure evaluation is reflected in the other two.

The immediate reaction level is observed while the training is being performed and is evidenced by observation of the learner's performance or as a result of direct tests of his learning.

The level of immediate outcome involves the validation by the learners and trainers, including the use of tests, at the end of the event in terms of satisfaction of the course objectives and the learners' personal objectives.

The intermediate level relates to the behaviour on the job as a result of the training, once the learner has returned to work and has put into practice whatever he might have decided in an end of course action plan.

The ultimate outcome level looks at the long-term effects of the training, whether the new skills have been maintained and the more organisationally oriented aspects of value.

ACTION PLANNING

Although the trainer may not be directly involved in the intermediate outcome level of evaluation, he can contribute towards it at the same time as he is obtaining one measure of immediate outcome assessment. It may be a truism that training is not performed for training's sake, but to satisfy the training need of the learner. But learners come to training courses with personal objectives in addition to the objectives of the course and it is useful for them to formalise their intentions at the end of an event.

This formalisation is normally referred to as Action Planning and commonly takes the form of a period of time devoted, at the end of a training course, to the learners considering what they have learned from the event and which new aspects they will be introducing when they return to work. In effect it is a contract with themselves to transfer some aspects of the learning to work.

One approach which I have found useful in the construction of an effective Action Plan has been mentioned earlier in connection with the interpersonal skills training course. The act of Action Planning can be presaged by a paired discussion activity in which the participants are encouraged to discuss what learning has emerged from the event and some views on how they intend to apply the learning. The value in this approach is that half-formed views and ideas can be bounced off the partner and clarified. An Action Plan would then be formulated, still with the facility of a partner with whom the various aspects included could be discussed.

The completed Action Plan has a number of uses. Primarily it exists as a written reminder to the learner that he intends to put certain aspects of the learning into action back at work. It also serves as a basic discussion document to be used at the learner's post-course debriefing session with his boss. But from a validation and evaluation point of view the Action Plan can be used as an instrument for immediate, intermediate and ultimate outcome assessment. If the Action Plan contains items which result directly from the course objectives, this inclusion is reasonable evidence of the validity of the course. The line manager and/or the manager-trainer can also refer to the action plan and its success or otherwise in implementation during any investigation at the intermediate or long-term level.

In a number of cases the trainer is very aware that when the learner returns to work his boss will take little or no interest in the outcome of the training event, but the Action Plan can be used in such cases as a point of entry. The learner, on return from the training, can actively seek out his boss with an invitation to see (and hence discuss) the completed Action Plan. Few bosses would be so churlish as to refuse such an invitation and could find themselves drawn into resulting action.

VALIDATION OF TRAINING

More direct methods than Action Plans are open to the trainer who wishes to validate, or more expressively, assess the value and effectiveness of his training. These involve assessment activities at both the immediate reaction and immediate outcome levels.

When the training is in progress, the subjective views of the trainer on how he feels the training is being accepted, can be supplemented by objective tests of knowledge or skill. In the case of knowledge tests, these can take the simple form of a series of questions related to what should have been learned, for example:

Name the elements of the management cycle.
What are the principal differences between McGregor's X and Y theories?

In the case of manual, technical or clerical skills, the trainees can be asked to perform practical tasks which will show directly whether they have mastered the necessary skills.

Testing becomes much more difficult in human relations practical training as there are so few *right* answers. An interview can be observed and the structure and behaviour can be assessed as good or bad, but if either assessment is challenged, so many times the trainer will be forced back to the position of 'In my opinion'. The problem is even more difficult to resolve in looking at more general interpersonal skills. In negotiating training there may be an ultimate answer in result terms to a negotiation problem, but there may be a number of ways to that end. And if the ultimate is not achieved, has the negotiator failed? He may have assessed the situation to the extent that *his* ultimate position is different and he has reached it.

Observational instruments such as Behaviour Analysis go a long way to providing an objective assessment of achievement, but they only present part of the picture. After all, a meeting leader may exhibit all the appropriate behaviour patterns of an effective leader, yet his leadership may have been a failure because of, say, the order in which he expressed his contributions, or the manner in which he made them. However, a final BA in an interpersonal skills course when compared with earlier ones can given an indication of how much movement there has been in the behaviour patterns and whether these have been appropriate or inappropriate. A BA of an interview can at least show objectively the ratio of open to closed questions.

Attempts at more objective tests are of little help to us as they are principally concerned with knowledge and the use of knowledge rather than the application of social skills. I have seen tests which offer a series of small case studies and require an answer in terms of what the learner would do. The responses may be textually correct, but there is no way of knowing whether they are considered responses, memory responses from the preceding training, or ones that the learner has assessed as being sought by the trainer.

Consequently the human relations trainer is forced into the position that an assessment at the immediate reaction level particularly, apart from the 'evidence' of such instruments as BA, must necessarily be subjective and based on his own assessment. The assessment of an experienced trainer is often correct, but if challenged he rarely has an objective, quantitative base to support him. However, we must not be too dismayed at the lack of objective approaches and the reliance on subjective assessments, after all human relations are themselves highly subjective.

IMMEDIATE OUTCOME LEVEL

When we reach the end of a human relations training event, assessment is no easier than at the reaction level. It may appear so to the onlooker from the written instruments which are completed by the learners. Even with these we have to accept their statements at face value. It is for this reason that such end-of-course validation sheets are referred to on occasions as the course 'happiness' sheets. But apart from the Action Plans referred to earlier, they are virtually all that is available to us.

The end-of-course validation questionnaire can take a number of different forms depending on what we are seeking to achieve with it. Commonly it seeks views from the learners on such topics as the value of the sessions, whether they were interesting or not, whether they were presented well or not, too long or too short, too many or too few visual aids and so on.

A number of different rating scales are available, some of which are more relevant to some forms of training, some to others.

One approach can be a simple, multiple choice approach in which the learner is asked to ring the choice nearest to his views.

I would not recommend this course   1
I would hesitate in recommending this course   2

I would recommend this course although with one or two
reservations   3
I would recommend this course   ④
I would enthusiastically recommend this course   5

Another approach which introduces the multiple choice is the
Likert type approach which asks the completer to state whether
he agrees more with a statement than he disagrees, or vice
versa. This approach is less restrictive than those which
demand categoric agreement or disagreement, although qualifications of strongly agree, agree, uncertain, disagree and
strongly disagree can be introduced. On the same question as
cited above, the questionnaire would look like:

This course can be recommended   (Agree)   Disagree
                              or
This course can be recommended   Strongly agree
                                                        (Agree)
                                                        Uncertain
                                                        Disagree
                                                        Strongly disagree.

Possibly the most common scale in use is the semantic
differential scale in which trainees are asked to rate subjects
sessions, activities etc. on a 5, 6 or 7 point scale connecting two
opposing evaluative statements.

Session: Introducing conflict.

Complicated |___|✓_|___|___|___| Simple
Enjoyable |___|✓_|___|___|___| Boring

All these approaches and others can be used to collect views on
individual parts of a course, on some selected parts of a course,
and on the course as a whole. One school of thought suggests
that the more questions that are asked, the more the information is given. My own experience, from both sides of the
questionnaire, suggests that participants find that extensive
questionnaires get in their way and consequently complete a
long and involved questionnaire superficially. Figure 12.1
shows an end-of-course questionnaire validation sheet I use

NAME _____

INTERPERSONAL SKILLS TRAINING

In order to maintain our learning events at the level required by you, our clients, we need to know to what extent the course has met your needs. Would you please complete the following as openly as possible.

Course objectives met   ⌊___⌊___⌊___⌊___⌊___⌊___⌊ Not met

My objectives met   ⌊___⌊___⌊___⌊___⌊___⌊___⌊ Not met

Course too long   ⌊___⌊___⌊___⌊___⌊___⌊___⌊ Too short

Tutor helpful   ⌊___⌊___⌊___⌊___⌊___⌊___⌊ Unhelpful

Tutor too directive   ⌊___⌊___⌊___⌊___⌊___⌊___⌊ Too non-directive

Course as a whole good ⌊___⌊___⌊___⌊___⌊___⌊___⌊ Poor

Would recommend   ⌊___⌊___⌊___⌊___⌊___⌊___⌊ Wouldn't

Which parts of the course did you find most helpful?

Which parts of the course did you find least helpful?

Are there any parts of the course you would omit?

Is there anything else you would have liked to have seen in the course?

Any other comments?

Figure 12.1   End-of-course validation

frequently for the interpersonal skills course when I am interested only in its general validation.

One approach I have found useful to extend the information given on review sheets, and to try to have the completers think more deeply about how they are scoring, is to add a probing question after the scale. If I am asking about the extent of learning I might have:

Learned a lot |___|___✓___|___|___| Learned nothing
Please state why you have scored the item in this way:

Another factor which must be taken into account, particularly with extensive review sheets, is the length of time to allow if they are to be completed effectively. If there are a large number of items on which the trainees have to comment, it is worthwhile issuing the questionnaire at the start of the course and suggesting that they should complete the sheets at the end of each day. The daily approach has the advantage on most courses over a completion after each session or activity in that completion would be less rushed. Also sometimes several sessions and activities link with each other and the learning is not apparent until after the last one of the series.

DAILY AUDIT

Whatever the subjectivity or objectivity of the end-of-course validation approach the result must of necessity be an 'after the event' statement. The training has been completed so the information is useful only in terms of saying how successful the training had been and giving some indications of possible changes for future courses.

But the caring trainer needs to know, as the event is progressing, how it is being received. Unless he is very unperceptive he will have some subjective feelings about this, but often these feelings are clouded by either a completely general view or by the signals coming from one strong member of the group. There are a number of ways of approaching a more current audit of reactions.

One way is to ask the course members to decide which

elements *they* would like to see in any validation/appraisal system for the course and which method they would use to rate the various aspects. In most cases the system produced is little different from the one the trainer would have produced – perhaps the words are different – but the members have a strong sense of ownership of the system and intend to make it realistic. Commonly a numerical rating is included and it is decided that 10 minutes are left aside at the end of each day for rating and recording the day.

A variant to this approach is to ask the group at the start of each day to write down three adjectives which describe the previous day. The group's words are then posted on a sheet of newsprint on the training room wall and discussed to the extent that the group wishes to discuss. If the discussion shows that a problem remains from the previous day, it can be clarified with little delay.

Another method I have used which highlights current problems is to ask the group to complete at the end of the day an audit questionnaire on the day. The questions are:

- which items raised today were most helpful to you?
- how will you apply these back at work?
- which concepts, techniques or activities were not helpful?
- why were they not helpful?

The comments to these, or other questions determined by the trainer, are collected and collated so that they can be discussed as a first activity the following morning, and again any emerging problems can be resolved as far as possible.

Course members accept well these approaches as they can see them as appraisals and validations in which they are involved and which can lead immediately to something being done about any emerging problems.

PRE-COURSE PREPARATION

Evaluation is basically the appraisal of whether an individual performs more effectively following the training than he did before the training. This statement implies that we, as the trainers, were aware of and measured the trainee's level of skill before he was exposed to the training. Unfortunately this is done rarely and we have the paradox of trainers trying to show that improvements have taken place during the training when there is no measure of what existed previously!

Evaluation must be one of the later stages in a complete system of training which follows a logical and progressive path. The start of this path must be an analysis of the task to be performed by the potential trainee. All aspects of the job must be determined and analysed in terms of the knowledge, skills and attitudes required to perform it effectively. Every job has problem areas and it is valuable to look at these areas where an effectivity gap may more likely exist. If a gap exists in these areas with the people who have to perform the job, a training need exists.

The identification of a training need or needs produces the base on which a training event can be planned and it is from these needs that a course as a whole or individual training sessions can be planned and prepared.

The scene is set for the trainees to come forward for training. The training objectives and session objectives have been identified from the general training needs. But, although most of the potential trainees fall within the general training needs, people can vary considerably and so can their individual training needs. This is the stage at which the pre-training level of knowledge, skills and attitudes must be determined. When we are dealing with new entrants to an industry, occupation or aspect of work, we can reasonably assume that the initial knowledge etc. is low or non-existent. It is very much more difficult when we are considering mature workers and their skill levels in human relations terms. Nobody starts at zero base and among the group one can expect to find skills right across the possible spectrum.

So, in order to assess at the end of the training how far each individual has moved along the continuum, we must know at which point they are starting. This is very difficult in human relations areas and in most cases all we can hope for is a subjective assessment. A typical approach is to ask the trainee, before coming to the training event, to complete a self-assessment questionnaire, identifying the level of skill in various areas related to the proposed training. For example, prior to attending an interactive skills programme, the learners can identify on a 5 or 7 point scale their level of skill in a number of specific skill areas. Or they can be asked to identify in the same way whether they see their skill levels as satisfactory or with a need to improve. If it is possible to do so, this subjective approach can be made more objective if the trainee's boss can be asked the same questions about the trainee.

At the end of the training event the learners are asked to complete the same questionnaire. The only difference on this occasion is in the version where they were asked to comment on their level – satisfactory or need to improve. In the end-of-course version they are asked to comment on whether their skills have improved or stayed the same. In the skill scoring approach, they are asked to rate themselves as at that terminal stage of the course. If for example, the learner initially scored himself 4 out of 7 on 'being aware of problem behaviour' and at the end of the course scored 6 out of 7, there had been an obvious movement in the right direction. Movement of this nature is reasonably objective validation of the effectiveness of the course and also of the improvement of the learner's skills.

There is however a possible contamination factor which can upset the apparent validation approach when this method is used. If we take the example cited above where for the particular skill the initial rating was 6 out of 7. This rating meant that the learner considered he was good at spotting behaviour problems in a group. However, at the time of the completion of the second questionnaire, the end of the course, a score of 5 out of 7 is given. This suggests that after a week of training during which there was considerable emphasis on this skill, his skill level had actually fallen, by 1 in the scoring system – a drop of 14%. In fact, what the individual is saying is that when he completed the original questionnaire he *thought* he was at that high level. The training showed him that he was nowhere near that level – more realistically he should have been at about 2 – but the training made him more aware (a) of his failings and (b) of awareness itself. So the change in scoring was really +4, a skill increase of 56%. But the two question-naires do not show this contamination of the assessments and a superficial examination of the audit suggests an ineffective approach.

In order to overcome the contamination effect Mezoff suggested the introduction of a third stage. He referred to the process as the PRE – THEN – POST test as opposed to the more normal PRE – POST test. Mezoff suggested that the end-of-course questionnaire should be completed as normal, but following this the learners should be asked to complete again the questionnaire they had scored at the beginning of the course. However, on this occasion they are asked to complete it on themselves as they were at the beginning of the course BUT in the light of the knowledge they now have of their skills as they really were at that stage.

I have tried this particular approach in the way suggested and the results were certainly significant. Three skill aspects will show what happened with one individual I have selected at random. Column 1 is the skill aspect; column 2 the self-rating out of 10 pre-course; column 3 the self-rating at the end of the course; and column 4 the revised pre-course rating.

(1)	(2)	(3)	(4)
Control of amount of talking I do as leader	5	8	3
Control amount of contribution I make as a member.	5	7	6
Thinking before talking	3	7	2

Taking the last skill as an example, before the course the learner felt he was not very good at controlling the amount of thinking he did before opening his mouth to talk – a score of 3/10. By the end of the course he felt his skill had increased quite considerably – to a score of 7/10, an increase of 4 scale points. But when he reconsidered his pre-course skill he gave it an even lower rating – 2/10; this produced an increase of 5 scale points over the course.

If the resources are available, the end-of-course questionnaire can be repeated some three to four months after the course when the learner has had the opportunity to practise the skills he learned, particularly the ones he identified in his

Action Plan. This follow-up can also act as a validation of the learning elements of the course – if they are not retained, is there any value in keeping them as part of the course? Again, objectivity can be sought by seeking the views for the second time of the learner's boss.

So, although validation or assessment of human relations training is fraught with difficulties and subjectivity, some approaches not only can be made but are worth while in reward terms. One must guard, however, against using the results in too absolute a manner.

REFERENCES AND RECOMMENDED READING

Davies, I.K. (1971): *The Management of Learning*. Maidenhead: McGraw-Hill. (Ch. 14 and 15).

Hamblin, A.C. (1974): *Evaluation and Control of Training*. Maidenhead: McGraw-Hill.

Kirkpatrick, D.L. (1976): 'Evaluation of training' in R.L. Craig (ed.) *Training and Development Handbook*. Maidenhead: McGraw-Hill.

Mezoff, B. (1981): 'How to Get Accurate Self-reports of Training Outcomes', *Training and Development Journal of the American Society for Training and Development*, 35 (9), September 1981.

Parker, T.C. (1976): 'Statistical Methods for Measuring Training Results', in R.L. Craig (ed.) *Training and Development Handbook*. Maidenhead: McGraw-Hill.

Rae, L. (1983): 'Towards a More Valid End-of-Course Validation', *The Training Officer*, October.

Rae, L. (1984): 'The Validation of Learning', *Journal of the Institute of Training and Development*. May.

Warr, P., Bird, M. and Rackham, N. (1970): *Evaluation of Management Training*. Aldershot: Gower.

Whitelaw, M. (1972): *The Evaluation of Management Training*, IPM Publishing.

13 The practice of human relations training

The overview of human relations training which has been presented in this book has described the range of methods and approaches available. I have also tried to demonstrate the complexity of this form of training and the level of skills needed by those who will be responsible for the training. Much of what has been described requires considerable skill and experience on the part of the 'trainer' and many of the approaches require a formal or semi-formal group to enable the experience to develop. However, this requirement is not universally true and much can be done on a one-to-one tutorial basis. In times of industrial and economic constraint there is a greater reluctance to look to group training schemes run by full-time trainers, particularly if the trainers are not in-company, and senior management looks carefully at what can be managed internally. Hence, in addition to full-time trainers, either internal or external, we have part-time trainers who perform much the same duties as the full-time trainer but on a more restricted basis and who also have another duty which they perform for the remaining part time. Finally there is the manager-trainer who, rather than having a separate training role, has to combine some elements of training with his managerial role.

FULL-TIME TRAINERS

The needs of the full-time trainer are relatively easy to recognise. In the same way that other forms of training demand certain knowledge, skills, abilities and attitudes, so does the human relations trainer. The basic trainer skills need to be present and almost automatic responses, but in addition to these are the factors which are needed more in human relations training than in the other, more 'technical' training. Although the trainer will still need to give formal input sessions on occasions, these will be less frequent than when he has to mount, control and take the feedback from an activity. But more than this, his intervention skills must be of the highest quality so that he knows when, and how, to intervene in order to convert a comment into an unstructured activity; when to keep quiet; when, sometimes quietly to leave the room and allow the group to progress without him; when to accept or reject the role of arbiter and so on. This approach demands not only a wide range of skills, but, as discussed at the beginning of this book, a personal and training philosophy which needs to be sincere, not divisive; an ability to encourage a learner-centred, not trainer-centred event; and the skill of behaving appropriately so that the learners can observe effective skills in operation.

The activities of the full-time human relations trainer will be as varied as there are shades of human relations, but they will fall somewhere within the range of approaches described in this book. The trainer's approach to his training activities or programmes will differ scarcely from those of his colleagues in other forms of training. This will certainly include:

1) *The identification of training needs.* Practice will vary from organisation to organisation in this approach as in some areas it will be the sole responsibility of the training department, in others identification will fall completely on the line management, and in others there will be a liaison between trainer and line manager. In practice it doesn't matter how this is done provided that:

- it is done
- it is done comprehensively and effectively
- action follows identification.

2) *Determination and statement of the learning objectives for the learning event.* Once the training needs have been firmly established, the general aims for the training can be readily

identified. But, in order that the training can subsequently be validated and evaluated, specific learning objectives must be identified and stated. Aims can be expressed in fairly broad terms – 'To improve the interviewing skills of middle-range managers in the areas of discipline and grievance'. Objectives, however, must be much more explicit and, so that they can be validated, must be couched in terms which will allow eventual testing. A number of words exist which are often used in statements of objectives, but which are so open to such a wide range of interpretation that they cannot serve in an objective. A list of words of this nature would include:

- to know
- to appreciate
- to understand
- to be aware of
- to consider
- to accept.

Words which are more closely related to objectives are action words which are precise and tell the reader, writer or learner what to expect. Such words include:

- to build
- to list
- to perform
- to write
- to read
- to solve

and will be made even more specific by the addition of quantitative measures. For example 'To solve quadratic equations so that 80% of the answers are correct'. Even this statement, specific though it may sound is not acceptable as a training objective as it is not made clear whether the 80% correctness refers to the total number of answers or to each answer.

It is obviousuly much more difficult to write specific objectives in these types of terms for human relations training and sometimes there will be a public objective in addition to an objective stated in training terms and retained by the trainer. The retention would not be for any divisive reason, for it may be that the learner would not be able to understand the objective until the training had been completed. For example, the public objective for an interactive skills course might include:

'To make the learner more aware of his behaviour in group situations and the effect of that behaviour on others. To give the learner the opportunity to practise behaviour modification so that aspects of his behaviour pattern become more appropriate.'

The related objectives retained by the trainer could be:

'To give BA feedback in terms of X categories as the result of the observation of Y activities.
To increase the building behaviour from 6 to 10% and reduce shutting out from 15 to 6%, etc.'

3) *The production of a learning event plan.* Once the overall learning objectives have been determined, the trainer knows where he is going and he can then construct a total event which will satisfy the objectives. At this stage the overall learning strategy will have to be decided. Will it be a course, a seminar, a workshop? What will be the balance between sessions and activities? How long will be necessary to reach the objectives? How many trainees will make an optimum/maximum/minimum course population?

The trainer will hope that not only will he produce answers to these and other questions, but that the answers will all be right. If they are he will have been very lucky in addition to being very skilful, for few new training courses are ever completely right from the first event.

4) *Determine session objectives.* In the same way that specific objectives were necessary for the whole event, so they are for each session or activity. What is it that the trainer is trying to achieve which will progress the learning, by including in the session? If a positive and very specific answer cannot be given, there will be serious doubts as to whether the session should be there at all. Sometimes, however, the session objective can be simple and not directly related to the training plan, although it will still have a specific purpose. If the training calls for a serious and very intensive involvement of the trainees, sometimes it may be necessary to introduce a session whose objective is simply to provide light relief.

5) *Production of session and activity methods.* The produc-

tion of an overall event plan followed the determination of the course objectives; similarly now that the individual session objectives have been determined, it can be decided how they will be achieved. Will the session be a formal input or an open discussion? Will it achieve the objectives better by being an activity? Structured or unstructured? One group or a number of groups? How will the feedback/appraisal be carried out?

6) *Other training arrangements.* It almost goes without saying that there will be many other considerations once the objectives, strategy and methods have been decided. Some of these will have cropped up naturally as other decisions were being taken. Which and how many tutors? How many trainees? Reservation of training and other accommodation. Arrangements for briefing documents, handouts and so on. Production of session briefs and visual aids for the tutors. Hiring of films, videos, equipment. The list is long indeed.

7) *The event.* But the great day comes and the event starts. Even then decisions may still be necessary. Having seen the group and perhaps their Learning Styles, how are they to be mixed for small group activities? Is the programme to be followed or in the light of X should we vary Y session/activity? Why did we ever start this!?

8) *Validation.* Whether any more extensive form of evaluation is to take place, as discussed in the last chapter some validation of the training will almost certainly be needed. Are end-of-course validation questionnaires to be used? What form should they take and how exhaustive should they be? When should they be issued? Should there also be an oral review?

9) *Review.* The final stage when the success of the event is considered against the objectives set. The trainer or trainers will review the course by reference to whatever validation information is available and consider their own views of what they saw occurring and how they reacted. Was the event too optimistic in its objectives or not optimistic enough? Which parts were more and which less successful and why? And certainly the starter question to the final section – what do we change?

Obviously for events which have been running for some time, all these stages will not be necessary, but certainly the final review stage must be included on every occasion. It is perhaps even more relevant for events which have been running for some time when there is the danger on a non-questioning, acceptance of the status quo settling in.

PART-TIME TRAINERS

The process described for the full-time trainer applies equally to the part-time trainer who will have more difficulties in practising it because of the constraints on his time. It also applies when the organisation is buying-in training from a trainer or consultant external to the company. The company must ensure that what is being offered in return for its money is what it wants, satisfies its own objectives and will be performed in a way that is not an anathema to the company's principles. If the company runs a tight operation with a benevolent autocracy as its style of management, it is unlikely that a sensitivity training approach would satisfy its needs, the more structured approach being more immediately relevant.

THE MANAGER-TRAINER

It is when we come to the role of the manager-trainer in human relations training that problems appear which are not as evident in the more technical modes of training. If someone doesn't know which button to push and the manager is the only one who does know, the manager's role is straightforward in telling/showing the other person which button to push. But human relations training is more complex and long term than this. Where does the manager-trainer fit in?

Mention has already been made of the manager's relationship with the training and development of his staff. At the very least he should be *concerned* about developing their skills and performance, and it is often quoted that one of the prime *responsibilities* of the manager is to ensure the training and development of all those he manages. The benefits to the manager are such that:

- there is more interest and job satisfaction for the employee
- the work is performed more effectively and efficiently
- the prospects of the individual employee are improved
- the prospects of the manager himself are improved
- a suitable successor is identified and developed accordingly so the manager may have no concerns when he is away.

There will always be, of course, managers who will not want to develop their staff, having the philosophy that:

- people do not need interest in their work, for they are paid to do that work
- effectiveness and efficiency are again what they are paid for
- let them work for promotion themselves – 'I had to'
- if they become too skilled, my job may be in jeopardy.

One hopes that managers with these attitudes are in the minority, but . . . . . .

However, in one sense every manager is also a trainer or at least responsible for ensuring that his staff obtain training. How can this situation be maximised when we consider needs in the human relations field?

In the first place, the attitudes of employees or subordinates are influenced strongly by the attitude and behaviour of their supervisors and managers, particularly senior managers. If the manager, whatever his motivation or real attitude, shows no overt interest in training and development, the assumption will be made that he is not. Consequently, individuals, unless they are personally very strongly self-motivated, will take a negative or at best a passive stance themselves. Even worse will be the case of the manager who, on the return of one of his staff from a training course, tells that individual to 'forget all that rubbish they've told you. I do it this way and that's the way it's going to be done'.

If, however, as has been suggested earlier, the manager discusses the proposed training at an early stage with the individual, has a pre-course and post-course meeting with him, and actively supports the implementation of the Action Plan, he is creating an atmosphere which is right for development. An atmosphere of this nature will not only ensure that learning is translated into productive reality, but also that the staff will think training and development and even be encouraged to take self-development action.

The liaison between the trainer and the manager in the identification of training needs has been mentioned and this must be a key aspect in the role of the manager-trainer. He is in a unique position to assess the training needs of at least his senior workers whom he can then train to identify the needs of their subordinates. He has a number of advantages over the trainer who is given the task of identifying training needs in that:

- he knows the people concerned
- he knows their skill levels
- he knows the jobs involved
- he knows the complexities and requirements of these jobs,

and therefore is already a long way along the path of training needs identification. Even so he will have to take positive steps to determine the needs accurately.

IDENTIFICATION OF TRAINING NEEDS

The identification of training needs is essentially a problem-solving situation which follows the classical approach:

Collect data —— Analysis ——Generation of possible solutions —— Selection of solution —— Action.

Numerous approaches to data collection, which is probably the key to the whole process, exist but the manager-trainer has the advantage of a reasonable amount of personal observation to support any other approaches.

The method which is probably used most frequently is for the manager to interview his subordinates for this specific purpose. The counselling interview approach is the one most likely to produce positive results although more formal or structured interactions can also give good results. Questionnaires can be used to obtain some information and are a useful way of obtaining information quickly from a large number of people so that the mass of data can be analysed. Other approaches include the Repertory Grid, the Critical Incident and Role Set Analysis methods, but the manager-trainer would have to ensure that he was sufficiently skilled to tackle the problem in this way. This approach to data collection may of course expose a training need for the manager himself. From the data collected the training needs will emerge and an assessment can be made of the most appropriate way of satisfying them.

The approach suggests the initiation of a special and separate series of staff interviews. Although this may be necessary on occasions, in many firms a continuing process exists which should be used for this purpose. This is the annual appraisal system with interviews which are held at every level in some companies and at specific levels in others.

Often the interview is based on a written report on the individual in which he is rated on his work over the year on a range of qualities or aspects of performance. The objectives of the interview are that the interviewee should become acquainted with the contents of the report – or as much as the organisation decrees he should be told – and then given the opportunity to discuss the assessments. Some part of this interview must be devoted to training. The assessments themselves may identify some areas of weakness which, following discussion, identify specific training needs and approaches. Additionally, as the interviewee is given a lot of opportunity to comment and discuss, other training areas may be identified.

Ideally, if an appraisal system is in operation and all the processes proceed in an effective way, the systems affords an excellent vehicle for identifying and discussing training topics. Unfortunately all too often appraisal interviews are either avoided or handled badly so that the opportunity is lost. These negative approaches to the appraisal interview also unfortunately occur with individuals who would benefit most from a meaningful discussion – those with training needs and for whom something could be arranged.

COACHING

Coaching, which has been described earlier in some detail, is the ideal approach in which the manager-trainer can take an active part provided he has the necessary skills. He is the 'trainer' on the spot, with a relationship already established with the individual and real work is readily available for use in the coaching project. Apart from the constraints of time, which of course can be very real, the main reason why coaching can fail is the manager's lack of skill in the techniques. However, if the motivation exists, training for the manager is possible.

But the principal problem in coaching is if the subordinate's problem is one of human relations. It is relatively simple to arrange coaching projects if the problem is one of writing reports, delegating, planning or any of the more specific problems. It is much more difficult if the problem is one of interviewing attitudes, relationships with colleagues, telephone manner etc. In some of these situations, for example when the problem is one of presentations, interviewing or telephone contacts, simulations can be set up at work with the manager and/or others assisting with roles and/or giving feedback. Other problems are much more difficult, but may be solved by a series of counselling interviews in which the problem is talked through, almost on a therapy basis, and solutions offered and agreed.

MODELLING

Where coaching is too difficult or not appropriate, provided that the manager or someone else from the workplace or organisation can perform the task in an appropriate and effective way, modelling can be used.

Let us take an example of an individual's problem in negotiating skills. Apart from a course where the techniques would be learned and practice given in an artificial environment, other training possibilities are difficult. If the learner is sent out to negotiate for practice, the real life negotiations may fail for him, the company will suffer and he may learn nothing other than the confirmation that he is a poor performer in negotiations.

An approach which is akin to coaching can be used effectively in a case such as this. The manager-trainer can discuss the elements of negotiation with the learner in a one-to-one tutorial and also describe a negotiation into which he (the manager) will soon be entering. He will describe the issues involved and the techniques and approaches he will use, also the ploys he assesses will be used by the other party and how he will react to these. The learner will attend the negotiations as an observer and in effect is being asked to subsequently model himself on what he has seen of the skilled manager-negotiator. Subsequently the learner will prepare, under the guidance of the manager, for a real negotiation of his own, perhaps to be accompanied by the manager who will act as observer, only entering the negotiation if invited to do so by the learner or in an absolute crisis situation. The negotiation would then be followed by an appraisal by both the manager and the learner.

This approach can be effective in a number of areas, including the leading of meetings, staff interviews and the like. The essential element however, must be that the manager-trainer on whom there is to be modelling, must himself be highly skilled otherwise the modelling is less than effective.

SELF-DEVELOPMENT

But the most effective role of the manager-trainer can be in the development of an atmosphere at work conducive to encouraging his subordinates to want to develop themselves. His approach under these circumstances is to encourage this interest, counsel the learner in the most effective paths, assist in discovering methods of self-development and actively encouraging continuance of the approach.

Although most human relations training appears to be through courses and group events of some nature and by very experienced and skilled trainers, the manager as trainer can help his staff to develop on the job. Learning achieved in this way is more likely to be applied and maintained than if it came about through a training course, however expert the training course. Training courses *are* important and useful as one aid in an individual's development, but I hope that this book has shown that there are other aids which should also be considered.

REFERENCES AND RECOMMENDED READING

Annett, J., Duncan, K.D., Stammers, R.B. and Gray, M.J. (1971): 'Task Analysis', *Training Information Paper* No. 6. London: HMSO.

Boydell, T. (1970): *A Guide to Job Analysis*. London: BACIE.

Boydell, T. (1976): *A Guide to the Identification of Training Needs*. London: BACIE.

Boydell, T. and Pedler, M. (1981): *Management Self-development*. Aldershot: Gower.

Davies, I.K. (1971): *The Management of Learning*. Maidenhead: McGraw-Hill.

Mumford, A. (1971): *The Manager and Training*. London: Pitman.

Pedler, M. and Boydell, T. (1983): *Self-Development for Managers*. Manpower Services Commission.

Pedler, M., Burgoyne, J. and Boydell, T. (1978): *A Manager's Guide to Self-Development*. Maidenhead: McGraw-Hill.

Rae, W.L. (1984): 'Management Self-Development.' *Journal of the Institute of Training and Development*. October.

Stewart, V. and Stewart A. (1978): *Managing the Manager's Growth*. Aldershot: Gower.

Warr, P. and Bird, M. (1968): 'Identifying Supervisory Training Needs.' *Training Information Paper* No. 2. London: HMSO.

Woodcock, M. and Francis, D. (1982): *The Unblocked Manager*. Aldershot: Gower.

Woodcock, M. and Francis, D. (1982): *Fifty Activities for Self-Development*. Aldershot: Gower.

Index